The Postcolonial Novel

The Postcolonial Novel

Richard J. Lane

polity

First published in 2006 by Polity Press

Polity Press
65 Bridge Street
Cambridge CB2 1UR, UK.

Polity Press
350 Main Street
Malden, MA 02148, USA

ISBN-10: 0-7456-3278-5
ISBN-13: 978-07456-3278-
ISBN-10: 0-7456-3279-3 (pb)
ISBN-13: 978-07456-3279- (pb)

A catalogue record for this book is available from the British Library.

Typeset in 10.5 on 12 pt Bembo
by SNP Best-set Typesetter Ltd, Hong Kong
Printed and bound in India by Replika Press Pvt. Ltd.

For further information on Polity, visit our website: www.polity.co.uk

Contents

Preface and Acknowledgements   vi

1   Introducing the Postcolonial Novel in English:
    Wilson Harris's *Palace of the Peacock*   1

2   The Counter-Canonical Novel: J.M. Coerzee's *Foe* and
    Jean Rhys's *Wide Sargasso Sea*   18

3   Alternative Historiographies: Chinua Achebe's
    Things Fall Apart   32

4   National Consciousness: Ngũgĩ wa Thiong'o's
    A Grain of Wheat   47

5   Interrogating Subjectivity: Bessie Head's *A Question of Power*   59

6   Recoding Narrative: Margaret Atwood's *Surfacing*   71

7   The Rushdie Affair: Salman Rushdie's *The Satanic Verses*   83

8   The Optical Unconscious: Arundhati Roy's
    The God of Small Things   97

Conclusion: Ending with Joy Kogawa's Obasan *and
Phyllis Greenwood's* An Interrupted Panorama   109

Notes   115

Bibliography   133

Index   144

Preface and Acknowledgements

This book is written for readers who are encountering postcolonial literatures for the first time. I take an historical approach, examining some (and only *some*) of the key novels in the western reception and reading of postcolonial literatures. I read the novels closely, often quite conventionally, to enable beginning readers to engage with the texts themselves and with some of the critical debates that emerged from study of these texts. A more sophisticated theoretical discourse is used at times, but my basic thesis is that such a discourse was developed because of the groundbreaking work of the novelists (not the other way round). This book is written to encourage more advanced debate, in the process of which this text will be necessarily critiqued, abandoned or cast aside. My privileging of a few key novels may appear arbitrary, if not oppressive, yet the selection is made precisely because of the impact that these novels not only once had, but *continue to have*. In other words, while other selections can be added to, or even replace, these novels – for example, if one were to construct a history of feminist postcolonial literatures, or Marxist postcolonial literatures, and so on – I still contend that these novels were of immense importance to the development of the diverse ways in which we 'do English', to steal Robert Eaglestone's phrase; in other words, to the ways in which *we still 'do English'*.[1] I have focused on the novel genre because of the ways in which postcolonial novels in English have had a rapid, global impact via the international book market. As academic postcolonial departments have become more established in universities throughout the world, a huge amount of research has been produced with focus on other genres, revealing how more performative texts (poetry and drama), for example, and new hybrid texts/genres are of immense importance for indigenous peoples around the world. My focus on the novel genre is in no way meant as an ignoring or forgetting of other genres and emerging modes of writing; elsewhere I have paid particular attention to the immensely creative and powerful resurgence of contemporary Canadian First Nations drama and ritual.[2]

I could not have written this book without the support of my wife Sarah: I dedicate this book to her. I am indebted to John Thieme, who introduced me to the study of postcolonial literatures, and to Deborah Madsen, who has continued to support my research in this area. For research support at the University of Debrecen, thanks go to Tamas Benyei, Nora Sellei and Peter Szaffko; in England, Andrea Drugan, Rod Mengham and Robert Eaglestone were of particular assistance; in Canada Sherrill Grace continues to inspire, and for an alternative perspective on the literatures of the Pacific Northwest, thanks go to Laurie Ricou. Some of my research for this book was first presented at the University of Turin, where I received much support from Carmen Concilio. I would also like to thank the staff of the British Library, London, the Koerner Library and Main Library of the University of British Columbia, Vancouver, and Malaspina University-College Library, Vancouver Island. Joseph Jones, Librarian Emeritus at the University of British Columbia, was also of great assistance.

1 Introducing the Postcolonial Novel in English

Wilson Harris's *Palace of the Peacock*

A NOTE ON BEGINNINGS

All of the novels discussed in this study have had a strong impact upon contemporary literary critical thought either in the field of postcolonial studies or more generally in literary studies and beyond. This book focuses on the postcolonial novel in English[1] because it also explores the diverse ways in which postcolonial novels have engendered a rethinking of theory in the English-speaking academic communities of Europe and North America. This is not to argue that such a rethinking is necessarily the most important – or the only – consequence of the publication of these particular novels; rather, it is merely *one* of the outcomes of postcolonial literary production, albeit a decisive one for those involved in the criticism of literary texts. Subsequently, the critical discourse used here is tied in with and in many cases traced 'back' to its literary precursors, rather than the literary texts being presented as mere 'examples' of theoretical concepts. Such a tracing is (it is hoped) not done too naïvely, i.e., it is achieved with an awareness of Nietzsche's, Foucault's and Said's work on 'genealogy' and 'beginnings' – that is to say, an awareness that 'the metaphysical "origin" is privileged, mythical and transcendent, asserting a point of universal truth, whereas the secular "beginning" is contingent, ceaselessly re-examined (and re-begun), restructuring and animating new ways of conceiving the world.'[2] The question of 'precursors' is thus one which may appear strangely reversed to those versed in the complexities and densities of literary theory: to put it simply, in this critical book, the novels take priority.

PALACE OF THE PEACOCK: A FIRST READING

Beginning, then, again . . . is to begin, always, with a novel: in this chapter, Wilson Harris's *Palace of the Peacock*.[3] Wilson Harris was born in British Guiana in 1921; the country is now called Guyana after gaining independence on 26 May 1966. Harris emigrated to England in 1959, but his fiction remains deeply rooted in the transformational possibilities of the landscapes and peoples of Guyana. Because of the experimental and challenging nature of Harris's writing, the first main question asked in this study is: 'how do we read *Palace*?' The opening section of the first chapter narrates the death of an otherwise unidentified 'horseman', followed by a strange reversal – the first-person narrator (the 'I') declares that 'The sun blinded and ruled my living sight but the dead man's eye remained open and obstinate and clear' (19). The living narrator appears to have lost sight, while the dead 'horseman' keeps his 'eye' open. Whose vision will narrate this novel, or to ask this another way, who will be the focalizer? As Jakob Lothe summarizes: 'If the narrative perspective is *internal* [inside the story world], the point of orientation will as a rule be linked to a character. The reader has no choice but to see the fictional events with the eyes of this character.'[4] But what if there is a situation where the narrator is a character inside the story world, presenting that world through the eyes (or seeing eye) of another character? In this case we would say that the other character is the focalizer.[5] In the second section of chapter one of *Palace*, the narrator dreams of a surreal and schizophrenic mode of vision: 'I awoke [in the dream] with one dead seeing eye and one living closed eye' (19). Now the opening section appears to be repeated by the dream, where the narrator has somehow internalized the dead man's open eye, the 'one dead seeing eye'. Suddenly, the horseman appears in the dream, and we learn more about the two modes of vision or focalization: 'And we looked through the window of the room together as though through his dead seeing material eye, rather than through my living closed spiritual eye' (20). The juxtaposition of 'dead' with 'seeing' and then 'living' with 'closed' creates an interpretive friction when compounded by the opposition of 'material' and 'spiritual' eyes. The phrases 'dead–closed–material' and 'living–seeing–spiritual' would appear to make sense. Perhaps the *actual* phrases used – i.e., 'dead–seeing–material' and 'living–closed–spiritual' – signify the differences between a material and a spiritual vision, where the former deals with externals and objects, the latter with the internal world of visions, dreams and the soul.[6] 'Closed' could thus mean 'solipsistic' or 'hermetic' (sealed in) yet intensifying the spiritual; 'open' could thus mean 'sensuous' yet unthinking. We read on to try to decipher further, only to learn that the narrator has given the 'horseman' a name – Donne[7] – and that Donne is abusive towards another character, called Mariella. Again there is a repetition of being blinded, but this time, it is Mariella's gaze that does the damage: 'She was staring hard at me. I turned away from her black hypnotic eyes as if I had been blinded by the sun, and saw inwardly in the haze of my blind eye a watching muse and phantom whose breath was on my lips' (21). Not only does Mariella's gaze have the power to blind, but she is responsible for killing Donne. After this dream sequence, the narrator wakes in a 'blinding light' (21). We discover that Donne is the narrator's brother, and that he is still alive; Mariella appears to be in a troubled relationship with Donne, and the encroaching blindness of one of the narrator's eyes is a 'fact' in the narrative present (the waking sequences). By the end of the chapter, all of the contradictions and repetitions of the first sections appear to be resolved, although in explaining and clarifying his own dream state, the narrator once again repeats the basic narrative of vision and blindness.

What is this opening chapter of *Palace* about? We might now think that we can distinguish between dream sequences and waking sequences. But returning to the opening section of the chapter, it also appears to be written in the narrative present, and it is not framed by any devices to indicate that it is describing a dream, a fantasy or a vision: 'A horseman appeared on the road coming at a breakneck stride. A shot rang out suddenly' (19), and so on. There are two sentences in this first section that do not appear to make much sense: first, 'The shot had pulled me up and stifled my own heart in heaven'; and second, 'The sun blinded and ruled my living sight but the dead man's eye remained open and obstinate and clear' (19). The phrase 'pulled me up' could mean 'startled me, made me rise from a sleeping or resting position' – but that seems a weak interpretation of a phrase that is far more powerful once conjoined with 'and stifled my own heart in heaven' (whatever that might mean). The statement 'The sun blinded and ruled my living sight' is possibly understandable, except for the fact that the narrator is looking down at a dead man, so it appears to refer to a general case (the sun always blinds and rules the narrator's sight) rather than the specific instance of performing *this* particular action. The narrator is not just writing, in this opening section, in the narrative present, he is not just referring to the events he is apparently witnessing and partaking of; there is an overlayering of information, the information that concerns the present events being overlayered by the information that makes bigger, but less comprehensible claims about the narrator's heart and sight.

By the end of the chapter we can reassess this opening section of *Palace*: it may simply be the dream itself, or it may be something more powerful than a dream, such as a prophetic vision. We are still not sure. Are we, as readers, prepared for such an indeterminate text? Can we trust this narrator? Is the way in which he presents us with ambiguous and indeterminate fragments of dreams and other unidentified sequences a sign that he is an unreliable narrator? Writing one year after the publication of *Palace*, Wayne C. Booth argues that '[w]hen the novelist chooses to deliver his facts and summaries as though from the mind of one of his characters, he is in danger of surrendering precisely 'that liberty of transcending the limits of the immediate scene' – particularly the limits of that character he has chosen as his mouthpiece.'[8] Further, 'it is enough to say that a fact, when it has been given to us by the author or his unequivocal spokesman, is a very different thing from the same "fact" when given to us by a fallible character in the story.'[9] The transition in Booth's argument, from fact to "fact", reveals that the stable world of the author's 'unequivocal spokesman' gives way, with the unreliable first-person narrator, to a fluid world of uncertainty and lack of direction. Thus, as Andrew Gibson summarizes a whole batch of concerns related to this transition identified by Booth: 'Novels can no longer offer directives which tell us about the way people are and how to discriminate amongst them.'[10] Or to put this another way, the first-person narrator in *Palace* does *not* appear to offer the reader a stable perspective from which 'the truth' of the situation(s) being narrated can be measured. Does this matter? Contemporary readers are often familiar with more than straightforward realism, i.e., with: self-reflexive and playful genre fiction; postmodern novels that suspend all certainties and eschew grand narratives; magic realism; multimedia texts, and so on; in other words, the move from conventional realism to the fictionality of fiction, fabulation or metafiction.[11] What appeared dangerous to Booth may now appear not exactly normal, but certainly not unexpected.[12] But that is not to say that *Palace* is not unsettling or disturbing, especially as the brief reading above is just *one* way of attempting to interpret the first chapter. Where the above brief reading ended was with the certainty that narrational ambiguities had been cleared up: there is a dream text (the murdered Donne, whose sight *may* provide focalization, etc.) and there is a real text, however it is defined (say, the perspective of the narrator), but at the least the real text is seen as being an *awakened* state. And so the reader reads on.

Chapter two begins with a description of a map: 'The map of the savannahs was a dream. The names Brazil and Guyana were colonial conventions I had known from childhood' (24). The map is instantly questioned and undermined by the narrator as it is given the status of a dream or a set of 'colonial conventions'; the map represents a fantasy, projected onto a land before eyes were even set on it by the colonizers, such as the map of the Pacific Northwest in Jonathan Swift's *Gulliver's Travels*. Who designed the map? Which colonizers? Was it the Spanish explorers, or the Dutch – their first settlement of Guyana was in 1616 – was it the Dutch West India Company, or was it the British, who settled from 1746, the French, who gained power in the region in the 1780s, or the British again, who controlled 'British Guiana' from 1831 to 1966? Is it possible to strip away the colonial mapping to find an essential country underneath? Or would this be an effacement of the hybrid ethnic groups that are an integral part of the cultural make-up of the nation? To put this another way, the economics of Guyana under colonial powers involved producing wealth through slavery, indenture and the concomitant economic migration: all of the peoples historically involved in this process create or contribute to a complex national identity. The narrator of *Palace* appears to acknowledge this complexity by clinging to the 'colonial conventions' even as they are questioned by giving them such a name:

I clung to them [the colonial conventions] now as to a curious necessary stone and footing, even in my dream, the ground I knew I must not relinquish. They were an actual stage, a presence, however mythical they seemed to the universal and the spiritual eye. They were as close to me as my ribs, the rivers and the flatland, the mountains and heartland I intimately saw. I could not help cherishing my symbolic map, and my bodily prejudice like a well-known room and house of superstition within which I dwelt. I saw this kingdom of man turned into a colony and battleground of spirit, a priceless tempting jewel I dreamed I possessed. (24)

The 'colonial conventions' which, claim, interpret, irrevocably change and map the country are in competition with a personal bodily response to the country, the merging of organic geological features with individual physiology. The phrase 'heartland' links intimately with love of this land at physiological and spiritual levels, which merge to form the 'symbolic map'. From the latter perspective, the 'colonial conventions' are 'mythical' – yet they also function as 'an actual stage, a presence'. In other words, current-day actors involved in this part of South America still perform their actions with more than a colonial backdrop; it forms the very stage 'boards' – or ground – upon which they tread. The increasing sense of unreality interwoven with points of reality that Harris so beautifully builds throughout the opening pages of *Palace* is something that also concerned the Algerian activist and intellectual Frantz Fanon. In Fanon's *The Wretched of the Earth*, he describes 'a zone of occult instability',[13] which reaches a point whereby this interweaving needs to be forcefully resisted:

After centuries of unreality, after having wallowed in the most outlandish phantoms, at long last the native, gun in hand, stands face to face with the only forces which contend for his life – the forces of colonialism. And the youth of a colonized country, growing up in an atmosphere of shot and fire, may well make a mock of, and does not hesitate to pour scorn upon the zombies of his ancestors, the horses with two heads, the dead who rise again, and the djinns who rush into your body while you yawn. The native discovers reality and transforms it into the pattern of his customs, into the practice of violence and into his plan for freedom.[14]

Fanon's ghosts are 'superstitions' and indigenous ways of perceiving the world that can be reclaimed and transformed at the moment of resisting the forces of colonialism. While the narrator of *Palace* does not advocate violence, he does narrate the violence characteristic of Donne, and the geological 'violent din' (25) of the rapids being negotiated on the river journey. 'Reality' and 'unreality' are complex deliberately unstable reference points for Harris, whereas Fanon wants to end such instability once and for all in the name of direct action. Harris approaches the 'colonial conventions' from an aesthetic perspective, whereas Fanon approaches them from the perspective of the political activist – it is important to distinguish between the two discursive modes (even given the fact that they sometimes share rhetorical strategies and devices).

The introduction of the river journey and the crew in *Palace* is evocative of one of the most contested novellas of postcolonial studies, Joseph Conrad's *Heart of Darkness*. As John Thieme notes, *Palace* follows in Conrad's footsteps by taking its protagonists, a mixed crew representative of the various ancestral strands of the Guyanese population, or more generally of the crew of mankind, on a journey upriver into the country's continental heartland. . . . In one sense . . . the interior journey of *Palace of the Peacock* retraces that of *Heart of Darkness* and there are clear Conradian echoes, for example, when the Kurtz-like protagonist Donne remembers a house he has built 'with the closeness and intimacy of a horror and a hell, that horror and that hell he had himself elaborately constructed from which to rule his earth'. (130)[15]

By rewriting and recasting Conrad's novella, Harris is intervening in the western literary tradition and a contested vision of Africa. As Ania Loomba puts it:

There [in *Heart of Darkness*] Africa is a primeval jungle and a source of power and wealth which fascinates and maddens the colonialist hero Kurtz. . . . Marlow journeys down the river Congo, into the 'heart of darkness,' in search of Kurtz, whose experiences are recreated as simultaneously a journey into childhood, madness and Africa. Although several critics regard Kurtz's dislocation as a product of colonialist greed, and the novel as a critique of imperialism, it can be seen to rehearse the primitivism of classical psychoanalysis. Chinua Achebe (1989) called it 'a story in which the very humanity of black people is called into question'. In this novel as in much colonialist fiction, Africa is a place where the European mind disintegrates and regresses into a primitive state.[16]

The interpretive questions in Loomba's summary are balanced neatly between *Heart of Darkness* as an account of the inherent rottenness of the colonial enterprise in Africa (and beyond) and/or *Heart of Darkness* as a fundamentally racist depiction of Africa. For Edward Said, one of the problems of the novella, regardless of which side upon this interpretive divide critics fall, is that its representational structure is hermetic or self-enclosed:

. . . neither Conrad not Marlow gives us a full view of what is *outside* the world-conquering attitudes embodied by Kurtz, Marlow, the circle of listeners on the deck of the *Nellie*, and Conrad. . . . For if we cannot truly understand someone else's experience and if we must therefore depend upon the assertive authority of the sort of power that Kurtz wields as a white man in the jungle or that Marlow, another white man, wields as narrator, there is no use looking for other, non-imperialist alternatives; the system has simply eliminated them and made them unthinkable.[17]

This textual world, closed in and controlled, is what Said calls the representational 'circularity' of the novella: '. . . the perfect closure of the whole thing is not only aesthetically but also mentally unassailable.'[18] In *Palace*, Harris achieves not only an assault upon this representational circularity by producing another version of the now classic 'heart of darkness' journey, but he also resists countering Conrad with another monolithic or hermetic representational system. In other words, he counters Conrad by producing a text that is representationally fluid and open. Said calls the politics and aesthetics of *Heart of Darkness* 'imperialist' whereas the politics and aesthetics of *Palace* are 'postcolonial' – they work against the colonialist discourses embedded in the literary canon and they open up a complex, even contradictory, vision of a nation that has a history inextricably interlinked with colonial projects. Furthermore, the 'new' way of seeing that *Palace* explores in its opening pages becomes a way of also rereading the past, be that past Conrad's novella or the colonialist mapping processes. The relationship between the western literary canon and postcolonial novels as a critique and rewriting of that canon – known more technically as the production of counter-discourse – is explored more fully in the next chapter, but for the moment it is crucial to emphasize that the intertextual relationships between canon and critique are complex; as Thieme argues: '. . . if counter-discourse takes up an oppositional position, it runs the risk of locking itself into the very codes that it is contesting, because it allows itself to be defined in terms of them, albeit through negation.'[19] Thieme notes that there is an additional twist to Harris's writing back against Conrad: that Harris regards Conrad as being 'a writer who stands on the threshold of questioning "monolithic codes of behaviour"'.[20] In other words, not only does *Palace* exceed the hermetically closed representational circle by offering multiple narrational perspectives, but it locates in *Heart of Darkness* the *beginnings* of a critique of colonialism both thematically and at the level of 'form'. For a hint concerning the latter, Fredric Jameson, discussing Conrad's *Lord Jim*, suggests that '[a] case could be made for reading Conrad not as an early modernist, but rather an anticipation of that later and quite different thing we have come to call variously textuality, *écriture*, post-modernism, or schizophrenic writing.'[21]

Whether the crew are dead or alive in *Palace* may contribute to a feeling of schizophrenia; at times the crew are portrayed as merely doubling a previous group of men who happen to have had the same names (26), but then at other times, they discuss the pros and cons of being dead in such a way as to bring even further questions into play: 'He had told them secretly he was a wanted man now, wanted for murder if it was known he was living. And so he wished to stay dead, he shouted, though he was perfectly alive' (56). If the reference to 'colonial conventions' at the beginning of chapter two is indicative of an actual historical context within which and through which the novel is written, then is there some kind of context for this mysterious ghostly crew? T.J. Cribb examines Harris's own past as a surveyor in Guyana to get a sense of the scientific discourses and methodologies involved in mapping the nation – discourses and methodologies which Harris already exceeded in his day-to-day duties. For example, Cribb notes that '[t]he bulk of the work of surveying is repetitive routine and hard slog, recorded in thousands of readings of angles and distances in the Level or Field Books.'[22] Harris recorded such readings in his first expedition to the Guyanese interior in 1942, exceeding the mere recording of facts and figures:

to record, uniquely, the humbler members of the expedition who were assisting him, holding the gauging staffs while he took the observations. . . . At the head of page fifteen of the Level Book there appear the names: 'Moore, A. da Silva, W. Schomburgh.' . . . Then Rodrigues takes over the book and adopts Harris's method, so we find on 17th November 'A. Carroll, G. Vigilance, L. De Souza'.[23]

As Cribb says, not only does this surveyor's book contain the original names later used as characters in *Palace*, but it also indicates the importance of their 'basis in experience.'[24] Surveying, mapping and naming are intricately related processes, all of which are important for the colonial project of claiming land title (and the associated mineral rights, logging rights, etc.), de-legitimizing and re-designating land use (i.e., replacing one 'improper' system of land use with another 'proper' one as defined by the colonizers), and interpreting land within radically different cultural contexts. Two Canadian examples suffice here. First, Eden Robinson, in her novel *Monkey Beach*, explains the mis-naming, the doubling and displacements of the Haisla town of Kitammat where the events of the novel are situated. Thus, Hudson's Bay traders once used Tsimshian First Nations guides whose own name – Kitamaat – for the main Haisla First Nation town means 'people of the falling snow,' and this is the name that the Hudson's Bay Company used from thereon. Then, an additional confusion arose when the Alcan Aluminium company moved into the area in the 1950s and built a workers' town which they called 'Kitimat.'[25] From a Haisla First Nation perspective, their own naming system – a key component of cultural identity – has been doubly displaced. The second example involves two competing names for the twin peaks of mountains overlooking the Canadian city of Vancouver: either 'The Lions' or 'The Two Sisters'. The first name refers to the Landseer Lions, the sculptures in London's Trafalgar Square, and the second name refers to First Nations mythology and culture. The fact that 'The Lions' is the name used today indicates the colonial recoding of the landscape.[26] In both of these examples, the processes of naming are not simple, and they do not simply draw upon empirical data – instead, they function according to chance (the guides happened to be Tsimshian that day, not Haisla) and power (the power of colonial companies to rename the environment). In writing from the position of a surveyor, Harris is rooted in multiple perspectives of the land from the very start; he reveals how surveying data, which is based upon empirical fact, can be used for myriad purposes, one of which is the writing of *Palace*. The crew – with their names based upon Harris's personal history in his surveying days – become as characters in a novel not just doubled, but somehow indeterminate *to themselves*. The journey into the interior, which in *Heart of Darkness* and the counter-discursive rewritings of it is seen as a psychological journey, is further rewritten by Harris via the technique of montage. In other words, the crew literally see alternative identities juxtaposed. This occurs most strongly as they re-experience the rapids that (may have) killed them the first time round, but it also occurs in summary and statement made by the narrator. Thus 'it looked the utmost inextricable confusion to determine where they were and what they were, whether they had made any step whatever towards a better relationship – amongst themselves and within themselves – or whether it was all a fantastic chimera' (84). The substantiality of the crew derives from the montage form, the 'chimera' given substance through the crew's continual dialectical interweaving of past, present and the hoped-for future. This dialectical interweaving can also be thought of as a 'dialogue with the past'[27] where 'history as progress' is questioned, undermined and recast, but always with an awareness of historical complexities and as a way of teasing out new readings of the nation's formation. The image of the dead crew climbing a cliff punctured with 'windows' through which they can peer is a poetic vision[28] of the dialectical interweaving found throughout the novel, and this leads on in the narrative to the final 'mystical vision', which is redemptive while also being, materially speaking, an expression of failure. As Thieme argues: 'The mystical vision of community and integration symbolized by the palace of the peacock at the waterfall remains an aspiration rather than an attainment.'[29] In relation to the material question, Thieme argues further that '[a]s European conquistadores, Donne and his crew, who die many deaths, fail to reach the El Dorado, but on another level they do arrive at the legendary golden city, achieving a sense of spiritual and psychic harmony through a syncretist vision of an Arawak Christ that draws on natural elements common to both settler and indigene cultures.'[30]

What does the word 'syncretist', used above, mean? Deriving from 'syncretism', the word literally means a joining of forces. Originally used in theological writing, but also in secular theatre criticism, the transfer of the term to postcolonial literature is viewed with some suspicion.[31] Ashcroft, Griffiths and Tiffin define the term as one 'sometimes used to avoid the problems some critics have associated with the idea of hybridity in identifying the fusion of two distinct traditions to produce a new and distinctive whole'.[32] The most important word in the construction of Harris's syncretist vision in *Palace* is 'dreaming': it is the one word that connects and maintains all of the contradictions and ambiguities in the text, yet it still enables the 'fusion' of literary, national and historical traditions to remain continually in process. The etymological root of the word 'dream' takes us back to Old English and the meaning 'song'; quite late in the novel, there is a direct quotation of a fragment of a sacred song, or *Psalm*: 'It is better to be a doorkeeper in the house of the Lord' (109). Prior to this direct quotation there are further allusions to this Psalm – Psalm number 84 – the huge wall of rock over which the waterfall pours can be thought of as the edge of a 'shield' or a plateau; there are countless references to the power of the sun; a swallow flies in and out of the room that Donne peers into, where the carpenter (or Messiah figure) works: all allude to key components of the Psalm, where the Christian God is compared with the sun and a shield, and a swallow nests in the Temple.[33] This biblical song or poetry is part of Harris's syncretist vision: in general, to dream means different things, in different times and cultures; to take just a few possible meanings, dreaming can be a core component of indigenous spirituality (e.g., Australian aboriginal dreamtime), it can be regarded as being out-of-touch with rational reality (the common meaning of 'daydreaming' in the West), it can be a way of receiving prophetic visions and command-ments (e.g., Jacob's dreams in the Old Testament) and it can be a process open to psychoanalysis (Freud's infamous *The Interpretation of Dreams* being an unsurpassed example of such an interpretive process). To disentangle ever so slightly the syncretist web, it is crucial to examine who, or what, is doing the dreaming in *Palace*. The first-person narrator describes not only his own modes of dreaming but also that of others; the word 'dream-ing' is used to describe the actions of people and objects, such as 'a million dreaming miles away' (20), 'the dense dreaming jungle' (924), 'Wishrop's dreaming eternity' (33), 'the sudden dreaming fury of the stream' (62), 'one sudden leering dreaming eye' (86), 'this dreaming return to a ruling nothingness' (101) and the references to a 'dreaming shoulder' (111, 112 and 114). How can objects dream? If the action of dreaming itself is syn-cretic, that is, a fusion of different meanings, then objects can indeed 'dream', be they read as symbolic, as having visionary significance, or as a mystical notion of the influence of landscape on the human psyche. Such a reading of *Palace* does not stray away from its own positioning as a post-colonial text. The character named Donne is an undoubted allusion to the English metaphysical poet John Donne (1573–1631), and thus carries not only the associated baggage of John Donne's expeditions with the Earl of Essex to Cadiz and the Azores,[34] but also the fact that as Dean of St Paul's he famously preached on the benefits of colonization of the new world. As he said to 'the stockholders of the Virginia Company',[35] referring to New England: 'You shall have made this Island, which is but as the Suburbs of the old world, a Bridge, a Gallery to the new; to join all to that world that shall never grow old, the Kingdom of Heaven. You shall add persons to this Kingdom, and to the Kingdom of heaven, and add names to the Books of our Chronicles, and to the Book of Life.'[36] The colonizers of the Americas dreamt not just of potential riches but also of the oppor-tunity to escape from religious intolerance and persecution in Europe; as history, unfortunately, continually repeats itself, we have since recognized that such an escape for one group of people can lead directly to the displacement and persecution of other indigenous groups.

Guyana, where *Palace* is set, has a doubled identity, with the Arawak (largely coastal-based) and Carib (based in the interior) communities ini-tially engaged in internal struggle and displacement. The early colonizers played off diverse strengths and weaknesses in these two communities, exacerbating earlier conflicts between them. We have here a clue, however, to a new strength: that of the cross-cultural energies and diversity that emerge from this history. Relating this notion of hybridity more technically to Harris's writing (both fiction and non-fiction), Ashcroft, Griffiths and Tiffin argue that his process-based texts are thus similarly cross-cultural:

Although Harris finds the apparent meaning of 'the word' constantly 'deferred' in a sense, and his critical practice involves the explosion of the text from the site of a 'fissure' in its apparently seamless texture, such 'deferrals' and 'fissures' are not for him, as for Derrida, the inescapable characteristics of language and textuality itself, but the ambi/valent 'limbo gateway' . . . to the de-imperialization of apparently monolithic European forms, ontologies, and epistemologies.[37]

This complex sentence needs some unpacking, given that it makes a number of assumptions about knowledge of deconstructive theory and other philosophical terms. The biblical tradition of the early colonizers and theorists of Empire, such as that found in the extract above from John Donne's sermon, generates what Ashcroft et al. are calling a 'monolithic European form' – that is to say, the increase in knowledge ('epistemology') and an engagement with the world through modes of being ('ontology') – which does not recognize the value of difference and diversity. This 'monolithic' form is fundamentally based upon the word-of-God, the *logos*; by utilizing logocentric discourses yet also keeping their meanings open and exposed to difference, indeed transformed by difference, Harris offers a way of countering 'imperial' modes of behaviour and thought. But why the mention, in the above quotation, of Derrida? In part, this is because Harris's methodologies appear *deconstructive*, where deconstruction is thought of as a way of revealing the potential openness of apparently closed systems such as imperialist or monolithic texts or philosophies. The relation between the historical emergence of a powerful new theory and a literary text is central to this study; often, literary texts are quoted or sampled as mere exemplars of a particular theory, but Ashcroft, Griffiths and Tiffin notice something different:

Harris's extensive fictional explorations, which have culminated in his recent theoretical writing, chronologically overlap Derrida's investigation of the limitations of the western philosophical tradition, and the resulting development of his theory of language '*différance*'. Harris's earliest novel, *Palace of the Peacock* (1960) predates Derrida's translation of Husserl by two years and the French publication of *Of Grammatology* . . . and *Writing and Difference* . . . by seven years. The relation between the two is therefore not one of influence but of a separate, similar, though finally diverging approach to the problem of language and meaning.[38]

This argument for the primacy of the literary text, as a crucible for developing radical new ways of thinking and writing, is essential if postcolonial literatures are to be regarded as culturally autonomous. Another related example of text-with-theory is the one drawn by Bart Moore-Gilbert in his engaging study called *Postcolonial Theory: Contexts, Practices, Politics*. Moore-Gilbert tantalizingly suggests some parallels between Wilson Harris and the postcolonial theorist Homi K. Bhabha: 'Harris's model of an experimental style characterized by the play of "infinite rehearsal" (whether in fiction or criticism), by comparison, is akin to Bhabha's conception of the "performative" . . . Harris's work seems to provide a crucial stimulus to the emergence and development of the concept of the "third space" in Bhabha's writing.'[39]

HOW THIS BOOK PROCEEDS

What have we learnt from this brief engagement with *Palace of the Peacock*? First and foremost, that the postcolonial novel in English can challenge our preconceptions or expectations about the ways in which novels are, or can be, written. Second, with this example, we experience either directly or indirectly (depending on our prior knowledge) some of the ways in which postcolonial novels 'write back' against the literary canon – this process will be explored in much more detail in the next chapter. Third, through even a minimum of critical and contextualizing study, we realize that the postcolonial novel engages with historical situations, and the ideas and systems of thought that are used to interpret those situations. This third point can become immensely complex, and new critical terminologies have been developed to explore and account for it, terminologies that are sometimes grouped together under the rubric 'postcolonial theory'.

The development of postcolonial theory within universities has its own relatively complex history. As John McLeod notes: 'One important antecedent for postcolonialism was the growth of the study of Commonwealth literature',[40] which was

a term literary critics began to use from the 1950s to describe literatures in English emerging from a selection of countries with a history of colonialism. It incorporated the study of writers from the predominantly European settler communities, as well as writers belonging to those countries which were in the process of gaining independence from British rule, such as those from the African, Caribbean and South Asian nations. Literary critics began to distinguish a fast-growing body of literature written in English which included work by such figures as R.K. Narayan (India), George Lamming (Barbados), Katherine Mansfield (New Zealand) and Chinua Achebe (Nigeria). The creation of the category of 'Commonwealth literature' as a special area of study was an attempt to identify and locate this vigorous literary activity, and to consider via a comparative approach the common concerns and attributes that these manifold literary voices might have.[41]

Critics have charted the rise of 'Commonwealth' literature in the USA, with one of the earliest courses being 'English 70: The Literature of the British Dominions and Colonies', offered by A. Bruce Sutherland at Pennsylvania State University in 1942.[42] One related issue here is that the conception of what the 'Commonwealth' actually consists of has radically changed – e.g., shifting from a reflection of British and other related colonial powers to that of independent nationhood with shared economic concerns. From a literary perspective, McLeod and others have argued that the term was still largely anchored by the primacy of English literature and the English language even as geopolitical realities and relationships shifted. As McLeod puts it: 'Commonwealth literature, then, was really a sub-set of canonical English literature, evaluated in terms derived from the conventional study of English that stressed the values of timelessness and universality.'[43] McLeod identifies this method of (sub-)classification of Commonwealth literature as stemming largely from a liberal humanist approach to the arts, whereby an official canon was perceived as setting the ('universal') standard against which all other literatures would be measured. Such a vision of universal values as embedded and expressed within certain literary texts has been regarded by some critics as liberatory and by others as repressive; what is certain is that there is a definable correspondence between the growth of colonial power and the study of centrally defined canons as classified by the purveyors of that power. In other words, a cen-trally based notion of aesthetics – meaning a strictly defined core set of values within art-works – dominates those 'peripheral' societies that have only recently been introduced to western languages and concepts via colonialism.

We can gain a sense of the problematic side of this 'core set of values' by briefly examining one such approach to these diverse emerging litera-tures. In the introduction to *The Commonwealth Pen*, A.L. McLeod surveys the various Commonwealth countries and the quantity and quality of their literatures; while the dominance of one language – English – is seen as an important factor in the assessment that '[i]n bulk, Australian and Indo-Anglian literatures are much more considerable than any other Common-wealth writing, just as they are in quality',[44] the more noticeable value judgement concerns ethnicity, where the editor notes that '[i]n South African fiction, as in West Indian and West African writing to a lesser degree, the problems of race relations are the substance of much writing.'[45] While he does examine why this focus is important, A.L. McLeod also asserts that '[m]ere race and color problems never produce good literature. These problems have to become submerged in more universal themes.'[46] What is troubling about such an assertion is that it reveals that local issues – or 'problems' – are thoroughly devalued by a liberal humanist critic taking this approach, unless the specifics of such issues/problems are sub-sumed by some bigger or wider 'universal' (read 'western' or 'Eurocentric') theme. In other words, the most important local issues, for some unwritten reason, cannot produce 'great' works of art according to the critics who once took this approach to 'Commonwealth' literature. This is not a minor point or quibble, since it leads to comparative and deeply problematic state-ments such as the following:

The characters in Olive Schreiner's *The Story of an African Farm*, for instance, have genuine, human attributes and the book is a good novel because the author deals with human and universal values, just as E.M. Forster does in *A Passage to India* and Joseph Conrad does in *Heart of Darkness* or *Nigger of the Narcissus*, where Jim is the amalgam of many kinds of man, and not just a black man.[47]

This is a striking instance not just of the liberal humanist desire for 'universal values' – that is to say, values constructed and created by those at the centre of aesthetic and other forms of power – but also an example of how indigenous identity is seen as somehow not an adequate base for expressing those values: 'just a black man' in other words, not a 'universal' man. The Algerian activist and intellectual Frantz Fanon, mentioned above, pondered these sorts of questions in his book *Black Skin, White Masks* (1952); for Fanon, the question of *why* black identity was effaced from a colonialist and humanist perspective was central, and he utilized a number of disciplines to answer it, ranging from Marxism to psychoanalysis and existential philosophy (especially the philosophy of Karl Jaspers and Jean-Paul Sartre). In his chapter 'The Fact of Blackness' the exotic, racist identification of the black person or subject is analysed as being a way of classifying indigenous peoples as a rarity or a surprise, an interruption to the normativity of everyday whiteness in the spaces of colonial power and existence. In recasting and reorientating such a racist identification, *Black Skin, White Masks* is a powerful antidote to the liberal humanist version of the more extreme statements that Fanon examines.

The liberal humanist and colonialist perspective embedded in the study of 'Commonwealth' literatures of the sort briefly touched upon above is criticized and in many respects dismantled by the *general* rise of contemporary theory across the humanities that took place in the 1960s and beyond (structuralism, deconstruction, feminism, postmodernism, etc.), a dismantling that can be more specifically located in relation to the literatures under study in this book via a number of key critical texts, such as Edward Said's *Orientalism* (1978), Gayatri Spivak's 'Can the Subaltern Speak?' (1988) and Bill Ashcroft, Gareth Griffiths and Helen Tiffin's *The Empire Writes Back: Theory and Practice in Post-Colonial Literatures* (1989). The rise of postcolonial theory (based on colonial discourse analysis, e.g., the work of Frantz Fanon, and then transforming itself into more theoretical modes of writing, e.g., Bhabha's work based largely on the theorists Jacques Lacan and Michel Foucault) brings another set of problems, grouped around the notion that for many people around the world the term 'postcolonial' continues to anchor their cultures to the colonial era. Ato Quayson offers a concise 'working definition for Postcolonialism', being a subject always in process, one that 'involves a studied engagement with the experience of colonialism and its past and present effects, both at the local level of ex-colonial societies as well as at the level of more general global developments thought to be the after-effects of empire'.[48] Embedded in this useful definition is the question of levels: the local societal level and the general global level. Taken in isolation, a particular postcolonial essay or book may appear to focus on one of these levels to the detriment of the other; taken as a whole, *and* as an ongoing process of study, development and modification, postcolonial theory and criticism covers a wide range of peoples, local and specific customs, cultural and ethnic differences, and so on, *as well as* interrelated global changes, such as mass migration, the importance of the western city space in the generation of hybrid identities, and other widespread developments. Thus the site of postcoloniality is as dispersed and as varied as is imaginable. As Quayson suggests: 'A growing concern among postcolonial critics has also been with racial minorities in the West, embracing native and African Americans in the US, British Asians and African Caribbeans in the UK and Aborigines in Australia among others.'[49] As Deborah Madsen writes in the introduction to a collection of critical essays called *Post-Colonial Literatures: Expanding the Canon*: 'The motive driving these individual writings and the book as a whole . . . is the desire to revise and expand the post-colonial paradigm to accommodate the contributions of such colonized peoples as Native Americans, Chicano/as, Afro-Hispanic and African-American Peoples.'[50] In opening up the new postcolonial canon with such a strategic move, Madsen also foregrounds the diversity of critical languages being used, although one constant has been the turn to psychoanalytical discourse, from Fanon, through Bhabha and beyond: for example, in the introduction to *Postcolonizing the Commonwealth: Studies in Literature and Culture*, editor Rowland Smith notes the 'repeated use of metaphors, rhetorical terms and phrases from psychoanalytical theory' utilized by the various contributors.[51] The at times theoretical density of much postcolonial criticism has led to accusations of a distancing from the diverse peoples and cultures under study; in other words, the production of 'high' postcolonial theory is accused of being another form of colonialism. The rejection of the critical term 'postcolonial' can be read in this light, as, for example, Native author and critic Thomas King argues, from a North American context:

While post-colonialism purports to be a method by which we can begin to look at those literatures which are formed out of the struggle of the oppressed against the oppressor, the colonized and the colonizer, the term itself assumes that the starting point for that discussion is the advent of Europeans in North America. At the same time, the term organizes the literature progressively suggesting that there is both progress and improvement. No less distressing, it also assumes that the struggle between guardian and ward is the catalyst for contemporary Native literature, providing those of us who write with method and topic. And, worst of all, the idea of post-colonial writing effectively cuts us off from our traditions, traditions that were in place before colonialism ever became a question, traditions which have come down to us through our cultures in spite of colonization, and it supposes that contemporary Native writing is largely a construct of oppression. Ironically, while the term itself – post-colonial – strives to escape to find new centres, it remains, in the end, a hostage to nationalism.[52]

King's overriding point is that indigenous cultures do not need defining from a Eurocentric base; in other words, for King, postcolonial theory always places indigenous subjects and texts in a defining relationship with fundamentally Eurocentric nationalism and ideology. To put this another way, King argues that there was – and is – life outside of the postcolonial interpretive text. Does King offer some alternative terminology for the critic to use? He suggests that the terms 'tribal, interfusional, polemical and associational' all function more accurately to describe open and autonomous Native literatures in North America (King crosses the American/ Canadian border in his work). He argues that these terms

> tend to be less centred and do not . . . privilege one culture over another; they avoid the sense of progress in which primitivism gives way to sophistication, suggesting as it does that such movement is both natural and desirable; they identify points on a cultural and literary continuum for Native literature which do not depend on anomalies such as the arrival of Europeans in North America or the advent of non-Native literature in this hemisphere.[53]

All of these points work overall to reorientate the reader's relations with the text, teasing apart Eurocentric notions of temporal and cultural origin and priority. Nonetheless, there are other ways of achieving the perspective that King advocates, and the next chapter examines how counter-discursive writing disrupts and reorientates notions of literary and cultural progression. King has been quoted here at length as an important example of a writer who entirely rejects the postcolonial label; perhaps one other impetus for this rejection is the fact that he is a creative writer, and that he attempts to resist the critical labels that descend upon the literary text after the fact. His replacement terms 'tribal, interfusional, polemical and associational' are not meant to be a new *universal* language of indigenous writing; rather, they are culturally specific terms that do not need Eurocentric conceptual systems for validation or even to be brought into existence. Nonetheless, there are other issues that need to be foregrounded, such as the fact that many contemporary American and Canadian Native writers use English – and the written word, not oral delivery – as their primary mode of cultural expression; tied in with the indigenous production of powerful literary works in contemporary genres, and the ways in which these works have had an impact on *non-indigenous* North American cultures, then there are obviously productive crossings between the adjacent realms or cultures within Canada. The term 'postcolonial' may then still be useful both in describing the impact of contemporary indigenous literatures upon western modes of expression and in teasing apart the mechanisms which facilitate such a process in the first place. Judith Leggatt presents a similarly dynamic notion of the postcolonial

> as a process, an ongoing attempt to find means of cross-cultural communication that escape the repressive hierarchies of colonial encounters. This urge includes everything from academic and philosophical analysis of the colonial processes (for only by understanding colonialism can we move beyond it); to explicit discussions of possible methods of decolonization; to artistic attempts to express the traditions

of cultures such as Hindu, Cree, Maori, or Yoruba in new languages, such as English, and new forms, such as the novel; to attempts to understand the implications of these artistic endeavors for the cultures, languages, and media, all of which have undergone a process of translation.[54]

Sticking with the metaphor of 'crossings', none of the processes in Leggatt's list work entirely in isolation: there is a constant interpenetration of literary production and critical understanding. In this book, the emphasis is upon the ways in which the literary has impacted upon the critical; but of course, the 'crossings' are still at work, and critical terms and tools are utilized and explained where necessary. Postcolonialism, then, is understood in this study as what David Punter has called 'a matter of a complex reading, a complex listening, whereby the plethora, the multitude of voices can be heard even as they speak the melancholy inevitability of their loss'.[55]

2 The Counter-Canonical Novel

J.M. Coetzee's *Foe* and Jean Rhys's *Wide Sargasso Sea*

Two slender novels that emerged from two different cultures – South Africa and the Caribbean – have become foci for the process of 'writing back' against the western literary canon. J.M. Coetzee's *Foe* (1986) writes back against Daniel Defoe's *Robinson Crusoe* (1719) and Jean Rhys's *Wide Sargasso Sea* (1966) against Charlotte Brontë's *Jane Eyre* (1847).[1] In this chapter the literary relations between these four novels and the impact Coetzee and Rhys have had upon postcolonial theory will be explored. One overriding question will be: how wide a discursive field does the process of 'writing back' cover? In other words, when a novel is in a critical and creative relationship with another novel, can we draw larger lessons from that relationship? Ashcroft, Griffiths and Tiffin make this point in their entry on 'counter-discourse' in their *Key Concepts in Post-Colonial Studies*:

A term coined by Richard Terdiman to characterize the theory and practice of symbolic resistance.
. . .
. . . his term has been adopted by post-colonial critics to describe the complex ways in which challenges to a dominant or established discourse (specifically those of the imperial centre) might be mounted from the periphery, always recognizing the powerful "absorptive capacity" of imperial and neo-imperial discourses. As a practice within post-colonialism, counter-discourse has been theorized less in terms of historical processes and literary movements than through challenges posed to particular texts, and thus to imperial ideologies inculcated, stabilized and specifically maintained through texts employed in colonialist education systems.
    The concept of counter-discourse within post-colonialism thus also raises the issue of the subversion of canonical texts and their inevitable reinscription in this process of subversion.[2]

The phrase 'inculcated, stabilized and specifically maintained' refers to those ideological elements of a text that often readers do not notice – not because people read incorrectly, but because these ideological elements are presented as natural and exist in the background of the text or as a substrate upon which the text is built. Counter-discursive writing, the above extract argues, challenges 'particular texts' first and foremost, and through these specific challenges, the wider set of colonialist values maintained by canonical texts are also brought under critique. Yet, even given this clinical way of analysing the situation, it is crucial to point out that we are also considering canonical texts that have been enormously successful, much loved by readers, and continually in great demand. These subjective evaluations also play a part in the relationship between canonical and counter-discursive novels, between the old and the new. The suggestion is that postcolonial counter-discourses also re-engage the reader with, and reinvigorate, the reception of canonical texts. Are there other ways of describing this relationship between old and new? Is the relationship 'dialectical' or 'dialogic'? Is it 'agonistic' or purely 'critical', 'disruptive', even 'deconstructive'?[3] Or is the relationship more complex than any of these terms signify? These descriptors can be placed into two groups, where the first group could be called the 'unidirectional' (meaning: moving in one direction only). In the unidirectional group, gathering 'critical, disruptive, deconstructive', the new text is regarded as performing a powerful critique of the old, with the ideological values of the new text also being an improvement over those of the old. The second group could be called 'bidirectional'[4] (meaning: moving in either direction to and from the old and new texts). In the bidirectional group, gathering 'agonistic, dialectical, dialogic', the new text is in a more dynamic relationship with that of the old: the new text may still be regarded as massively critical of the ideology of the old, but it also engages in a 'two-way' process, whereby its new readings add to the experience of reading particular canonical novels (ironically, the liberal humanist notion of 'richness' in canonical literature is in some ways thereby reinvigorated). In this latter sense, the canonical novel is *not* seen as totally obliterated by the postcolonial critique, yet the colonial values revealed and rejected still provide a powerful lesson. Elsewhere, I have suggested that another term may be used for the relationship under discussion: that of 'embroiling narratives'.[5] Why use this additional term, especially as it has some negative connotations? The word 'embroil' derives from the French *embrouiller,* in turn from *brouiller,* to mingle, confuse.[6] Embroil means to involve someone in trouble, conflict or argument, or to throw affairs into a state of confusion or disorder.[7] In each of these definitions, there are positives and negatives: 'to mingle', 'to argue' and 'to disorder' can be regarded as positive strategies for postcolonial novels interrogating the colonial canon, but 'to confuse', 'cause trouble' or 'cause conflict' may be seen as being radical and aggressive. The *Oxford English Dictionary* adds to the latter with the additional meanings of 'to throw into uproar or tumult' and with an obsolete usage, 'to set on fire, burn up'. I use the term 'embroiling narratives' for counter-discursive novels precisely because both possibilities – those of radical critique and those of violent rejection and destruction – are brought together. It is up to the reader to decide how far a counter-discursive novel has gone, not just by engaging with a critical survey, but, more importantly, by engaging with the literary texts themselves.

READING FOE

Daniel Defoe's *Robinson Crusoe* has become for many readers the archetypal colonialist island tale. The narrative tells the story of a shipwrecked man who diligently constructs an ordered world in the midst of his isolation, structured by a mercantile mind-set, and served eventually by his enslaved islander called Man Friday: 'Defoe's hero is a prodigal son who is saved by his own hard work and God's mercy, an adventurer who can narrate his past and present with detailed certainty.'[8] *Robinson Crusoe* has been repeatedly analysed as a key text intertwining the rise of the English novel in the eighteenth century with the rise of the mercantile classes in England. Most notable in this line of argumentation is Ian Watt's *The Rise of the Novel* (1957), where Watt argues that *Robinson Crusoe* provides a 'unique demonstration of the connexion between individualism in its many forms and the rise of the novel'.[9] More importantly, for postcolonial responses to Defoe's novel, there are the critical readings which situate Crusoe within the expansion of western economic empires: '. . . Crusoe effectively develops an embryonic plantation economy, staffed by a one-man subservient labour force in the person of Man Friday, albeit without the benefit of a market in which to sell his produce.'[10] Said regards *Robinson Crusoe* as having inaugurated the English novel with this story of the founding of a 'new world' ruled and claimed 'for Christianity and England'.[11] It is within these contexts that J.M. Coetzee, a South African writer, wrote his own creative response to *Robinson Crusoe* with the novel *Foe*.[12]

Foe opens with the first-person narrator saying, 'At last I could row no further' (5). The narrator slips overboard with exhaustion and swims towards a 'strange island' to be greeted eventually by a black man who does not speak. The utopian fantasies of the readers of travellers'' tales are undercut by the narrator:

> . . . the words *desert isle* may conjure up a place of soft sands and shady trees where brooks run to quench the castaway's thirst and ripe fruit falls into his hand, where no more is asked of him than to drowse the days away till a ship calls to fetch him home. But the island on which I was cast away was quite another place: a great rocky hill with a flat top, rising sharply from the sea on all sides except one, dotted with drab bushes that never flowered and never shed their leaves. (7)

We learn that the black man is called Friday, perhaps expected all along from our prior knowledge of *Robinson Crusoe*, but with the same knowledge we might not expect the narrator to be called 'Susan Barton', and a rough-looking man whom she meets to be called 'Cruso'. Gayatri Spivak points out that 'Coetzee's Susan Barton is also Defoe's Roxana, whose first name is Susan. (There are other incidental similarities.)'[13] This is an important observation given that *Roxana* is a novel about female autonomy and sexual economies set in a time when married women had no power or rights within marriage beyond the highly restrictive inheritance laws. Susan

Barton describes Cruso's 'encampment', consisting of a hut and a garden on the top of a flat hill. Susan tells Cruso her story, explaining her lineage, her search for her daughter abducted and conveyed to the 'new world' and her abandonment by mutineers; she concludes by writing, 'With these words I presented myself to Robinson Cruso, in the days when he still ruled over his island, and became his second subject, the first being his manservant Friday' (11). The later undermining of Susan's verisimilitude by the character 'Mr Foe' is foreshadowed by her own comments concerning Cruso's contradictory stories of his own life: 'So in the end I did not know what was truth, what was lies, and what was mere rambling' (12). Susan is shocked to discover that Cruso no longer desires to leave the island, and that a combination of 'indifference to salvation', habit and 'the stubbornness of old age' are keeping him firmly in place (14). She is again surprised when she discovers that Cruso keeps no record of his time, no journal or even carvings or notches to record the *passing* of time. Spivak sees this disengagement from record-keeping, or, more precisely, book-keeping, as a disengagement from 'capitalism' and a re-focus within the text on 'gender and empire'.[14] Stories, however, are also commodities, and they can constitute a 'capital investment' that can be later realized, as the captain of the vessel that eventually rescues Susan makes clear: 'It is a story you should set down in writing and offer to the booksellers. . . . There has never before, to my knowledge, been a female castaway of our nation' (40). Susan's problem is that the economies of fiction are controlled by men. In the early stages of the novel, however, She regards the story of the island as a potential *memorial*, a marker that will survive their death, and remind people of their existence. The memorial is also a supplement to living, faulty memory, writing being regarded as something permanent and far more reliable than the human mind, but Cruso simply responds to this notion by saying, 'Nothing I have forgotten is worth the remembering' (17). Once again, the issue of verisimilitude arises, with Susan arguing that forgetting effaces specificity; in other words, if the small details of everyday life are forgotten and not written down, the 'island tale' becomes composed of archetypal generalities, becomes not just like every other island tale, but one that is not believed to be truthful. This is an interesting theory because one of the most powerful debates during the rise of the English novel concerned 'truthfulness' and competing definitions of 'realism'. The move from archetypal French Romances to English tales of everyday life was projected as providing a more realistic mode of writing. Defoe's *A Journal of the Plague Year* (1722) is a classic example of the new realism, whereby a novel is regularly mistaken for an eyewitness account in part because of the journal format. Susan makes the observation that '[t]he truth that makes your story yours alone, that sets you apart from the old mariner by the fireside spinning yarns of sea-monsters and mermaids, resides in a thousand touches which today may seem of no importance' (18); her observation could easily be about any of Daniel Defoe's novels. Cruso rejects the entire argument and simply says that what he will leave behind as his memorial will be the terraces and walls that he has been so monotonously constructing.

Language is the focus of the first part of *Foe*. After the debate concerning memorials, or narrative versus stone structures, Susan realizes that Friday has been taught an extremely small vocabulary to respond to, one which is purely functional for his role as slave: 'How many words of English does Friday know?' Susan asks Cruso; he replies: 'As many as he needs' (21), meaning as many as he needs to get work done. As I have noted elsewhere, there is direct reference here not only to the language theories of the eighteenth century but also to the parodies of those theories:

Swift, in particular satirised the concept that 'excess' words could be removed, leaving the 'user' with exact equivalences. This is taken to extremes with his 'Scheme for entirely abolishing all Words whatsoever', which Gulliver encounters in 'the grand academy of Lagado', where it is suggested that 'since words are only Names for Things, it would be more convenient for all men to carry about them, such Things as were necessary to express the particular business they are to discourse on.'[15]

There is an equivalence in *Foe* where Friday performs the stripped–down language of commands; in other words, he can only 'speak' by manipulating objects. Eighteenth-century philosophers were concerned with understanding the origin of languages, their theories often starting with so-called 'primitive' races and basic emotional responses and needs translated into simple tongues. Such interpretive notions of the Other, 'primitive' and 'simple' with only basic needs, would be countered by the notion of the Other as excessive, filled with uncontrollable desires, and dangerously unstable. Both modes of interpreting the Other, even though contradictory and based upon fundamentally flawed empirical research, were brought together in justifying the enslavement of entire peoples. When Susan learns that Friday has no tongue, Cruso explains it away by saying that 'slavers' have cut it out: '. . . perhaps they grew weary of listening to Friday's wails of grief, that went on day and night. Perhaps they wanted to prevent him from ever telling his story: who he was, where his home lay, how it came about that he was taken. Perhaps they cut out the tongue of every cannibal they took, as a punishment' (23). The fact that Friday has been enslaved and abused is of no concern to Cruso. In explaining the removal of the tongue there is a double projection of the Other, always already a cannibal (a threat to order and stability) yet always already denied a voice, a story of his own, which would no doubt dispute the official imposed history of his life. Friday is not a person here, but a *topos*, a constant, constructed theme or concept; he is 'a set of references, a congeries of characteristics, that seems to have its origin in a quotation, or a fragment of a text, or a citation'.[16] Friday is defined by the discourses of colonialism, i.e., endlessly cited and circulated misinformation about the Other, a slave who Cruso thinks is better off under a so-called 'lenient master' (23).

In the second, longest section of the book, the format changes to a mixed journal and epistolary mode. Susan and Friday have survived their rescue from the island, but Cruso has died. Susan is now known to be married to Cruso, under the advice of the rescuing ship's captain, and she is lodging with Friday in London (he has a bed in a cellar). Susan's texts are all addressed indirectly or directly to a writer called Foe (a play on the name Defoe,[17] and also, of course, a word that means 'enemy'). Her adoption of the journal/epistolary mode is not only mimetic of *Robinson Crusoe's* journal, but it is also a direct parody of the 'sentimental' eighteenth-century novels of Samuel Richardson, the most well known being his *Pamela* (1740), a novel innovative in its attempt to represent immediacy, i.e., writing of events as they happen or immediately afterwards. Susan is now trying to get Foe to rewrite her 'limping' narrative, to 'set it right' (47). The irony in this section of *Foe* is that as Susan denies her abilities, she writes a fascinating narrative of her time in London and an intriguing description of the writer, who maintains his distance from her. Susan is fascinated by the diverse contents of Foe's storage chest, which contains the raw materials for his literary productions, including 'a multitude of castaway narratives', which again appears to demean her own account, though she is quick to add that 'most of them, I would guess, [are] riddled with lies' (50). For Susan, the question of authenticity makes her own castaway narrative more important than those others that have been embellished and fictionalized in advance. But without the supplementary embellishment of the novel writer, she feels that her own existence is ghost-like, without substance, and this is an issue which will be re-encountered in the next section on *Wide Sargasso Sea*. There is the possibility that Susan's insubstantiality is an effect not just of Coetzee's narrative strategies and literary devices, but also due to her intertextual relationship with *Robinson Crusoe*; where, in *Foe*, Susan says that she felt like 'a ghost behind the true body of Cruso' (51) this may also be read as the potentially adjacent statement, almost identical but a repetition with a difference: she felt like 'a ghost behind the true body of Robinson Crusoe'. Susan is caught up in a plot that already exists, a type of predestination,[18] but she is also disruptive of that plot, embroiling it by making undecidable a series of otherwise clear-cut oppositions: authentic and inauthentic stories, well-written (lies) and poorly written (truth) texts, multiplicity (the myriad castaway narratives) and singularity (her narrative), the actual (stone memorials) and the projected (the memorial that Cruso did not write). The second part of the novel thus gains a surreal quality the more it attempts to narrate what 'actually' happened: both the accounts of the island life and Susan's everyday accounts become more and more bizarre. In the latter, Susan encounters a young woman who claims to be her lost daughter, a dead baby girl, and Friday becomes like a child to her; Foe goes into hiding when the bailiffs come after him, and Susan and Friday initially occupy his empty house before setting off for Bristol, where Susan intends on releasing Friday back into freedom and

Africa. At Bristol she learns that all she will achieve is to send Friday back into slavery, as she cannot find an honest seaman who will take him home. In this second section of the novel a dream-like quality (Susan's projections of the past and the future) becomes even more foregrounded with a short sequence in which Susan takes her *doppelgänger* (the women who claims to be her daughter and also claims the name 'Susan Barton') into Epping Forest:

In the darkest heart of the forest I halt. 'Let us rest again,' I say. I take her cloak from me and spread it over the leaves. We sit. 'Come to me,' I say, and put an arm around her. A light trembling runs through her body. It is the second time I have allowed her to touch me. 'Close your eyes,' I say. It is so quiet that we can hear the brushing of our clothes, the grey stuff of hers against the black stuff of mine. Her head lies on my shoulder. In a sea of fallen leaves we sit, she and I, two substantial beings.

   'I have brought you here to tell you of your parentage,' I commence. 'I do not know who told you that your father was a brewer from Deptford who fled to the Low Countries, but the story is false. Your father is a man named Daniel Foe. He is the man who set you to watching the house in Newington. Just as it was he who told you I am your mother, I will vouch he is the author of the story of the brewer. He maintains whole regiments in Flanders.' (90–1)

It is not clear if this part of the narrative describes one of Susan's dreams, because immediately after it she wakes 'in the grey of a London dawn' (91). The two paragraphs juxtapose two ontological frameworks: the first, that of verisimilitude and 'substantiality' constructed through minor everyday details (the projected or asserted paradigm of the new English novel); and the second, that of falsehoods, fiction, lies and 'insubstantiality' (how the new English novel was actually written). Susan herself partakes of the realization of substantiality via sensuality, by simply touching, and later kissing, her *doppelgänger*, and then she partakes of a de-realization as she tells this impostor that the stories of her childhood are fabrications, constructed by Foe. The great irony here is that Foe takes over Susan's story, but she herself – thought of as Roxanna – is a character from another Defoe novel.[19]

   The third section of the novel finally brings Susan and Friday into contact with Foe. This section is the most obviously self-reflexive, with Foe and Susan having a debate about fictionality, ownership of narrative, and the possibilities of Friday finding a language of his own. The section also foregrounds questions concerning gender and the role of the 'female muse', the latter seen as partaking of a sexual economy both desired by the male author and also feared as an attack upon masculine control and dominance. Spivak notes that Susan 'wants to "father" her story into history, with Mr. Foe's help'.[20] It is not entirely clear whether Coetzee is problematizing this notion, and for Spivak this opens up a space for critique: 'Coetzee has trouble negotiating a gendered position; he and the text strain to make the trouble noticeable. This text will not defend itself against the undecidability and discomfort of imagining a woman.'[21] If *Foe* writes back against the canon, then the question of gender becomes central; in some ways this makes the interaction with *Roxana* more crucial than that of the interaction with *Robinson Crusoe*, and the 'ease' with which two male authors represent female protagonists needs further analysis. Spivak provides this analysis with her questioning of the tropes deployed by Coetzee: 'Is that authoritative word *father* being turned into a false but useful analogy (catachresis) here? Or is Coetzee's Susan being made to operate a traditional masculist topos of reversal and making Foe "gestate?" We cannot know.'[22] The indeterminacy, I argue, is an effect of embroilment, precisely a disruption of the opposition that Woolf most famously argued for in *Robinson Crusoe*, with the separation of 'the important and lasting side of things' from 'the passing and the trivial' when it comes to Defoe's representation of women.[23] The third section of the novel has received much critical attention concerning the attempt to teach Friday how to communicate through written English. Friday appears supremely resistant to this attempt, which may be read as a resistance to being given the language of colonialism and of reinterpretation (i.e., it is the language which calls or interpolates the Other as 'a cannibal' or 'a savage', and so on).[24] Thieme notes parallels here between Susan and Marlow in Conrad's *Heart of Darkness*, where Friday's story is a 'puzzle or hole in the narrative' (121) which can also be read as 'an absence in the signifying systems with which she [Susan] is familiar, in much the same way as the anonymous African's of *Heart of Darkness* belong to a discursive universe that lies beyond Marlow's comprehension. She appreciates that he is a colonial Other who has been constructed from outside because of his lack of access to language.'[25] The novel resists a liberal humanist resolution or closure, moving, in the fourth and final short section, to a condensed and overdetermined section of text. The location and the time of the final narrative appear to be highly unstable. How is this possible? The first-person narrator appears to be observing Susan, Foe and Friday in their room, but the characters are old and fragile, as if they had died: 'The skin, dry as paper, is stretched tight over their bones. Their lips have receded, uncovering their teeth, so that they seem to be smiling' (153). This mysterious first-person narrator listens close up to the sleeping Friday's mouth: '. . . I begin to hear the faintest faraway roar: as she said, the roar of waves in a seashell; and over that, as if once or twice a violin-string were touched, the whine of the wind and the cry of a bird' (154). Bizarrely, from the mute Friday, come the sounds of the island. But then, in a new part of section four, there appears a shift in time: 'At one corner of the house, above head-height, a plaque is bolted to the wall. *Daniel Defoe, Author*, are the words, white on blue, and then more writing too small to read' (155). The blue plaque is a marker from contemporary times of the place where Defoe lived in London; such plaques are common across the city. But the narrative *Foe* is contemporaneous with Defoe's life and times (the eighteenth century), so how can the narrative

suddenly shift to the twentieth century? The narrative appears to be repeating itself, with the first-person narrator again entering the room where
Foe, Susan and Friday are lodging. The narrator just has time to read a
letter from Susan before suddenly slipping overboard, the juxtaposition of
the room and a boat being immediate and shocking. The narrator is now
surrounded by 'the petals cast by Friday' (155), in other words, the ritual
that Friday performs on the island, described earlier in the novel. From
blue plaque to Foe's room to Friday's ritual, the time has shifted from the
modern day, back to the eighteenth century and then back to an earlier
plot sequence within *Foe*. Anachronisms continue, with the narrator diving
into a wrecked ship, the seawater thick with mud 'like the mud of Flanders,
in which generations of grenadiers now lie dead' (156). The time has
shifted, via this analogy, to the memory of the First World War, and
then to a vision of Susan Barton drowned, swollen with water, and then
Friday, out of whose mouth watery syllables emerge in a powerful but slow
stream (157).

The imagery of this final section of the novel is reminiscent of Samuel
Beckett's play *Not I* (1973), where 'Mouth' bursts forth a stream of words,
while 'Auditor' is mute, making gestures only, in an adjacent, possibly
connected realm.[26] The analogy is not as far-fetched as might at first seem,
since the play is about the imposition of authorship upon one's subjectivity
in a form of torture (the gendered performance itself), and a form of displacement and denial of voice (the so-called Auditor). This works well
given Spivak's concern with what she calls *Foe's* message, where 'the impossible politics of overdetermination (mothering, authoring, giving voice to
the native "in" the text; a white male South African writer engaging in
such inscriptions "outside" the text) should not be regularized into a blithe
continuity, where the European redoes the primitive's project in herself.'[27]
From a pedagogic perspective, this leads to four interpretive possibilities
suggested by Spivak:

1. Correcting Defoe's imagination of the marginal in comradeship
2. Reinscribing the white woman as agent, as the asymmetrical double of
   the author. (I think the problems with the figure of 'fathering' mark this
   asymmetry)
3. Situating the politics of overdetermination as aporia
4. Halting before Friday, since for him, here, now, *and* for Susan Barton, *and* for
   Daniel Foe, that is the arbitrary name of the withheld limit.[28]

These four points can be thought-through again as counter discursive possibilities. Thus, the correction of Defoe's representation of the 'marginal in
comradeship' is given a limit by Coetzee, one in which the counter-
discursive result is that the representation of the Other is deferred for
another time and place. The 'asymmetrical double of the author' functions
counter-discursively to reveal that authorship and authenticity are always
already over-compensated for in the power struggles that are the domain

of auto/biographical discourses. Recognition of the 'aporia' (the irresolvable contradiction) of the 'politics of overdetermination' is to hold narratives and their historico-political contexts open for further indigenous counter-discursive analysis. Finally, the 'arbitrary name' Friday, which stands in for the 'withheld limit', is recognized as the (Lacanian) Real of the text. Thieme puts this more clearly:

> Through this labyrinthine series of twists and turns . . . [*Foe*] refuses, however, to do one thing: to speak for black subjectivity. All three endings of *Foe* conclude with Friday seemingly on the threshold of entering into language, but in each case his utterance is left outside the verbal mode of the fiction, with the white South African author who is finally its originator demonstrating his sensitivity to the need to give voice to silenced black subjectivity, but refusing to attempt to render such discourse himself.[29]

To 'halt before Friday' is thus to hand over the task of postcolonial representation, simultaneously dismantling some of the codes and conventions of canonical aesthetics, which continue otherwise to situate a western vision of indigenous peoples.

READING WIDE SARGASSO SEA

As a work of counter-discursive force, Jean Rhys's *Wide Sargasso Sea* has been called 'one of the canonical texts of postcolonial studies'.[30] Summarizing a wide range of postcolonial readings, John J. Su notes that '[p]revious criticism has explored how the novel's intertextuality succeeds in "breaking the master narrative" of *Jane Eyre* specifically and the British imperial project more generally by giving the suppressed Bertha Mason a voice, giving her a different name (Antoinette), relocating the action to the West Indies, and changing the frame of reference.'[31] The technical term which is used in this quotation for the relationship between the two novels is 'intertextuality' – that is, a process that describes the ways in which texts are composed of allusions to, memories of, and characters, images and quotations from other texts. In counter-discursive writing, intertextuality is used in an obvious or pronounced way, creating parallels between texts, telling the story again from a different angle or perspective, rewriting conclusions and the ethics of a text, critiquing either subtly or overtly the canonical text(s) in question. Clearly, these processes just described are complementary and may take place in an overall intertextual relationship to a lesser or greater extent. Put another way, counter-discursive writing is a 'critical constellation', to use a term from Walter Benjamin: a clustering of related concepts and processes. Ashcroft, Griffiths and Tiffin note that the 'subversion of a canon is not simply a matter of replacing one set of texts with another. This would be radically to simplify what is implicit in the idea of canonicity itself.'[32] The point being made is that 'the canon' is not simply composed of particular texts, but is 'a set of reading practices';[33]

counter-discursive texts are directly intertextual (e.g., there might be a character drawn from one novel present in the later novel) and represent a mode of reading, that is, contribute to and guide the 'reading practices' of the new postcolonial canon. Is such a process restricted purely to postcolonial studies? Wider ethical processes are at work whereby 'narrative assists ethics'.[34] Su summarizes three main ways in which this assistance takes place: '. . . first, it [narrative] provides a description of the world that we could not otherwise have, thereby making us more likely to empathize with the values and needs of others . . . second, it acts against the abuses of ritualized commemoration by offering the opportunity of "telling otherwise" . . . third, it exposes the ambiguities and aporias of any ethical project.'[35] In the following summary of *Wide Sargasso Sea*, I will be examining how the novel and its readers generate an ethical bond with *Jane Eyre*.

The unnamed 'I' who narrates the first section of *Wide Sargasso Sea* is Antoinette, the first wife of Rochester, hidden away in the attic in *Jane Eyre*. The opening sentences of Rhys's novel are a series of negations: 'They say when trouble comes close ranks, and so the white people did. But we were not in their ranks. The Jamaican ladies had never approved of my mother.'[36] The negative word 'trouble' is enhanced by the negation of being outside of the closed ranks, and being the subject, indirectly, of disapproval. This series of negations, a kind of 'absolute negativity',[37] foreshadows Antoinette's formation as a subject via Rochester: 'In her relationship with Rochester, Antoinette, unlike Jane Eyre, can make sense of her experiences only through a ceaseless chain of negations. Before she can assert herself she must engage in a long and losing battle to make Rochester unlearn what he already knows about her.'[38] The negations continue via the ironic naming of the landscape: Antoinette's neighbour Mr Luttrell commits suicide, leaving his property called 'Nelson's Rest' untended; the allusion to Viscount Nelson (1758–1805) is unmistakable, thus giving the opening paragraphs an echo of Britain's colonial past in more ways than one, although Antoinette then compares her garden to the Garden of Eden, recruiting an even more canonical text as her guide. As Sylive Maurel argues:

Named after one of Britain's heroes who fought the Napoleonic wars and opposed the abolition of the slave trade, Lutrell's plantation is a clear inscription of the Empire's coercive power and of the colonizer's self-proclaimed legitimacy: after territorial conquest, he is entitled to a well-earned 'rest'. . . . 'Nelson's Rest' is then a case of misnaming through which Jean Rhys exposes what David Punter calls 'the colonial arbitrary', the imposition of arbitrary labellings on the reality of the colony, which, Jean Rhys intimates, is yet another form of violence.[39]

The negations continue with the description of the character Christophine, who speaks differently ('Not adieu as we said it'), whose songs are different ('Her songs were not like Jamaican songs') and who is not like other women (20). The fact of her 'blackness', however, switches from negative to positive, and then becomes a sign of her power, foreshadowing her later use of magic. While critics such as Spivak focus on Christophine's commodification, Maurel stresses the potential power that Christophine has in the wider indigenous community: '. . . thanks to her occult and awe-inspiring activities as obeah woman, she is a figure of power.'[40] While both Antoinette and Christophine are inserted into the text through their apparent absolute negativity, this process reveals their role within the narrative as 'a structural rather than marginal issue' in their diverse culutures.[41]

One way of reading this shift toward the structural is via the gothic mode; counter-discursive postcolonial writers do not just write back via character and plot, but also via genre. The gothic novel has long been noted for its performance of gender: '. . . moving from early eighteenth-century stereotypes of the heroine to twentieth-century interrogations of domesticity and patriarchy, the Gothic has always enabled discussion and representation at various levels of female sexuality, transgression, and gender-based boundary blurring.'[42] What Rhys has achieved is the wresting of a 'gothic' character out of her subservient and marginal position in *Jane Eyre* (echoed and shadowed by the apparent notion of Christophine), recasting the gothic genre as a postcolonial mode of writing. It is essential to stress, however, that the metaphor of 'embroiling narratives' still holds with *Wide Sargasso Sea*: the ghosting of characters, their apparent doubling and shadowing of one another, reveals that the gothic retains its ability to disturb and thrill the reader, even when it is used strategically. An example early on in the novel is that of Antoinette's friendship with the young girl called 'Tia'. Tia wishes to gain possession of some coins and challenges Antoinette to perform a somersault underwater; Antoinette takes up the challenge and then gets the following response: 'Tia laughed and told me that it certainly look like I drown dead that time. Then she picked up the money' (24). The statement appears to indicate that Tia wanted Antoinette dead so that she could take the money; she takes the money anyway and then derides Antoinette after she has been insulted by her, called a 'cheating nigger' (24). Tia turns the tables, putting Antoinette in her place in terms of economics and race, then silently stealing Antoinette's dress, becoming a more successful and sharper *doppelgänger*. Tia returns to haunt Antoinette in the third and final section of the novel, with its 'sudden and sweeping accretion of hybrid Jamaican images in the final segment culminating in the vision of the black girl Tia and a single, terrified utterance of her name'.[43] As Romita Choudhury argues: 'It is as if Antoinette has glimpsed the failed possibility of achieving a composite identity. In this moment of exteriority, it cannot be forgotten that she has once before seen her own bruised and bloody face in that of Tia.'[44] The uncanny shifting of identities between Antoinette and Tia, and the 'failure' of the composite identity (i.e., the isolation of being divorced from community and indigenous culture), is foreshadowed in the projection of Bertha Mason as the 'inhuman' in *Jane Eyre*. There are a myriad ways of reading Charlotte

Brontë's depiction of Bertha Mason, but one powerful, uncanny image is that of the vampire, transmuted in *Wide Sargasso Sea* into the figure of the zombie. In *Jane Eyre*, the power of the western interpretive gaze is indicated in the competing descriptions of Bertha Mason (Jane regards her as a vampire; Rochester regards her as a beauty);[45] in *Wide Sargasso Sea*, the switch to the zombie metaphor shifts the text from one driven by exterior interpretation to that of direct and indirect control of interior subjectivity. Now there are competing 'controllers': Rochester and Christophine, the latter performing obeah or magic, which leads to a chiastic embroiling of conscious and unconscious:

> . . . the various narrative dislocations of the novel function primarily as a conve-
> nient figural representation of the permeable boundaries of the characters' uncon-
> scious, and the sudden shifts in focalization provide an aesthetically useful osmotic
> shock to the actual process of reading insofar as they serve to reinforce the more
> pervasive thematics of destabilization. But significantly, the scrimmage for control
> of the unconscious process in the intratextual realm of character is also repeated
> in the intertextual relation of *Wide Sargasso Sea* and *Jane Eyre*. Indeed, of all the
> elaborate parallels between the two novels, the most interesting doublings concern
> the dreams of the central characters and the ways in which the dreams of Antoi-
> nette and Rochester encroach upon the dreams of Jane and vice versa.[46]

The 'intratextual realm' of *Wide Sargasso Sea* is precisely the uncanny doubling and ghosting that occurs throughout the novel, which can be thought of as the embroiling of characters just as the *intertextual* realm is an embroiling of narratives. *Wide Sargasso Sea*, while in many respects unravelling from a radically different or other perspective an otherwise preordained story (its canonical forebear), is a powerful, moving novel in its own right.

THE IMPACT OF *FOE* AND
WIDE SARGASSO SEA

Coetzee and Rhys have produced an extensive body of fiction and non-fiction that has influenced the ways in which critics read postcolonial literatures. This influence extends in myriad directions, including crucial advances in feminist criticism. As Carine Melkom Mardorossian argues concerning *Wide Sargasso Sea*, 'the novel itself played an important role in the evolution of feminist critical trends.'[47] Other critical intersections include theoretical advances and debates concerning the political representations of events and regimes, such as the colonialist project in general or more specific instances and structures, such as apartheid South Africa. While some critics have argued *against* Coetzee for not appearing to directly represent South Africa from the perspective of the dispossessed, others argue that he does achieve this via sophisticated strategies of writing, thus: 'Coetzee's art seeks for itself the task of bearing witness to "the abundance of real suffering" engendered by apartheid – and more broadly by the history of colonialism, the larger context within which Coetzee has insisted South African apartheid must be understood.'[48] What both of these quotations suggest is that while critical readings of *Foe* and *Wide Sargasso Sea* have transmuted over the years, the novels themselves remain key texts. Mardorossian's analytical survey of feminist criticism and *Wide Sargasso Sea* reveals these transmutations, although she does argue that they cannot be solely explained 'as a result of the complexities of her [Rhys's] work':[49]

The interpretation of feminist novels as the struggle of a heroine against oppressive patriarchal forces was soon scrutinized and criticized for positing a distinctive and essential female condition and ignoring the varied circumstances of women's oppression. Such First World and Eurocentric bias was particularly salient in 1970s feminist readings of *Wide Sargasso Sea* that represented Rhys's West Indian protagonist as facing the same sexist constraints and ideologies as the heroine of Brontë's imperial narrative. Antoinette Cosway and Jane Eyre were seen as two sides of the same coin: both victims of the workings of a homogeneous system of sexual domination. By the mid-80s, however, the recognition that race, ethnicity, class, and nationality functioned as interlocking systems of oppression and formed a 'matrix of domination' . . . disrupted the monolithic category of Woman these readings postulated. A new paradigm examining the articulation of gender along the axes of race, class, and nationality emerged and effectively displaced previous interpretations.[50]

The ambivalences in Rhys's novel, read as deconstructive or poetic imagery, or simply signifying an uncertainty or even replication of images and structures of oppression, are such that the jury is still out: 'What has now become a subject of debate among Rhys critics . . . is whether Rhys herself meant to highlight the ways in which racist assumptions permeate her two main characters' perceptions of the black Creoles or whether these stereotypical notions are present in the text because the author herself – albeit unconsciously – adhered to them.'[51] Nevertheless, while *Wide Sargasso Sea* may have come under recent fire, it still remains a 'cult text' (to use Spivak's phrase) for feminist and postcolonial debate precisely because it, like *Foe*, is such a 'strong instance' of a mode of 'literary resistance'.[52] One of the dangers, however, in comparing and contrasting two such instances is that their differences will be effaced or subsumed into a general reading driven by theoretical demands rather than close reading and the reading experience itself. This chapter ends, then, with Samuel Durrant's insistence that *Foe* and *Wide Sargasso Sea* are fundamentally different, since Coetzee 'does not attempt to recover the voice of the colonized other'.[53] Durrant argues that *Foe* is an attempt to 'remember the silencing' of the Other, where Susan bears witness to this silencing.[54] Two counter-discursive novels can thus share writing-back strategies, articulated, however, in different ways: the *mise-en-abyme* of representation in *Wide Sargasso Sea* (articulated through various 'waves' of feminisms) does, in my reading, share some affinity with the paradoxical but absolutely necessary remembrance of silencing in *Foe*.

3 Alternative Historiographies
Chinua Achebe's *Things Fall Apart*

Reflecting on the personal significance of Nigerian novelist Chinua Achebe's *Things Fall Apart* (1958), critic Simon Gikandi notes that for him it represented a 'transformative' moment that has wider implications:

> . . . there is consensus that *Things Fall Apart* was important for the marking and making of that exciting first decade of decolonization. There also seems to be consensus that the production of the novel, as well as its reading and (re)reading, and its circulation within the institutions of education, came to define who we were, where we were, and as Achebe himself would say, where the rain began to beat us.[1]

Gikandi realizes, and confesses, that his response is generational, in other words, that his personal *experience* of the 'irruption into the world'[2] of this transformative novel is different to that of younger scholars and readers, and to those who argue for a more complex causal structure to African literary history. For Gikandi,

> . . . the more I reread the works of such figures as René Maran, Amos Tutuola, Paul Hazoumé, and Sol Plaatje, the more I am convinced of their significance in the foundation of an African tradition of letters. Still, none of these writers had the effect Achebe had on the establishment and reconfiguration of an African literary tradition; none were able to enter and interrupt the institutions of exegesis and education the same way he did; none were able to establish the terms by which African literature was produced, circulated, and interpreted.[3]

Critical debates concerning the extent to which the publication of *Things Fall Apart* is a postcolonial 'inaugural' moment may reach one consensus: that the novel continues nearly four decades later to serve as a fascinating and powerful entry point into 'African' writing in English.[4] Such a task, however, not only places enormous demands upon the novel – i.e., what readers want to learn from the novel – but it also leads to intense debates concerning the *types* of knowledge that a fictional work can or should communicate to its readers. In turn, this leads to further debates about the mode of knowledge delivery, especially in relation to the ways in which postcolonial novels assert difference from colonial or external accounts of African culture. The genre of realism has become central to these debates, where realism claims to represent the everyday world (non-literary discourses, events and experiences) faithfully and accurately, and has to be continually recoded from an indigenous perspective, discarding and reject- ing colonial or external bias and ideological distortion. This competition in effect for the rights to realism reveals its inherently unstable and perfor- mative nature.

Ato Quayson notes how '[t]he assumption that realism shares a com- munity of values with other non-literary discourses was particularly impor- tant in the general conceptions of the role of literature in the newly emergent African nations.'[5] In other words, an entire range of writings which rejected colonial rule needed to have the authority to counter and override *imposed notions* of African peoples and place; without recourse to an empirical basis, it is possible that these new writings would not have made such an impact. But, as Quayson points out, such a recourse to the empirical has led in some instances to a reductive critical approach to Achebe's novels:

The confidence Achebe expresses in the realism of his early novels was shared by his critics and led to several critical formations which sought to elucidate the rep- resentationalist aspects of his work. The critical tendency that seemed to take the novels most evidently as in a one-to-one relationship to reality was that which sought to recover anthropological data about the Igbos from the novels. . . . Pre- ceding from such a premise, it is not difficult for . . . [such critics] to conclude that there is very little scenic description [in *Things Fall Apart*] related to the building of mood and atmosphere in the Western sense, and that Achebe's descriptions are used directly for functional rather than for aesthetic purposes.[6]

The stress on 'realism', then, while strategically important within an his- torical context, should not blind the reader to the rhetorical devices or the poetics of Achebe's novel. This conundrum – the precise relationship between a strategic mode of writing, realism and historical veracity or recovery, and the exploration of indigenous belief systems – was explored from a Marxist and Existentialist perspective by Frantz Fanon. In *The Wretched of the Earth* (1961) Fanon calls the above conundrum a 'cultural matrix',[7] indicating that the intellectual or artist writing on the eve of independence has an agonistic relationship not just with his or her colonial education/culture, but also with his or her indigenous education/culture. This agonistic relationship, according to Fanon, goes through three phases: (1) the rejection of indigenous culture in favour of apparently more sophis- ticated Eurocentric or western models; (2) a return to indigenous culture but from an external perspective; and (3) the production of an authentic, new work, which integrates indigenous culture and the lessons learned from actual nationalist struggles. As Fanon puts it: 'When a people under- takes an armed struggle or even a political struggle against a relentless colonialism, the significance of tradition changes.'[8] Fanon's three phases are typically Marxist or Hegelian, consisting of a thesis, antithesis and synthe- sis. The thesis is that the colonialist 'native' is alienated; the antithesis is that the colonialist–educated native's return to tradition is external and alienated; the synthesis is that the perspective or experience of the thesis and antithesis can be transformed by being involved in revolutionary struggle, concomitantly producing a new literature which emerges from the new existential or direct experiences of the rejection of colonialism. Neither a simplistic nostalgic or idealistic return to a past, nor an embracing of the colonial perspective *per se*, a new postcolonial stance is adopted which is not utopian but realistic. The key phrase, in relation here to the study of Achebe, is Fanon's 'the significance of tradition changes'. To return to Simon Gikandi's essay on Achebe, it is possible to re-read his notion of the 'inauguration' of an African literature via *Things Fall Apart* not as purely idealistic hyperbole, but as an existential experience, that is to say, one that triggered a change of personal direction:

> For reading *Things Fall Apart* brought to me the sudden realization that fiction was not merely about a set of texts which one studied for the Cambridge Overseas exam, which, for my generation, had been renamed the East African Certificate of Education; on the contrary, literature was about real and familiar worlds, of culture and human experience, of politics and economics, now re-routed through a language and structure that seemed at odds with the history or geography books we were reading at the time.[9]

READING *THINGS FALL APART*

Introduced immediately to the protagonist of the novel, the reader is also plunged into the workings of his Umuofian society: 'Okonkwo was well known throughout the nine villages and even beyond.'[10] The reasons for his fame are revealed: he has brought honour to his village by winning a wrestling match with a great wrestler called 'Amalinze the Cat', and he has wealth, three wives, two titles, and has 'shown incredible prowess in two inter-tribal wars' (6). It is important to pay close attention to *how* the narrator presents this information: in-between being told of Okonkwo's wrestling skills and his other achievements is interpolated a narrative concerning his father, a man who was a failure in life through laziness, ending heavily in debt at his death. Okonkwo's success is thus not only contrasted with, but contextualized by, the story of his father's failure; the two narratives are intertwined, and later the reader learns that this is an early foreshadowing of Okonkwo's ultimate downfall. The first chapter of the novel reveals not just information about character, but also the way in which such information circulates and is added to by a primarily oral culture. The technical name for this process (as written) is parataxis, which literally means 'to arrange side-by-side'. Okonkwo's story is arranged side-by-side with his father's, embedding Okonkwo in a familial structure, where one's ancestor's actions are as important as the events or present-day reality. But there is further arrangement of information in the opening chapter: not just characterization, but cultural information. Rather than suggesting that the novel is presenting an anthropological account of

Umuofian culture, it can be seen that this contextualizing material is the substrate or ground upon which the actual story and its characters are being constructed. Ato Quayson theorizes the text's structural complexities, arguing that it has two simultaneous levels:

> At one level, the novel concerns itself with a description of Umuofian culture and its subversion by the contact with Western imperialism. This level of the novel can be perceived as metonymic of an Igbo or African reality. In Jakobsonian terms, the narrative progresses metonymically, with narrative elements selected for attention because they exist in discernible contiguous relation to one another. Significantly, however, the text frequently departs from the overarching narrative of the fall of Okonkwo and the division of the clan to pursue numerous anecdotes and digressions that are demonstrably not related to the main narrative but embody subtle qualifications of it. Furthermore, within the context of the unfolding events, the narrative generates a secondary level of conceptualization that can be seen as symbolic/metaphorical. This level subtends the metonymic text but gathers around itself all the antinomies associated with metaphor: ambiguity, contradiction, irony, and paradox.[11]

Put more simply, at the first level the story progresses in a linear fashion, but is interrupted by digressions – the parataxis – which add subtlety and amplify the reader's knowledge of the society depicted. At the second level, however (that of the generation of symbolic meaning), there is a certain marking-off or bracketing of the first level, suggesting that the interpretation of the text's realism must be supplemented and almost supplanted by the rhetorical strategies of the symbolic text. Quayson performs such an interpretation by examining the representation of gender in the novel:

> . . . in totally focalizing the narrative through Okonkwo and the male-dominated institutions of Umuofia, the novel itself implies a patriarchal discourse within which women, and much of what they can be taken to represent in the novel, are restricted to the perceptual fringes. In spite of this demonstrable patriarchy, however, Okonkwo is at various times ironized by the text suggesting the inadequacy of the values he represents and ultimately those of the hierarchy that ensures his social status.[12]

An example of the 'levels' at work in the representation of women and the patriarchal discourse of the novel is Okonkwo beating his wife for not returning home in time to cook his meal. He beats her mercilessly, even though interrupted by his other two wives, who alert him to the fact that it is the 'Week of Peace' prior to the planting of the yams, and that he is breaking a taboo with his violence: 'His first two wives ran out in great alarm pleading with him that it was the sacred week. But Okonkwo was not the man to stop beating somebody half-way through, not even for fear of a goddess' (21). Okonkwo's violence is gendered: he does not fear his wife, and neither does he fear a 'goddess'; the breaking of the taboo – that violence should not occur during the Week of Peace – is represented as a particularly masculine occurrence. Okonkwo is punished, however, via the judgement of the priest of the earth goddess Ani. Okonkwo retains his outward appearance of invincibility while inwardly 'he was repentant' (22). The village then debate the crime that he has committed and the merits of harsher and lighter punishments. The representation of gender in this passage is more complex than first appears. Okonkwo *appears* to be punished for his 'masculinist' breaking of a 'feminine' rule. However, the punishment is revealed to be inordinately light, and the priest concurs that Okonkwo's wife 'was at fault' (22) in her actions. Furthermore, while inwardly repentant, Okonkwo's hard exterior is what is presented to the community as a whole, who will interpret his reaction to his punishment accordingly. The apparent critique of male aggression in this passage thus masks the overarching patriarchy that lays down the law and fails to deal adequately with its transgression, even though the goddess Ani is later portrayed as 'the ultimate judge of morality and conduct' (26). The overall symbolic effect generated by the passage reveals that there are checks and balances within the organizational structure of the community, checks and balances that can constrain male aggression; the closer reading reveals that such a symbolic reading is in itself suspect (from a feminist perspective) because of the ongoing pattern of resistance to constraint, manifested by Okonkwo.

Critics have long debated the balance of history and myth presented in *Things Fall Apart*. The novel's three main parts appear to take the reader from a pre-colonial-contact world, through initial contact (in the form of Christianity) and then to post-contact, with the suicide of Okonkwo and the breakdown of indigenous belief and governance systems. In a formal sense, this tripartite structure could be regarded as representing the larger-scale history of colonialism; focusing more closely on the actual text, the customs and belief systems it explores and represents, the tripartite structure specifically explores events in Nigeria. Some critics, such as Wole Ogundele, have argued that *Things Fall Apart* actually portrays a 'culture' rather than a history: 'As such, the narrative weight is more on filling a cultural canvas with the way it was than on dramatizing the historical evolution of that way.'[13] Again, focusing on the tripartite structure of the book, Ogundele notes that the novel is heavily weighted to the first part, with its thirteen chapters (compared with six chapters each for parts two and three), the significance being that the novel is weighted toward cultural description and analysis:

Part one is about religious beliefs and the rituals and festivals that go with them, about social norms and etiquette, even about the cultural economy of agriculture. It is also about political and social institutions, prominent among which are marriage and family. All these are grounded in daily rounds of activities and human emotions presented through the narrative technique of verisimilitude. There is also a strong element of psychological realism to the characters, for the author is able to step out of his own time most of the time, enter into their minds, and present their world from their own perspective. All these give the novel the exterior of a factual narrative. In short, we have in this first part a narrative of the way of life of a pre-colonial African society that appears to be very historically authentic.[14]

In analysing the novel from a narratological perspective, Ogundele registers the balance between interior and exterior perspectives. From the 'interior' perspective, the reader gains access to the individuals who form part of a community; but, apart from Okonkwo, there is no extended psychological or existential analysis, precisely because of the fact that everyday life is a communal event, and personal decisions *always* have a corporate impact – *and vice versa*. An example is the exchange system developed for correcting a 'wrong', most vividly portrayed early on in the novel by the murder of Ogbuefi Udo's wife in the Mbaino market. Rather than endure a war which they fear that they would lose, the Mbaino offer a young woman and a young man to the people of Umuofia, the young man living for three years with Okonkwo. In this instance, the murder of a woman has led to the possibility of conflict between two entire communities. An individual's misfortune has the potential to impact upon a huge number of people. The community responds by sending two other individuals, who become in effect scapegoats, and the communities are safe. But the story does not end there. After three years the 'Oracle of the Hills and the Caves' (40) demands that the young man, Ikemefuna, should be killed. Okonkwo takes part in his murder, and afterwards regrets this decision. The apparent senselessness of Ikemefuna's death, ostensibly for the continuation of the communal good, impacts upon the individuals once again. There are various ways of interpreting this circuit of integration between the individual and the community. One way is to think of this as reflecting the harmonious and organic rhythms of the community. As David Carroll argues, such rhythm is expressed through Achebe's 'sensitive' control of narrative voice: 'The voice is that of a wise and sympathetic elder of the tribe who has witnessed time and time again the cycle of the seasons and the accompanying rituals in the villages. This measured tone of voice implants in the reader's mind the sense of order, perspective, and harmony whose later destruction is most poignant.'[15] But is this an historical voice? Carroll argues that what is important here is not so much where on an historical index this narrative appears (i.e., closer to 'myth' or closer to 'history'), but rather the way in which the narratological strategies are radically different from the codes and conventions of European fiction. Thus, Achebe's narrator is a 'mediator' between the views of the individual and those of the community, whereas canonical European fiction creates 'individual introspection' as the norm.[16] Why is this such a crucial point to make? Because an historical account of the Umuofian way of life, presented from a European perspective, utilizing European modes of analysis and representation, is precisely what Achebe is resisting. Carroll calls the tribal perspective a 'dialectic', that is to say, the constant negotiations between individual and community are portrayed by Achebe as dynamic and in process. Referring to the incident of the *egwugwu* (masked spirits) and their role in resolving a marriage dispute, Carroll notes that '[d]espite the ancient formulae, the ritual exchanges, the apparently inflexible ceremony, this is a very fluid system of negotiation.'[17] It is worth unpacking further this incident in the novel, and Carroll's notion of a dialectic.

The marriage dispute is not *simply* narrated in *Things Fall Apart*; it is preceded not just by the reconstruction of the ceremonial and ritualistic aspects of the gathering of the people and the *egwugwu*, but also by an interpretive narrative voice:

Large crowds began to gather on the village *ilo* [green] as soon as the edge had worn off the sun's heat and it was no longer painful on the body. Most communal ceremonies took place at that time of the day, so that even when it was said that a ceremony would begin 'after the midday meal' everyone understood that it would begin a long time later, when the sun's heat had softened. (62)

With this interpretive narrative voice, the dialectic is already underway: tradition says a meeting will take place at a certain time; reality is that the meeting takes place at a later (cooler) time of day. In the very next paragraph, again the narrator interprets for the reader: 'It was clear from the way the crowd stood or sat that the ceremony was for men' (62). Then we are given the description that follows this interpretation. An iron gong sounds, and a 'powerful flute' blasts out a high-pitched note: 'Then came the voices of the *egwugwu*, guttural and awesome' (62). The women and children respond with a momentary 'backward stampede' and the reader is given to understand that this gendered response is part of the ceremony. Thus, after letting the reader know that this is a purely male ceremony, and that no women have ever seen inside the *egwugwu* house, the narrator comments that 'Okonkwo's wives, and perhaps other women as well, might have noticed that the second *egwugwu* had the springly walk of Okonkwo' (63–4). In other words, the dialectic here is the gendered exchange of action and reaction, the outward appearance of fear and ignorance, matched by the inward certainty and knowledge of the women. But this is not to say that the apparent or visible role the women play is of no consequence for the power structures of the Umuofian world. Eventually, the masked spirit Evil Forest asks Uzowulu, the aggrieved husband in the dispute, to present his case:

'That woman standing there is my wife, Mgbafo. I married her with my money and my yams. I do not owe my in-laws anything. I owe them no yams. I owe them no coco-yams. One morning three of them came to my house, beat me up and took my wife and children away. This happened in the rainy season. I have waited in vain for my wife to return. At last I went to my in-laws and said to them, "You have taken back your sister. I did not send her away. You yourselves took her. The law of the clan is that you should return her bride-price." But my wife's brothers said they had nothing to tell me. So I have brought the matter to the fathers of the clan. My case is finished. I salute you.' (64)

Uzowulu presents his case in economic terms: he makes it clear that he paid the correct bride-price for his wife, that he paid in full and is therefore not a debtor to his wife's family, and he argues that if his wife's family have taken her away from him permanently they should return the bride-price to him. Evil Forest makes no comment beyond the form statement: 'Your words are good', which is immediately balanced by the statement: 'Let us hear Odukwe. His words may also be good' (64). Odukwe verifies the stoy that his brother-in-law, Uzowulu, was beaten up and his wife removed, and that the bride-price has not been repaid. But Odukwe takes another tactic, refusing to couch the events in purely economic terms. He says: 'My in-law, Uzowulu, is a beast. My sister lived with him for nine years. During those years no single day passed in the sky without his beating the woman' (65). Odukwe tells how Uzowulu assaulted his pregnant wife, causing a miscarriage, and how later she had to flee her husband to save her own life. Evil Forest then gathers more witness statements, and the *egwugwu* go back to their house to consult with one another. The judgement is cunningly simple: Uzowulu is to return with his in-laws to his wife with a pot of wine, and he is to beg for her return, but spliced in with this judgment is the more important one that '[i]t is not bravery when a man fights with a woman' (66), which, coming from the *egwugwu*, is a powerful command for Uzowulu's future behaviour. Carroll argues that there is a 'refusal to rely upon absolute principles of law'[18] in the justice of the *egwugwu*; in other words, the needs of the community are balanced with that of the disputants. The decentred approach to justice, and the needs of the wider community, is both a strength and a weakness: in the next section of the novel, the beginnings of colonial rule, prefaced by the arrival of Christianity, are facilitated precisely by the flexibility of Umuofian society, which allows (at least in the first instance) the co-existence of another ideological group.

Critics have been concerned with how far *Things Fall Apart* is 'historical' in the widest sense. I have been suggesting that what is more important than where we place this novel on some kind of myth–history continuum is the reorientation that takes place in the first part of the novel, whereby the reader is taken out of a (possibly) Eurocentric frame of mind and into the Umuofian frame of mind, to gain insight into Igbo life. Wole Ogundele argues that part one of *Things Fall Apart* cannot be historical because 'the time markers and other indices suggest a more mythical . . . narrative.'[19] This is a narrative which portrays a 'fictional' society where 'mythical stasis, rather than social stability, prevails'.[20] There are two ironies in Ogundele's argument: first, it is argued that the fictional insight into interior subjectivity in the first part of *Things Fall Apart* makes it less historical; and, second, the foregrounding of the first part's fictional status is deemed problematic, even though the book is a novel! But there are some important issues concerning postcolonial history being raised by Ogundele: how far, with the reorientation of the reader's perspective through insight into the Igbo world, where mythical figures and ritual dominate, can the novel make larger or more universal historical claims? For Ogundele, there is an historical turn in the novel, although it is one that introduces *colonial history*, taking the reorientation of part one and reversing it:

> But then, things do begin to change in part two; narrative time speeds up; time markers become more definitive. Chapter fourteen opens this part with Okonkwo's reception by his mother's people. By the next chapter when his friend Obierika visits, he is already in his second year of exile. . . .
> In part three, events career down a steep slope, and narrative time literally skips long tracts of time. Obierika is used in chapter twenty to give a highly compressed account of how far things have fallen apart prior to Okonkwo's return. Three brief chapters later, we are somewhat surprised to learn that he has been back many years. In the next, he silently berates his community for having listened to Egonwanne 'five years ago'. Time as experienced in the novel has decisively changed from the cyclic one in the first part to a linear one. That change carries with it the undertones of a world rushing to an apocalyptic end constituted by four pivotal events and their cause-and-cumulative effect relationship.[21]

What are these four events? Ogundele summarizes: 'the "killing" of an *egwugwu*; the destruction of the [Christian] church; the arrest and detention of Umuofia's elders; and Okonkwo's killing of the District Officer's messenger'.[22] The difference between these events and the events in the first part of the novel are profound. To take one example, Okonkwo's accidental killing of another man, which has led him into temporary exile, is not an irrevocable event because the Umuofian society has inbuilt checks and balances, or customs, which can deal with the occurrence. Again, this process is one of exchange: 'It was a crime against the earth goddess to kill a clansman, and a man who committed it must flee from the land' (87). The crime is gendered, classed as either male or female: 'Okonkwo had committed the female [crime], because it had been inadvertent. He could return to the clan after seven years' (87). Okonkwo is not destroyed by his exile, just significantly delayed in his acquisition of wealth and titles. Events in the later sections of the novel do, however, appear irrevocable, at the level of either the individual (leading to Okonkwo's death) or the society (the intrusive colonial disruption and destruction of the indigenous way of life). It is through accelerating narrative time, and through juxtaposing different ways of measuring time, that Achebe creates the profound feeling of unease in the later parts of the novel. Okonkwo as a 'tragic hero' also crosses two worlds, and his own impatience with the organic, rhythmic time of his indigenous culture, where time itself can be exchanged (i.e., loss of life compensated for by the time of exile, which is a loss of life experience within the community), is ironically met with the accelerated time of colonialism and modernity, where things are now falling apart or changing too quickly.

Closer analysis of the narratological strategies that Achebe utilizes in the different sections of *Things Fall Apart* reveals that the accelerated time of parts two and three are not as straightforwardly progressive as might first appear. This is key to competing understandings of what an 'historical narrative' actually looks like. Ogundele's statement that '[t]ime as experienced in the novel has decisively changed from the cyclic one in the first part to a linear one'[23] is undoubtedly true. But the 'linear' time of parts two and three is actually composed of repetition, foreshadowed in part one. This repetition reveals not a homogeneous colonial power but precisely a heterogeneous power, hard to pin down, and highly effective in its destructiveness. Another way of putting this is to say that the irruption of *colonial* history in the novel does not simply occur once; it occurs again and again, amplifying itself each time, but essentially repeating itself. The founding moment of colonialism is thus a dispersal, not a unified origin, and this will be crucial for colonialism's success in overtaking different cultures through different means. Thus colonial intervention within Africa is different to that within India, in turn different to that within Canada, and so on. This mechanism is subtly revealed by Achebe.

Critics have long pointed to the foreshadowing of colonialism in the first part of the novel and the jokes that accompany it at a betrothal ceremony. The men are discussing the strange habits of their neighbours, where customs are turned upside-down. Obierika says, 'It is like the story of the white men who, they say, are white like this piece of chalk' (51) and who 'have no toes' (52) – i.e., they are wearing shoes. These strange features – white skin and a lack of toes – are turned into a punning joke, when Machi says that he sees one of them frequently called Amadi: 'Those who knew Amadi laughed. He was a leper, and the polite name for leprosy was "the white skin"' (52). This foreshadowing of the irruption of colonialism is complex. Comparing the white men to a piece of chalk is given further significance by the narrator's informational point that Obierika 'held up a piece of chalk, which every man kept in his *obi* [living quarters] and with which his guests drew lines on the floor before they ate Kola nuts' (51–2). In other words, the analogy is composed not just via colour, but also by the very act of boundary-marking: the 'white men' will be eventually given the worst land on which to build their church, not only outside of the home, but outside of the community as a whole; however, the boundaries of what constitute inside and outside will be redrawn by the colonialists, so that their site of danger becomes a site of power. The second analogy, between white men and lepers, created via the polite term for leprosy, 'white skin', creates another possibility: that the colonialists are themselves a disease that will spread rapidly across the land. This foreshadowing works in another way, in that the Christian church will welcome the outcasts of Igbo society as a way of gaining a foothold and expressing moral superiority. As noted, this foreshadowing is not necessarily the foreshadowing of a single event: the irruption of colonialism takes place through repetition and difference. In part two of the novel, Okonkwo discovers that a neighbouring clan has been wiped out. The story begins with the appearance among the Abame of a white man 'riding an iron horse' (97). The elders of the village consult their Oracle and are told that this stranger will 'break their clan and spread destruction among them' (97). The white man is killed and his 'iron horse', or bicycle, is tied to the sacred tree. The Oracle also compares the white man to a locust scouting out for the ones that will follow. Next, three white men appear, observe the bicycle and leave; then the men return on a market day with accomplices, and massacre virtually the entire clan. The discussion that follows this narrative brings back a memory to Obierika: 'We have heard stories about white men who made the powerful guns and the strong drinks and took slaves away across the seas, but no one thought the stories were true' (99). This adds to the complex structure of the irruption of colonialism in the novel: first, a foreshadowing, then an appearance, followed by another appearance, then a third appearance which is the massacre, followed by a reassessment of stories heard earlier. The arrival of Christianity takes a similar structure with, first, two years later, a summary of events: 'The missionaries had come to Umuofia. They had built their church there, won a handful of converts and were already sending evangelists to the surrounding towns and villages' (101). Obierika visits Okonkwo to let him know that his son Nwoye has joined the new church. This leads to a narrative repetition and expansion of the summary:

The arrival of the missionaries had caused a considerable stir in the village of Mbanta. There were six of them and one was a white man. Every man and woman came out to see the white man. Stories about these strange men had grown since one of them had been killed in Abame and his iron horse tied to the sacred silk-cotton tree. And so everybody came to see the white man. (101–2)

While there is undoubted temporal acceleration in this part of the novel, the novel also clearly functions via repetition. Here, the murder of the first white man and the fact that his bicycle was tied to the sacred tree is repeated; this is also an immediate repetition and amplification of the opening of chapter sixteen. As with the earlier foreshadowing, the humour of the pun is echoed here, with the humour generated by the bad translations of the Igbo man who speaks a different dialect: 'Instead of saying "myself" he always said "my buttocks"' (102). The humour is sustained throughout the passage, and lightens the actual subject matter: that the indigenous religious system is being countered with the colonial Christian system. The reception of the missionaries, while humorous, is not straight-forward, as the narrator reveals the differences between Okonkwo's and his son Nwoye's responses. First, Okonkwo is convinced that the mission-aries are mad. This response is countered with a radically different one from Nwoye:

But there was a young lad who had been captivated. His name was Nwoye, Okonkwo's first son. It was not the mad logic of the Trinity that captivated him. He did not understand it. It was the poetry of the new religion, something felt in the marrow. The hymn about the brothers who sat in darkness and in fear seemed to answer a vague and persistent question that haunted his young soul – the question of the twins crying in the bush and the question of Ikemefuna who was killed. He felt a relief within as the hymn poured into his parched soul. The words of the hymn were like the drops of frozen rain melting on the dry plate of the panting earth. (103–4)

The response here has been brewing a long time: Nwoye has been mal-treated by Okonkwo over many years for not being in his eyes masculine enough; furthermore, Nwoye has questioned what he perceives as unneces-sary cruelties in the Umuofian belief system. But the narrator in section one of the novel has revealed that the Umuofian belief system is highly flexible, not completely anchored to fixed laws, and open to a wide range of interpretations and applications. In other words, given a more influential role in the society as an adult man, Nwoye would stand a chance of address-ing some of the concerns he feels. However, the psychological battering he has received from his overly aggressive and ambitious father has led Nwoye to seek solutions from another belief system entirely. As Achebe puts it: 'Nwoye's callow mind was greatly puzzled' (104). In other words, Nwoye's immaturity, in part caused by the way Okonkwo has dominated him, is puzzled by this alternative and foreign belief system bringing him great relief.[24]

The repetitions in the novel continue: the missionaries preach in the market-place (echoing the massacre in the market-place), and eventually are given a piece of the evil forest on which they build their church. Ironi-cally, the plan, which should lead to their destruction within four days because the evil forest is a place of sinister forces and the powers of dark-ness, leads instead to proof that the missionaries can have 'victory over death' (105). When Okonkwo returns to Umuofia the church has already established itself there, as has a new form of government. The earlier scene where the two belief systems are debated is repeated by the white mission-ary, Mr Brown, debating religion in Umuofia with Akunna. Mr Brown, however, has to leave for health reasons, and another missionary replaces him, the Reverend James Smith. The new missionary takes a radically different approach to Mr Brown: 'He saw the world as a battlefield in which the children of light were locked in mortal conflict with the sons of dark-ness' (130). Once again, this is a repetition, a new arrival of Christianity, of colonialism in a different guise. However, with the unmasking of an *egwugwu*, by the zealous convert Enoch (an act which breaks a sacred taboo by the removal of the spirit mask to reveal the person underneath), the Christian church is destroyed in the ensuing uproar, leading to the inter-vention of the District Commissioner and the eventual downfall and death of Okonkwo.

There are a number of critical ways in which the myth–history con-tinuum, and the uses of realism in *Things Fall Apart*, can be reconfigured to escape a binary, either/or – style reading of the novel. John Thieme uses two useful terms in a brief discussion of Achebe: 'revisionist fictional histories' and 'the construction of an alternative historiography'.[25] Rather than regarding colonialism, in the second and third parts of the novel, as an inauguration of a 'proper' historical narrative, regardless of what is being said by that narrative (i.e., how critical it is of colonialism and Christianity used as a colonial tool), Achebe manages to present two alternative but interlinked historiographic perspectives. Thus the supposed 'progressive' historical perspective of parts two and three is revealed actually to be composed of repetition and amplification, whereby colonialism constantly performs a finite set of internal values (presented as 'universals') in heterogeneous but related ways. Study of how these repetitions work in the latter parts of the novel reveals not just an alternative historiography, but a *historicity* that prevails across all of the parts of the novel. By 'historicity' I draw deliberately, as Fanon repeatedly does, upon Karl Jaspers' work, and the notion that historicity is a synthesis of freedom and necessity, one founded upon contingency.[26] The perspective of historicity is one where individual existence is constantly and inevitably bound to change, exposed to contingency, regardless of the efficacy of the belief system in place which protects the community as a whole. As Slavoj Žižek notes: '. . . there is always something traumatic about the raw factuality of what we encounter as "actual"; actuality is always marked . . . as impossible.'[27] Part one of *Things Fall Apart* foreshadows change, in the trauma of Okonkwo's encounter with actuality, and also sets and the scene for his downfall, both in terms of his familial character formation and the accidents that befall him.

THE IMPACT OF *THINGS FALL APART*

Achebe's narration of the downfall of his central protagonists, in *Things Fall Apart* and *Arrow of God* (his 1964 novel, which has been the subject of a similarly vast critical literature), has continued to resonate across the decades since their publication.[28] Writing in 2001, in a homage to Chinua Achebe in his seventieth year, F. Abiola Irele contextualizes the local reception of his work among the 'young, aspiring bearers of an emerging modern culture' where 'the creation of a national literature that reflected the new shape the African world was assuming became a major concern.'[29] Taking a retrospective view, Irele argues that:

In the more than forty years since its publication, *Things Fall Apart* has lost none of that compelling force upon our attention that derives not only from its engagement with the colonial encounter, but also from its reformulation of the inherited imperial language, a reformulation that lent a special expressiveness to the novel's enactment of a decisive moment of the African experience.[30]

How accurate is this assessment? Some recent critical examples back up Irele's assertion, in diverse ways. While critics still debate *Things Fall Apart* at the level of character, plot, theme and structure, perhaps more importantly the novel has facilitated a deeper understanding of the complexities of the colonial encounter. For example, the potential *vulnerability* of ethico-religious difference as expressed via indigenous cultures is acknowledged and explored by Achebe; in other words, acknowledging the vulnerability of ethico-religious difference can be a stage on the way to reasserting that difference, and a way of ensuring that strategic safeguards are later put in place precisely to protect it. One of Achebe's tasks in *Things Fall Apart*, as Adewale Maja-Pearce has argued, is to show how 'the spiritual values of pre-colonial Africa were in no way inferior to those of Europe, merely different.'[31] Clayton G. MacKenzie builds upon this argument to suggest that this 'difference became a source of vulnerability'.[32] As MacKenzie explains: 'The religious codes and practices of Umuofia, unchallenged for centuries and perhaps millennia, had not evolved strategies for adaptation or confrontation. Like the sacred python, no one ever thought their sacredness would ever be challenged.'[33] The indigenous polytheistic system comes up against monotheistic (colonial-)state-sanctioned religion, and a reversal of 'norms' takes place: 'The real power of missionary proselytization lay in the breaking down of community norms. The evil forest became no longer evil; the outcasts became no longer outcasts; the objects and rituals of traditional sacrament were destroyed.'[34] So, it is not being suggested that there is some inherent weakness in indigenous spirituality; rather, it is an unpreparedness for the brute force of monotheism that is problematic. The violence of colonialism is not the only violence explored by Achebe; David Hoegberg has called *Things Fall Apart* 'one of the most influential fictional statements on violence in a colonial setting'.[35] A structural approach to the novel reveals the types of violence explored by Achebe:

Although Achebe powerfully criticizes the violence of British colonial practices, the British do not enter the picture until after Achebe has explored the internal workings of Igbo culture. . . . Okonkwo is frequently violent, but Achebe's statements about the relations of culture to violence are better seen in the actions and beliefs of the group as a whole. Since the majority of Igbo in the novel tend to be less violent than Okonkwo, those forms of violence they do condone and enact are especially revealing of the widespread cultural forces that foster violence. . . .

[The example of the 'Week of Peace'] shows that in the not-too-distant past the conditions for questioning and constructive change of violent traditions were present in Igbo society.[36]

To put this another way: the dynamic Igbo society can be observed only by paying close attention to glimpses of historical change in the novel, and the ways in which tradition is portrayed from multiple perspectives not as a dead weight, but as a vital, developing body of wisdom and action.

Achebe's *Things Fall Apart* has also triggered important feminist research. In other words, the colonial encounter is not perceived as something that happened in a 'gender-neutral' domain; instead, gender roles constitutive of indigenous and invader societies come into contact and conflict. While early feminist accounts of *Things Fall Apart* argued that the novel was inherently sexist, more recent feminists have turned to a closer reading of Achebe's texts to recover 'inscriptions of women's oppositional narratives of resistance to both the Igbo masculine tradition and its patriarchal discourses'.[37] To give one example from Kwadwo Osei-Nyame's recent study of the novel: 'In reading about the fearless Ekwefi and especially after our familiarity with her struggle with Ezinma in their mutual triumph in the 'war' of childbirth, the narrative foregrounds the emasculation of Okonkwo at precisely the point where it constructs alternatively viable significations around the women.'[38] While Achebe's novel appears phallocentric, there are moments of contradiction that enable the emergence of feminist counter-discourses, or points of entry into the text whereby oppositional voices may be heard – perhaps the most intriguing being Biodun Jeyifo's recovery of Okonkwo's mother.[39] It is this openness to other voices – and perhaps the multiple 'endings'[40] – that keeps Achebe's novel alive, leading Neil Ten Kortenaar to argue that *Things Fall Apart* is 'the most influential text to come out of Africa'.[41]

4 National Consciousness

Ngũgĩ wa Thiong'o's *A Grain of Wheat*

As a study in arrested decolonization, Ngũgĩ wa Thiong'o's novel *A Grain of Wheat* (1967) arguably remains unsurpassed; through complex and sensitive character development, and a narratology that functions to build a form of community writing, the novel explores the eruption of independence ('Uhuru') in Kenya, gained on 12 December 1963. The struggle for independence is revealed in the novel to be complex and contradictory, liberating and imprisoning; the central protagonist, Mugo, appears to be a hero, but in reality is a traitor, and Mugo's narrative is also symbolic of the ways in which decolonization can be arrested or even transformed into neo-colonialism. Mugo's narrative has intertextual links with Joseph Conrad's *Under Western Eyes*, but critics have long since shown how Ngũgĩ develops a unique, powerfully tragic and original protagonist in the *character* of Mugo, partly because of the ways in which he is inextricably linked with the emergence of a new nation and a new community.[1] Kofi Owusu notes that Ngũgĩ 'employs a narrative strategy that allows his characters to pick up and pass on the narrative thread in a way that is obviously intended to suggest that the narrative is as much theirs as it is the author's'.[2] The image of the 'thread' is derived from early on in the novel: after one of the community leaders, Warui has spoken, there is a silence: 'Each person seemed engrossed in himself as if turning over the words in his mind. The woman cleared her throat, an indication that she was about to take up the thread from Warui.'[3] The implication here is that none of the characters within the novel should be considered entirely in isolation; they are implicated in, and contribute to, the independence of their nation, and, as such, are deeply interrelated.

A Grain of Wheat opens with Mugo lying on his back, dreaming and feeling nervous. He dreams of a drop of water that is suspended above him, slowly gathering in size, and picking up soot from the roof as it draws towards him. Mugo wants to close his eyes or move out of the way, but he can do neither: 'He tried to move his head: it was firmly chained to the bed-frame' (1). His own body refuses to obey his will to escape the drop of water, but then the power of his despair enables him to wake up. This powerful existential opening to the novel (*existential* because it is the power of despair that *moves* Mugo) creates a finely balanced tension: between immobility and mobility; imprisonment and freedom; the world of dreams and fantasies and the waking world of reality; and finally between a nihilist and a an affirmative will-power. Later on in the novel, the reader learns the long-suspected truth: that Mugo actually betrayed a leading revolutionary called Kihika, who had visited Mugo after assassinating the District Officer, a man called Thomas Robson, or Tom the Terror. The arrival of Kihika to Mugo's hut, and the latter's response, contrasts with Mugo's earlier fantasies that he would somehow become a Messiah-like figure:

[Mugo was] . . . revelling in the dreams he loved, dreams which often transported him from the present to the future. He had come to see in them a private message, a prophecy. Had he not already escaped, unscathed, the early operations of the Emergency? Kenya had been in a state of Emergency since 1952. Some people had been taken to detention camps; others had run away to the forest: but this was a drama in a world not his own. He kept alone, feeling a day would come when horns, drums and trumpets would beat together to announce his entrance into the new world. (187)

The problems with Mugo's fantasies reflect neatly the external misunderstandings concerning Kenyan community. To explain further, on closer reflection, Mugo's Messiah fantasies reveal a detachment from society, with his belief that the bad things happening in society are taking place in a world separate from his. The central phrase here is that he 'kept alone' in an adjacent sphere of activity: tending to his crops, going through the motions of a model citizen, but fundamentally isolated. In temporal terms, Mugo has rejected the time of the crisis that society is experiencing (i.e., the crisis of colonialism and its violent rejection, and the concomitant increase in repressive counter-measures) in favour of the time of prophecy, where he merely waits for 'destiny'. Egocentrically, the destiny for which he awaits is his entry back into society, but this time as some kind of indeterminate saviour announced by 'horns, drums and trumpets'. How does this make Mugo's vision akin to external misunderstandings? Kofi Owusu argues that close analysis of point of view and narrative strategy can explain such a mechanism where the novel, 'in its entirety, gives a forceful impression of an implied "they" against whom "we" react'.[4] Owusu gives some powerful examples: '"They" say, for example, that "another Mau Mau terrorist had been shot dead" (6), when "you" and "I" – in effect, "we" – know that the person "murdered," Gitogo, is innocent. What "they" call "detention camps" are what "we" see as "concentration camps" (90)'.[5] In other words, the external perspective is that of the colonists, attempting to denigrate the quest for independence and freedom. The community or social perspective of the novel – the 'we' – reveals not some idealized, perfected indigenous society, but one that is fundamentally human, with all of the concomitant contradictions and problems, yet still moving unstoppably towards transforming the ideals of independence and freedom into everyday realities. From Mugo's isolated perspective, the process whereby those ideals are transformed is messy, troubling and problematic. He wants to rely on some undefined transcendent force, some external agency, that will eventually put everything right. But such a reliance is also a denial of the injustices which the community suffers daily. As such, Ngũgĩ posits the revolutionary over the Messianic; given that British colonialism and missionary activity were bedfellows, this distinction is crucial for the novel, even though biblical text permeates the entire narrative. Owusu regards the narrative strategies that reveal the differences and shared values of isolation and colonialism as also being important for questions concerning authorial identification:

These observations, almost inevitably, raise some of those questions which have bedevilled the criticism of African literature for decades: for whom does the African writer write? On whose authority is a story told? Is it on the authority of the author as an individual artist or the author who, as spokesperson, gives expression to a communal, collective consciousness?

The author of *A Grain of Wheat* gives the impression that he is writing on behalf of, and communicating with, his people. (His decision, after publication of his fourth novel in English, to write in his native Gikuyu is in consonance with this stance.)[6]

The question remains: how does Ngũgĩ write through and for community? How does he allow the narrative 'thread' to be taken up? The reading that follows attempts to begin exploration of these questions.

READING *A GRAIN OF WHEAT*

After Mugo's dream that opens the novel, we ironically witness him thinking about time repeating itself: '. . . the day ahead would be just like yesterday and the day before' (2). We learn that he has experienced time in this repetitive way in detention, although at this early stage in the novel, we have no idea why he was detained. Mugo goes through the rhythms of daily life, but is puzzled by a question asked of him by Warui, a village elder: 'And how is your hut, ready for Uhuru?' (2). Mugo begins to perceive that something is different on this day, that the villagers are looking at him and talking to him in a different and strange way: 'Why are people suddenly looking at me with curiosity?' (4). Mugo's walk takes him past an 'old woman' whose son Gitogo was killed by soldiers. Ngũgĩ narrates the scene from three perspectives: those of the woman and her son; of the other people frightened by the appearance of guns and tanks; and, in one sentence, of colonial rule: 'Another Mau Mau terrorist had been shot dead' (5). The injustice of the latter statement is shown by the sad scene that prefaces it, with Gitogo's innocence succinctly portrayed. Mugo's attempt to become close with the old woman had ended in failure, partly because of her piercing 'recognition' of him as a traitor, and partly because the thought of her touch revolts Mugo. He summarizes the situation to himself: 'Perhaps there was something fateful in his contact with this old woman' (6). Mugo's failure to become the old woman's son, symbolic or otherwise, and his revulsion at the thought that human touch may change his 'fate' are indicative of his detachment and isolation from human community. As with Conrad's protagonist in *Under Western Eyes*, it is precisely the signs of detachment, however, that the community misreads: Mugo's/Razumov's identities are, for the community, empty vessels which will be filled with their desires. Ironically, those desires include a need for salvation: the very Messiah-like role that Mugo fantasizes about. The narrative goes into flashback mode – a key narratological strategy in the book – with a brief account of Mugo's harsh upbringing at the hands of an alcoholic aunt. With the death of his hated aunt, however, Mugo is left feeling absolutely isolated and alone: 'Whom could he now call a relation? He wanted somebody, anybody, who would use the claims of kinship to do him ill or good. Either one or the other as long as he was not left alone, an outsider' (8). Again, ironically, just when Mugo appears apparently content with his isolated life and fantasies, the community come to him in the form of from the revolutionary Party, also known as the Movement, upsetting and worrying him; it is this visit that ends the opening chapter.

While chapter one deals with an isolated individual and the world perceived through his dreams, fantasies and fears, chapter two opens with 'the Movement', the origins of which, traced via the people, go back to the beginnings of colonialism and 'the day the whiteman came to the country, clutching the book of God in both hands, a magic witness that the whiteman was a messenger from the Lord' (10). Intriguingly, Ngũgĩ writes of the 'echo' of a distant past, heard when the story of the British Queen is told: 'It was many, many years ago. The women ruled the land of the Agikuyu. Men had no property, they were only there to serve the whims and needs of the women' (10–11). After a revolution that overthrows this matriarchy, there is still the story of the woman who 'became a leader and ruled over a large section of Muranga' (11). These two indigenous narratives constitute a framework within which the Queen's distant rule is made sense of; the framework gives way with initial disbelief to the strange symbols of Christianity, which provide the new language for interpreting colonial rule, followed by the rapid defiling and acquisition of sacred land by the colonists. At this point Ngũgĩ switches to narrate the resistance to colonialism: 'Waiyaki and other warrior-leaders took arms' (12). Even though these initial uprisings are violently quashed, it is Waiyaki's 'seed' or 'grain' that gives birth to the Movement. The peasant's revolt, led by men such as Harry Thuku (12), is again violently quashed, but yet again, another revolutionary leader emerges: the man who becomes known as 'Burning Spear' (14). Ngũgĩ switches narrative perspective at this point, with the rapid historical overview being replaced by Mugo's point of view at a meeting of the Movement, introducing at the same time the other main characters of the novel: Gikonyo, his future wife Mumbi and Kihika, the man whom Mugo will eventually betray:

'This is not 1920. What we now want is action, a blow which will tell,' he [Kihika] said as women from Thabai pulled at their clothes and hair, and screamed with delight. Kihika, a son of the land, was marked out as one of the heroes of deliverance. Mugo, who had seen Kihika on the ridge a number of times, had never suspected that the man had such power and knowledge. Kihika unrolled the history of Kenya, the coming of the whiteman and the birth of the Party. Mugo glanced at Gikonyo and Mumbi. Their eyes were fixed on Kihika; their lives seemed dependent on his falling words. (14)

Mugo, one of many important characters in the novel, defines himself as being outside of the community that admires Kihika; his reaction to Kihika's knowledge and vision is one of jealousy and hatred, but also, more importantly for his later actions, terror (15). John McLeod notes how Ngũgĩ follows 'Fanon's lead in making the people the subject for his novel, and the fortunes of the Thabai community can be read as a mirror of the fledgling nation as a whole'.[7] Kihika, unlike Mugo, not only speaks for the community, but also puts his words into action: 'Kihika lived the words of sacrifice he had spoken to the multitude' (15). Going into the forest to become a Freedom Fighter, Kihika's greatest success is the capture of a police garrison and transit camp, freeing prisoners and raiding the place for arms and ammunition. Although his demise is also narrated in the chapter, the thread is passed on again: 'The Movement . . . remained alive and grew, as people put it, on the wounds of those Kihika left behind' (17).

The two opposing chapters – the first presenting the reader with an alienated and isolated individual character sheltering from the community, the second presenting a more complex history and a community of individuals who will be transformed by Uhuru – do share some features. Most importantly, they share a sense of time as established by the emergency, as noted with Mugo's sense of repetition. As Simon Gikandi puts it:

A temporal moment that should be defined by rupture [Uhuru] becomes one of repetition. In this chapter [one], as for most of the novel, time is represented from the vantage point of the emergency – the primary referent against which individual and collective desires are measured. Indeed, Thabai, the central locality in the novel, is a creation of the emergency . . .; its sense of order is a reflection of the imperial power that created it in order to contain insurgency against colonial rule.[8]

This narrative 'vantage point' leads Gikandi to ask some key questions about the novel:

In *A Grain of Wheat*, even people's lives have come to revolve around the emergency which, in the process of narration, is unconsciously elevated to the status of the primal event of late colonialism in Kenya. The stories that the characters in the novel tell each other in an attempt to get a handle on their past revolve around the meaning of their lives during the state of emergency. But, like the state of emergency itself, this telling and retelling of worn out stories is a symptom of the tenuous nature of signification – and temporality – in Ngugi's novel: is this a novel about the recent colonial past or about the moment of decolonization in which it is set? Why is the central subject of Ngugi's novel also the one man who seems to be most distanced from its central events? How do we explain the structure of time in the novel, especially the paradoxical fact that a hundred-year history of colonialism is contained within a few days before independence?[9]

Gikandi argues that understanding Ngũgĩ's use of allegory and irony in the novel can help answer these questions.[10] However, in doing so, two novels in one emerge, held in exquisitely balanced tension by Ngũgĩ. Firstly, there is the ironic novel, where the reader is alerted 'to the discrepancies between the structure of the narrative and the experiences it represents'.[11] Secondly, there is the allegorical novel, where the reader is 'invited to identify with the grand narrative of nationalism and its desires'.[12] As Gikandi says: 'What makes this schema complicated, however, is that we cannot read *A Grain of Wheat* from one perspective without being cognizant of the other; we cannot read the novel as a radical critique of decolonization without considering its passionate identification with the ideals of cultural nationalism'.[13] The third chapter of the novel neatly reveals the tension of this schema, as a group of characters arrive at Mugo's home, for purposes that in the first instance are unspecified.

Chapter three opens with Gikonyo saying that the people have come to see Mugo about the Uhuru celebrations. The visitors are all highly respected members of the community, including Warui, whose life is considered 'the story of the Movement' (18). Warui argues that the village of Thabai must not only celebrate independence, but also honour the dead. For Mugo, the resurrection of the dead through celebration is a frightening thought, due to his betrayal of Kihika. Wambui takes up the thread from Warui, and says that: 'We too cannot forget our sons. And Kihika was such a man, a great man' (20). For Mugo, this naming of Kihika spells potential doom, and there is panic in his voice when he asks his visitors 'What do you want?' (20). The tension increases with a loud knocking at the door, and the entry of two Freedom Fighters, Lieutenant Koina and General R. The tension breaks with confused and broken speech, masked by the others, but written first from Mugo's perspective:

'Sit down – on the bed,' Mugo invited them, and was startled by the sound of his own voice. So old – so rusty . . . today . . . tonight . . . everything is strange . . . people's looks and gestures frighten me . . . I'm not really afraid because . . . because . . . a man's life, like mine, is not important . . . and . . . and . . . God . . . I've ceased to care . . . I don't . . . don't . . . The arrival of the two men had broken the mounting tension. Everybody was talking. The hut was animated with a low excited murmur. (20)

The fragmentation of Mugo's monologue, indicated by the incomplete sentences and ellipses, can be interpreted as the manifestation of a 'fragmented consciousness', one which 'prevents him from piecing together his experiences into a comprehensible pattern'.[14] Various psychoanalytical models could be brought to bear here, but Fanon's existential approach is probably most useful, because it argues that the colonial context must always be considered the overarching framework and cause of 'neurosis'.[15] As John Lutz suggests:

In the depiction of Mugo's underlying motivations, Ngugi illuminates the complex relationship between individualism, alienation, and colonial ideology by exposing how all conspire to produce the objective conditions under which power becomes the primary object of desire for colonizer and colonized alike. Working to disrupt any sense of community, place, or moral obligation, the process of colonial domination reproduces in the very subjects that it traumatizes a powerful impulse to brutalize and dominate other human beings.[16]

Mugo fears that the misinterpretation of his character, which he wears like a mask that covers the raw truth of his treachery, is about to be ripped away by the people in his hut. From the multiple conversations, the low excited murmur, emerges Lieutenant Koina's account to Wambui of how the Freedom Fighters made a sacrifice in the forest and then ate the meat afterwards in order to survive. Koina repeats the prayer said before battle as well as the Freedom song. For Mugo, the entire scene in his hut has become unreal: 'I'll soon wake up from the dream . . . My hut will be empty and I'll find myself alone as I have always been' (21). This undercutting of the prayer and the Freedom song, by calling their expression unreal, suggests not only that for Mugo the entire emergency period has been a nightmare, but also that he desires a normality that does not involve community demands upon the individual. Yet the latter is precisely what his visitors have come to make of him. Chillingly, for Mugo, they preface their demands with reminiscing and wondering about Kihika, especially the fact that his belief in prayer, his deep faith, did not help him when he walked into the trap that led to his death – the trap that the reader knows was set by Mugo. But instead of accusing Mugo, General R. praises him: 'I believe you were the man who sheltered Kihika on that night. That is why you were later arrested and sent to detention, is that not so?' (23). The praise is repeated by Gikonyo, who requests that Mugo will therefore lead the independence day ceremonies. Mugo does not answer this request, but the visitors leave him saying that he does not have to respond immediately. For Lieutenant Koina and General R., their most important task for Uhuru is to find out who betrayed Kihika; ironically, their other notion of Mugo is that he was not very important, and hardly ever mentioned by Kihika, which removes any suspicions of him that might remain from their uncertain notion of his actual 'heroism'.

Much of *A Grain of Wheat* is narrated via extended flashbacks – a narrative process that Gérard Genette calls analepsis. Ngũgĩ explores the meaning of historical consciousness – and all of its complexities and contradictions – through the range of characters who engage with, and attempt to make sense of, the past. Analepsis is therefore central to the novel precisely because it is the mechanism by which individual and collective historical consciousness intersect; a purely abstract historical consciousness can be one in which general nationalistic phrases abound, yet do not touch the people, whereas a purely personal reminiscence, divorced from society, can lead to a situation such as Mugo's solipsism. Ngũgĩ shows how his characters engage differently and complexly with the past, not just reliving and reinterpreting history, but making it. Gikandi argues that in this way, Ngũgĩ 'does not represent the past as a unified narrative; on the contrary, history is represented in the form of a conflict of interpretations, a conflict that takes three main forms: history as a repressed spectre that returns to haunt its actants, the past as an unsayable event, and the act of remembering as a narrative moment of forgetfulness'.[17] The characters of Mumbi and Gikonyo can be studied to understand Gikandi's schema further, from the early rival narrative (between Gikonyo and Karanja), to Gikonyo's detention (with narrative analepsis and his proleptic fantasies), to the shock of the current situation on Gikonyo's release (Mumbi has given birth to Karanja's child), and then Mumbi's later retelling of events to Mugo. In many respects, Gikonyo invents a ghost to haunt him over and over again, in the midst of his jealousy, as he bitterly fantasizes about the moment of conception of Mumbi's child. Furthermore, the failure of Gikonyo's 'precolonial expectations'[18] can be read allegorically as a failure of Uhuru: 'As Gokonyo's example shows so vividly, the restoration that was expected to justify the whole history of Kenya, especially the suffering people had to endure during the state of emergency, has not come about.'[19] From Mumbi's perspective – bearing in mind that she is cast as 'the symbolic mother of the nation'[20] – she is haunted by Gikonyo's rival Karanja, and the different pathway that he has taken. She once insulted Karanja and asked him, 'Why don't you wear your mother's skirt . . .? When others went to fight, you remained behind to lick the feet of your white husbands' (148). Karanja replies that it is the coward who lives because he is aware that the colonialists will win the battle. Karanja later uses his fantasy of total, permanent colonial domination to trick Mumbi, by suddenly surprising her with news of Gikonyo's impending release. As Mumbi says to Mugo: 'I completely lost hope of meeting him [Gikonyo] again on this earth, and lived on the memory of happy days before the State of Emergency' (149). The act of remembrance here is used to efface the present-day knowledge that she will never see her husband again, but Karanja disrupts and abuses this process of remembrance and forgetfulness and makes love to her. Mumbi's analepsis contradicts Gikonyo's overdetermined fantasy of her repeated betrayal – he imagines her making love to his rival every night in his absence; in the process, the reader realizes that her character is still that of the pre-emergency person whom Gikonyo and Karanja fought over, although now scarred by the emergency.

Gikandi, in an insightful and extended analysis of Mumbi and Gikonyo, notes in passing that the 'thread of life' is not taken up by Gikonyo in ways he predicted while under detention. *A Grain of Wheat* continually challenges those who take the community narrative thread, as personal fantasies give way to the needs and desires of the community as a whole. Readers of the novel must continually be aware of the 'network of person-to-person relationships' which Ngũgĩ presents via a 'technique of combining recollection and multiple foci [which] can lead to variations in interpretations and judgments about the way people behave'.[21] However, in taking Mumbi's story as an example of these variations, Delia Krause expresses some disappointment at Mumbi's revelation, suggesting that readers 'anticipate Mumbi's child as the result of her being forced to submit to the now-powerful Karanja – as a case of rape'.[22] Thus, because Ngũgĩ has constructed a certain character type, when Mumbi declares that she was 'full of submissive gratitude' (150), Krause argues that 'we are disappointed because this is not a plausible reaction, and not in keeping with Mumbi's character in the rest of the novel.'[23] However, there are three further issues that need consideration: firstly, the fact that Ngũgĩ's characters do *not* act in predictable ways (i.e., their actions often contradict external appearances); secondly, the fact that the overall hopes for the future, i.e., Uhuru, are undercut (and that future includes the reader's hopes for individual characters); and, thirdly, the precise textual phrasing that Mumbi uses, not just 'submissive gratitude' but '*I remember being full of* submissive gratitude' (150, my italics), in a novel in which memory is revealed to be complex, contradictory, uncertain and partial at the best of times. The final point being made is *not* that Mumbi's own feelings should be suspected, since it is clear that she is manipulated and tricked into an abrupt catharsis, or temporary unsettling of her established character; rather, Mumbi's 'recollection' may span a whole range of emotions, times and even places that intersect at the moment of conceiving her child. Read as a symbolic character, it would be a mistake to read her conception merely as a failure of characterization; the 'symbolic' child has been conceived by the 'mother of the nation' and a coward, a man who symbolizes in turn the type of person who will construct a neo-colonialism. As Joyce Johnson argues, Mumbi is the 'link between forces which tend to move in different directions. In this respect, she personifies the community itself.'[24] The reader's expectation of an assault occurring here, while predicted in terms of Mumbi's strength of character (i.e., her strength of potential resistance), may not take into account the opposing forces that converge in this moment; in other words, Ngũgĩ balances realism with symbolism, oppression and agency, not just to explore the pathways to neo-colonialism, but also to express a more Foucauldian notion of power, one which is characterized by micro-powers rather than a simplistic top-down action.

Reading *A Grain of Wheat* closely involves an awareness of the different versions of the novel, from its initial manuscript version called *Wrestling with God*, to publication of the first 1967 printed version as *A Grain of Wheat*, to its revision and republication in 1986. One of the changes from the early to the later version of the novel is a difference in emphasis upon the Christian religion and colonialism. Jacqueline Bardolph situates the writing of the novel biographically, historically and in a religious context:

Ngugi was educated in a religious context before going to university at Makerere. One must also underline that during the years of Emergency, the churches as a whole were on the side of the British government, in particular helping with the propaganda that described Mau Mau as terrorists, violent outsiders refusing Christian and human values for the sake of atavistic regression. The villagers, suspected of helping the forest guerrillas, and the inmates in detention camps, were subjected to intensive re-education, told to confess, to seek rehabilitation. Moral Rearmament was explicitly involved in the campaign to cultivate guilt feelings among the people, and pacifist Revivalist currents encouraged them to 'see the light' at public meetings.[25]

Bardolph argues that the 'Christian mode of narrative'[26] utilized by the novel comes under suspicion as Ngũgĩ developed as a writer and thinker; some of the changes made between the 1967 and the 1986 editions reflect this suspicion, for example, with the character of Reverend Jackson, who converts to Revivalism, preaching against the Freedom Fighters: 'In 1986, the church minister who has been an informer is justly executed. The recent version is firmly didactic and shows as far as possible the people as more conscious, more united.'[27] So why did Ngũgĩ utilize a Christian mode of narrative in the first place? The answer lies not just in his biographical circumstances, but in the ways in which the Kenyan people adopted a biblical discourse of emancipation and messianic redemption. Before converting to the Movement, this was the case for Kihika, who

was moved by the story of Moses and the children of Israel, which he had learnt during Sunday school – an integral part of their education – conducted at the church by the headmaster. As soon as he learnt how to read, Kihika bought a Bible and read the story of Moses over and over again, later recounting it to Mumbi and any other person who would listen. (85)

The community adopts the language and stories of the Bible precisely because of a perceived, shared set of values: 'The oppressed were the people of Israel, and Kenyatta was to be the Moses who would deliver them.'[28] Govind Narain Sharma is one of many critics who argue for the centrality of the Christian mode of narrative:

. . . it seems impossible to read and interpret *A Grain of Wheat* without taking into account the Christian myth, which not only constitutes the basic framework of the story and incorporates the author's message but also dominates his use of image and symbol. All the leading characters of the novel . . . make use of Christian concepts to express their dreams and aspirations, their lapses and fears.[29]

One such example, is Mumbi, and the way in which she initially portrays herself through biblical symbolism:

Her dark eyes had a dreamy look that longed for something the village could not give. She lay in the sun and ardently yearned for a life in which love and heroism, suffering, and martyrdom were possible. She was young. She had fed on stories in which Gikuya women braved the terrors of the forest to save people, of beautiful girls given to the gods as sacrifice before the rains. In the Old Testament she often saw herself as Esther: so she revelled in that moment when Esther finally answers King Ahasuerus' question and dramatically points at Haman, saying: The adversary and enemy is wicked Haman. (76)

Mumbi's vision of herself is syncretic, in other words, it involves 'fusion of two distinct traditions [here indigenous and Christian] to produce a new and distinctive whole'.[30] The revolutionary fervour that Mumbi expresses is one which mixes action and sacrifice, and may give the reader another interpretive framework within which to think through her response to Karanja (see above). Even though Mumbi does not join the Freedom Fighters, she is still 'fighting' for independence, personally and nationally. In the words of Bu–Buakei Jabbi:

Mumbi does not . . . go into the forest when the Mau Mau warfare breaks out. But her intuitions of self-sacrifice and of rescue are sufficiently realized in other aspects of her life and conduct, as in her matrimonial devotion despite suffering or her selfless efforts to save the necks of Karanja and Mugo, who had respectively jeopardized both her marriage and her brother's life.[31]

This is not to make of Mumbi a stereotypically passive wife; her tolerance threshold is eventually reached and she leaves Giyonko to his own bitterness, and to his own attempt at a fresh start. Further, it is important to realize that Mumbi also has a profound effect on Mugo, who has listened to her story. The latter suggests that it is essential continually to be aware of the form of the novel; Mumbi's story, like so many others in the novel, is not told in isolation – it is told to an audience, be it an audience of one. Mugo is 'cracked open' (172) by Mumbi's story and is driven back to the trench where he defended a woman who was being abused by guards; Mumbi has forced Mugo out of the 'limbo' (174) state in which he has lived most of his life.[32]

THE IMPACT OF *A GRAIN OF WHEAT*

Kenneth Harrow asserts that with the publication of Ngũgĩ's *A Grain of Wheat*, 'the African viewpoint on the struggle for independence in Kenya was given its fullest, most complex, and most moving expression. East African literature appeared to have finally come into its own with this novel which capped Ngũgĩ's burgeoning career.'[33] Critics have long debated the role of intertextuality and 'influence' upon postcolonial writing through

Ngũgĩ's novel: for example, countering the arguments for or against the influence of Conrad's *Under Western Eyes* on *A Grain of Wheat*, Byron Caminero-Santangelo suggests that 'part of the "originality" of Ngũgĩ's novel lies in his critical appropriation of Conrad's text into an evolving Kenyan culture'.[34] In other words, Ngũgĩ's novel is counter-discursive, radically reworking a canonical author from a Kenyan perspective. Other novels and key thinkers are intertextually examined by *A Grain of Wheat*; perhaps the most noted of these thinkers is Franz Fanon. But the situation concerning Ngũgĩ's relationship with Fanon's work is complex, as Simon Gikandi suggests:

> It is hard to say whether Ngugi started writing *A Grain of Wheat* after encountering Fanon's book, or whether he had already started working on it when he read *The Wretched of the Earth*. Nevertheless, the genealogy of the novel raises questions that are germane to its interpretation: does the (Marxist) aesthetic ideology of the novel mark a radical break with Ngugi's previous narrative and cultural practices? Does this novel initiate the socialist ideology and aesthetic that culminated in later works such as *Petals of Blood* and *Devil on the Cross*? Or is it a continuation of the cultural nationalist project . . . that reaches its apotheosis in the troubled temporality of decolonization?[35]

The complexities of Ngũgĩ's writing demand that there 'are no categorical answers to these questions'.[36] For Gikandi, this is also the case because of Ngũgĩ's 'conflicting intentions': 'The novel itself is caught between its author's desire to trace the history and consequences of cultural nationalism – and thus provide a paradigm for representing decolonization – and the imperative to proffer a cultural grammar for understanding the new post-colonial state.'[37] Such a new 'cultural grammar' is at times more postmodern than modern (for example, the multiple perspectives of the novel, and the play of competing signifiers concerning Independence/arrested decolonization) and this aspect of Ngũgĩ's writing has more recently intrigued scholars. Drawing upon the work of Henry A. Giroux, Kathy Kessler, for example, argues that '[i]n redefining concepts of difference and otherness, a task which . . . Ngugi wa Thiong'o participates in, we "step beyond the modernist celebration of the unified self, totalizing notions of history and universalistic models of reason".'[38] Kessler adds that even with his more Marxist stance, '. . . Ngugi's later fiction contributes to a shift away from the "Eurocentric notion of society that subordinates the discourse of ethics and politics to . . . an unproblematic acceptance of European culture as the basis of civilization, and a notion of the individual subject as a unified, rational self which is the source of all cultural and social meaning".'[39] The intersection here of the postcolonial and the postmodern may be a key reason as to why Ngũgĩ's writing continues to have relevance and interest for current-day readers.

5 Interrogating Subjectivity

Bessie Head's *A Question of Power*

The autobiographical imperative has long been recognized in Bessie Head's most successful novel, *A Question of Power* (1974). With the rise of highly theoretical approaches to literary studies in the late 1960s and early 1970s, the autobiographical genre came under intense suspicion, especially with its single-subject-centred view of the world. But important research in feminist and postcolonial criticism soon led to a realization that new ways of doing autobiography were emerging that countered mainstream, liberal humanist, largely Eurocentric approaches to subjectivity. As Linda Anderson writes, autobiographical writing 'by female and postcolonial subjects . . . has interrogated the ideological underpinning of autobiographical tradition and explored the possibility of difference as excessive and uncontainable'.[1] In *A Question of Power*, 'difference' is encoded in multiple ways (difference as 'excessive and uncontainable' is returned to below), and there is some consensus that this narrative of difference parallels key aspects of Head's life.[2] Born in Pietermaritzburg, South Africa, Head's Scottish mother was institutionalized for having a relationship with a black South African groom.[3] Head was born in the asylum hospital in 1937 and sent initially to a nursing home, and then fostered by a Boer family; both rejected her as a child because she was black.[4] Even at this early stage, there is a sense in which Head's identity, like the character Elizabeth in *A Question of Power*, is always at odds with other people's desires: neither white nor black South African (in the terms of the harsh racial identity laws of the time), still the authorities attempt to perform her 'white' identity for her, but she is rejected for clearly not being white *enough*; yet as a mixed-race child, she is also in an other hybrid space. Head regards being at odds with other people's desires as leading to intense secrecy; as Jacqueline Rose suggests: 'The first secret is an intimate, sexual, family secret, a trauma of begetting which speaks a whole history of racial division: apartheid as sexual apartheid as much as, if not before, anything else.'[5] Head was eventually fostered to a mother of mixed race. Her biological mother's true identity and circumstances were withheld, constituting another powerful secret; this secret, however, was finally disclosed. In 1964, after having worked as a teacher and journalist, Head moved to Botswana, where she spent the rest of her life.[6]

Manus Vicki Briault reads Head's novel, written in her self-imposed exile, as directly autobiographical:

A Question of Power, her greatest and most devastating novel, records her mental breakdown and her struggle back to sanity. It was written just after three years of internment in the psychiatric hospital in Gabarone, Botswana. Bessie Head had emigrated to Botswana on a 'one-way only' exit permit from South Africa in 1964. She was a stateless person, like millions of non-white South Africans who were refused passports and other accoutrements of citizenship. A foreigner, cut off from the many friends she had left behind . . . her early years in Botswana were marked by loneliness, instability as a refugee, and difficulty in getting accepted, being neither completely African nor completely European, in the narrow acceptance of the terms current at the time.[7]

The novel may be read as autobiography, but, as noted, contemporary theorists of autobiographical writing – drawing upon feminist and post-colonial writing – have recognized difference as 'excessive and uncontain-able'. *A Question of Power* thus becomes a conundrum: how to express something that may exceed representation? How to describe experiences, in other words, that question the very foundations of logic and order?

Head's novel is a powerful and transgressive mode of writing, precisely because she questions categories of 'acceptability' and conventional literary and generic form. Some early critics regarded this incessant questioning as simply flawed writing; as more sophisticated readings of *A Question of Power* were produced, critical consensus shifted in recognition that Head's writing of 'madness' was in itself highly complex and creative, revealing connections between personal and societal/political situations. As Jacqueline Rose puts it: 'For Bessie Head . . . inside the head is the place where you can make the links or points of connection – both deadly and of universal potential – which are invisible to the cultural, historical, and racial differentiations aboveground.'[8] Head challenges the reader to rethink assumptions made about colonial and postcolonial societies and their relationship to knowledge and power; in exploring the painful experiences of stateless-ness and disconnection from society, viewed through the lens of an individual who is suffering from mental illness, Head also challenges the reader's assumptions about indigenous knowledge. For example, indigenous theories of the spirit world are not the only models circulating in African society during the period of *A Question of Power*; partly through the influence of Fanon, western theories of the psyche, in particular those of Karl Jaspers and Jacques Lacan, also circulated. As Patrick Colm Hogan notes: 'It is worth keeping in mind . . . that at least some of Lacan's ideas were introduced to the colonial world by Frantz Fanon decades before they reached North American universities.'[9] Close reading of *A Question of Power* means being aware of the competing models of the psyche that circulate throughout the text, as well as the more literary structures and mythological frameworks that are also brought to bear on the subject of mental illness.

The literary-theoretical lines of communication of contemporary critics may find themselves challenged by Head's proleptic account of more recent obsessions. As Jacqueline Rose puts it:

Head writes a semifictional account of what she herself describes as a breakdown, in which there is in fact *too much* communication – voices inside the mind. It would be odd to respond to this extraordinary piece of writing as if channels, lines, wires – how things get transmitted – were not precisely the issue, something which the book shows as available for total, hostile sabotage.[10]

In reading the novel, then, it is important to adopt a critical stance which is open to being challenged by Head, one which is flexible enough to respond to the exploration and representation of the 'excessive and un-containable' even, if not especially, where the latter is at odds with how contemporary western and other critics *want* literature to be written. The sexual politics of the text – both interrogative and troubling from a feminist perspective – may burst the boundaries of current critical domains. As Desiree Lewis argues:

Head is read in terms of what the reader would like to see: the feminist writer who consistently subverts masculine authority (even though Head often cele-brated masculinity and authoritative male leaders). Or the socially committed writer who identifies clear-cut solutions to oppression (although Head was often preoccupied with spiritual sources and forms of liberation). Or the politically incorrect writer who 'failed' to sustain a feminist critique or social commitment (even though she probed injustices in extremely expansive ways). Or the writer of 'essentially African' works (despite the fact that she developed a universal vision and also drew self-consciously on writers like Boris Pasternack [*sic*] and D.H. Lawrence).[11]

The Lacanian interpretive model of madness that can be perceived in the novel (which is not to suggest that this is a consciously produced model[12]) may also offer clues for the novel's strong *critique* of patriarchy. It is also important to register the fact that the context of the novel's pro-duction – and setting – is as crucial as the exploration of the psyche, partly because the psyche is revealed by Head to be inextricably linked with the political situation within which her protagonist Elizabeth defines herself. Some critics have argued that all Head does is explore the personal and the psyche; but this critical move can be perceived as creating a 'false dichotomy between the public and private'.[13] James M. Garrett argues that the concept of the 'political unconscious' as developed by Fredric Jameson

allows us to do away with the dichotomies built up out of the political and the apolitical by eliminating the very possibility of the apolitical. So-called private responses are no longer seen as separated from the social and political context, but are themselves responses to that social and political context, part of the social and political dialogue that subsumes both the private and the public.[14]

READING *A QUESTION OF POWER*

A Question of Power is written in two main parts called 'Sello' and 'Dan'; the protagonist's journey through her mental illness involves her inter-actions with these two projections or male spirit-figures who haunt her, as well as her involvement in the external, material world – a world of gar-dening, community relations and healing. Some critics have found the shift into healing at the close of the novel too abrupt and not in keeping with the characterization that precedes it. This is an important criticism and needs to be answered in full, especially as it pertains to the two 'worlds' that appear to clash in the novel: the interior world of the psyche and the exterior, material world. Furthermore, in answering and rejecting this charge (that the novel is 'flawed'), simplistic models of mental 'health' can be shown to be critiqued by the novel. Joanne Chase sketches the prob-lematic from a negative perspective:

. . . two major flaws, one in content and one in style, detract from the persuasive-ness of the work. Because Elizabeth is said to come out of her insanity with a 'lofty serenity of soul nothing could shake,' (202) because she is presented as coming through hell with the treasure of knowledge of the universe, with absolute understanding of the nature of evil and good and God and man, Head could be accused of romanticizing insanity and coming up with a trivialized, seemingly tacked on 'message of the brotherhood of man.' . . . One's sense of the author's having tied everything up so neatly is more unsettling than the horror of the character's insanity. . . . Bessie Head does not skimp on the ugliness of insanity, but yet it seems a misrepresentation of the ordeal of the mentally ill to claim that it is creative and productive rather than simply a sickness like any other. The book enters the realm of fantasy and romance in its implication that only an irrational, visionary experience can lead to insight, rather than the hard spade work of the intellect.[15]

Ironically, it is such a perspective of 'insanity' sketched in this quotation that *A Question of Power* interrogates! In other words, Head rejects the reductive notion that mental illness is 'a sickness like any other' (think about that 'any other' category), just as she rejects the normative assump-tion that mental illness is merely a passive, victim-based 'ordeal' rather than an experience which in itself has the capacity to be 'creative and produc-tive'. As such, Head is one in a long line of important women writers who have critiqued the normative perspective that continually condemns the mentally ill to silence and solitude, a normative perspective that condemns women who stray too far across the boundaries of the socially acceptable to the category of the mentally ill.

In many respects, the originary story of Head's mother's incarceration is indicative of such a transgression being recoded as illness and an attempt by white society to hide away and silence female sexually and socially transgressive behaviour. Additionally, *A Question of Power* asserts the cre-ativity and productivity of the mentally ill, as a way of escaping from alternative systems of thought; the entire range of belief systems explored and challenged in the novel are like parts of a machine that Elizabeth switches on and off to see if they work *for her*. The belief systems may be categorized under the two main characters of Sello and Dan, and many critics do this for clarification of story and plot, but they are also merely machinic parts that do not add up to some transcendent whole. If anything, the ending of the novel is less romantic and more realistic, as the local indigenous community continues to be the site of healing. A key theoretical text of the early 1970s, Deleuze and Guattari's *Anti-Oedipus: Capitalism and Schizophrenia*, argues for alternative mental states as a machinic production; the notion of a human 'subject' is rejected in favour of 'desiring machines', which are not secondary to some transcendent system or deity, but rather primary, creating the real. Deleuze and Guattari's infamous statement that '[a] schizophrenic out for a walk is a better model than a neurotic lying on the analyst's couch' is a rejection of the Freudian concept of repression and the Oedipus Complex. Head, by exploring her protagonist's mental experiences via two male projections, similarly disrupts Freudianism and explores the primacy of 'phallogocentrism' in psychoanalytical discourses.[16]

The opening page of section one of the novel is a description not of the protagonist Elizabeth, but one of her projections, Sello. Sello is described as almost incidentally being African – because of his identification with 'mankind' in general – but also somehow making a universalist and empathetic statement with his assertion that 'I am just anyone.'[17] As the narrator says: 'It was as though his soul was a jigsaw; one more piece being put into place' (11). Given that Elizabeth will be ferociously attacked by the law of the phallus with the character of Dan, it may appear strange to open the novel with this assessment of Sello; as a self-projection on Elizabeth's part, reference to jigsaw pieces and 'soul-journeys' begins to be more comprehensible. The beginning of the novel is thus its closing and vice-versa in a structurally circular movement; as Sello-as-self-projection says:

Everything felt right with him. A barrier of solitude and bleak, arid barrenness of soul had broken down. He loved each particle of earth around him, the everyday event of sunrise, the people and animals of the village of Motabeng; perhaps his love included the whole universe. He said to himself that evening: 'I might have died before I found this freedom of heart.' That was another perfect statement, to him – love was freedom of heart. (11)

The circularity in the novel, with this connection between beginning and closing, does not, however, deny all progression; Elizabeth progresses through the novel from object to subject: 'To be a passive receiver of horrors is to become the abject, the undesirable. . . . It is precisely this passivity that Elizabeth attempts to escape through the written word and, as transmitter of horror to us, the readers.'[18] The triangular relationship between Elizabeth, Sello and Dan is described as a 'strange journey into hell' (12); this journey is in part caused by the two men demanding at different times that Elizabeth is 'abject', someone turned into a 'something' by being cast-away, cast-off and rejected. Julia Kristeva is careful to note that the abject only 'has one quality of the object – that of being opposed to *I*'.[19] In other words, it is a mistake to think of the abject as being devoid of any power whatsoever, because 'from its place of banishment, the abject does not cease challenging its master'.[20] For Head, the 'master' is the triangular relationship: there is undoubtedly a tension with patriarchy, but Elizabeth is also grappling with self-projected beings or spirits and the effects of her mental illness; she also produces a series of realities that she is in a dialectical relationship with, shifting her bonds back and forth between Sello and Dan. The dialectical relationship is shown early on in the first few pages of the novel, just after the narrator has said that '[b]oth men flung unpleasant details at her in sustained ferocity' (12). First, Elizabeth recognizes that Dan is 'her own hell'. Even though he had been in the middle of sexually and emotionally abusing her, sadistically asserting the power of the phallus over her 'absent' sex, this throws him off-guard, thus triggering a dialectical shift. Sello then says: 'Love is two people mutually feeding each other, not one living on the soul of the other, like a ghoul' (13). Of course, this shift does not mean that there is some kind of instantaneous catharsis, or anything else so simplistic, but it is part of Elizabeth's productive psychic journey: her 'madness' produces the two men, but it is clear that she has also been subjected to a patriarchal society that produces her nightmarish internalization of emotional and sexual abuse.

It is precisely the blurring between Elizabeth's material and psychic experiences that give the novel a nightmarish quality, with the nightmares including: 'ghostly apparitions, witchcraft, scenes of sexual excess and cannibalism, verbal violence, hallucinations which perhaps are not hallucinations at all . . . leaving the reader uncomfortably stranded between fiction and non-fiction readings'.[21] A purely thematic reading of the text would perhaps entirely miss the speculative character of much that occurs to Elizabeth, but a purely psychoanalytical reading would also perhaps over-privilege the speculative. Manus Vicki Briault suggests that to get a foothold in this dialectical, ever-shifting narrative, the reader needs to be aware of the narratological elements which constitute it. Thus, the identification at times of the narrator and protagonist, which can lead to confusion, can be mapped and articulated: 'The narrator is . . . apparently extradiegetic (outside the story), yet so subjectively consolidated with the protagonist, expressing insights and attitudes which clearly emanate from her, that she often seems homodiegetic (part of the story). From this emerges a confusion between first and third-person perspectives.'[22] There are stretches of narrative which appear most 'objective' and autobiographical (in terms of seeing parallels between Bessie Head and Elizabeth), where the narrator is clearly demarcated; there are also stretches where the blurring of first and third person has the above-mentioned effect. A useful term here for thinking through these narratological issues is that of 'narrated monologue', where, as Eleni Coundouriotis puts it, Elizabeth's psyche is 'embedded directly in the narration'.[23] Related to this is the term 'psycho-narration', where 'the narrator describes a character's mental state but tells us more than the character knows. Another way to formulate this is to say that the narrator has a greater awareness, a fuller articulation of the meaning of the character's experience, and in this way, assumes control over the character.'[24] An example of psycho-narration early on in the novel is during the meeting between Elizabeth and Medusa; as with Dan's taunting, Medusa flaunts her female sexuality in contrast with Elizabeth's perceived 'lack': 'Without any bother for decencies she sprawled her long black legs in the air, and the most exquisite sensation travelled out of her towards Elizabeth. It enveloped Elizabeth from head to toe like a slow, deep, sensuous bomb' (44). The shifting of senses in this passage – from sight to sensual, explosive orgasm – does not mean that Elizabeth can *stay* permanently in the realm of pleasure; Medusa is accusing her of lack, and proving this by an enveloping that when repeated leads to utter breakdown: '. . . Medusa's next assault pulled the ground right from under Elizabeth's feet. She fell into a deep hole of such excruciating torture that, briefly, she went stark, raving mad' (44). The interior perspective – that of the all-encompassing orgasm – is replaced by a narratorial telling: an external perspective. As Coundouriotis puts it: '*Psycho-narration* is one manifestation of the unsituated point of view where the narrator's knowledge is unrestricted because of his/her privileged placement in the text where all is visible. The internal point of view on the other hand is restricted (like narrated monologue) to the character's own knowledge.'[25] As she further argues, 'The difficulty of a novel such as *A Question of Power* is that it fluctuates somewhere between what Gérard Genette has called a *nonfocalized* and an *internally focalized* narrative.'[26] It is in the fluctuations that the reader is thrown off-guard; the ability to make sense of events in the novel is always countered by the fact that the experiences of mental illness exceed sense, and refuse to be pinned down. Head's narrative resists constantly 'Reason's progressive conquest'[27] as it works things out for Elizabeth; that is not to say that patterns, symbols and statements cannot be observed and commented upon, more that the '*repression of that* which [observers in the West] call madness'[28] is constantly evaded and avoided within the text.

Elizabeth's attempt to learn vegetable farming methods in the novel is not a separation from her 'soul' journey: the garden becomes not only the place in which she learns new skills for self-survival, but also the site in which societal, racial and colonial relations are worked out. In part one of the novel, she is sacked from her teaching job because of her breakdown; she is offered a chance to join a cooperative local-industries project in virtually any capacity, and she chooses to work with crops, which takes her first to the farmer's youth development work-group. Elizabeth compares the methods of the stuffy, boring and deeply conservative English farm manager with the more fascinating and human Danish families 'who made up the small group of disgruntled farm-instructors' (71). She quickly observes that the Danish families have brought an almost hermetically sealed environment with them from Denmark, 'down to the last ounce of petrol' (71), yet they are deeply dissatisfied with the local Batswana students, whom they feel are incompetent in comparison with their university-trained minds. The farm manager, however, works with the local people, and allows them to pass on their knowledge in a more traditional way:

> He had selected the most brilliant students, who quickly grasped scientific terms and formulas, and placed them in positions of responsibility over the others. They formed a second vanguard of teaching instructors, communicating in Setswana all the knowledge they had grasped ahead of the others. He never talked about the stupidity or illiteracy of the material he had to work with. (71)

Both approaches – negative and positive – can be seen as models of colonialism, the latter being more successful. But Elizabeth also observes the importance of autonomy from the colonial leaders here when she goes into the field to learn from 'Small-Boy' and encounters the ugly racism of Camilla, who Elizabeth eventually decides loves her home more than she loves people. The perfect order of the 'new methods' (73) in the gardens are described and explained to Elizabeth by Small-Boy, who also continues to work as Elizabeth takes notes from him. This model of industriousness and understanding of the local environment is rudely interrupted by the appearance of one of the Danish staff, Camilla:

> She came speeding towards them, her eyes, her hands, her walk creating a turmoil of distraction, shattering the sleepy, murmuring peace of the garden. All life had to stop and turn towards her. Her voice had an insistent command to it, yet it was no command of life. It was a scatter-brained assertion of self-importance. She stopped an instant at a bed and shouted to Small-Boy. . . .
> . . .
> 'I assist Gunner who is class instructor,' she said. 'He is away on holiday at present. I'm really a landscape gardener in my own country. If someone doesn't come down here during practical work time these trainees will just sit under the trees and play dice.'
> . . .
> All of a sudden, the vegetable garden was the most miserable place on earth. The students had simply become humiliated little boys shoved around by a hysterical white woman who never saw black people as people but as objects of permanent idiocy. (75–6)

The scene is one of abrupt reversal: the autonomy given to the local young men is revealed in their sense of industriousness and dignity. Small-Boy commands a perfectly functioning garden which becomes instantly dysfunctional with the invasion of a racist. The symbolism is clear, but none the less important for that fact. Camilla's actions are not simply some unconscious importing of another culture, they are deliberately geared to making the local people confused and humiliated: 'She flung information at her [Elizabeth] in such a way as to make it totally incomprehensible and meaningless, subtly demonstrating that to reach her level of education Elizabeth had to be able to grasp the incoherent' (76). Yet the opposite happens – Elizabeth judges her character with great insight and clarity, especially when she sees how Camilla lives: 'Elizabeth turned and stared at her incredulously. Houses were loved, not people' (78). Elizabeth does befriend another Dane who is about to leave the country, a woman called Birgette, who attempts to ignore Camilla's racist comments concerning literature. For Elizabeth's journey through self-reflection, leading to the writing of her experiences, this is a key, if quiet, moment. Camilla has been boasting of the advanced level of culture in her own country: 'In our country culture has become so complex, this complexity is reflected in our literature. It takes a certain level of education to understand our novelists. The ordinary man cannot understand them' (79). Apart from the absurdity of this hyperbolic statement, and its role in denigrating diverse African cultures and literatures, it also reveals a desire for a culture divorced from the common people – the 'ordinary man', as she puts it. Elizabeth becomes interested in the character of Birgette, an intellectual who negates Camilla's racism simply by saying 'I don't know anything about it' (80). Birgette and Elizabeth become close, and this enables both the describing of Elizabeth's 'Cape Gooseberry' project (her future fruit-growing and jam-making enterprise) and her feelings about Camilla:

She [Camilla] takes the inferiority of the black man so much for granted that she thinks nothing of telling us straight to our faces we are stupid and don't know anything. There's so many like her. They don't see the shades and shadows of life on black people's faces. She's never stopped a minute, paused, stood back and watched the serious, concentrated expressions of the farm students. There's a dismal life behind them of starvation and years and years of drought when there was no food, no hope, no anything. There's a magical world ahead of them with the despair and drudgery of semi-desert agriculture alleviated by knowledge. (82–3)

The friendship with Birgette helps Elizabeth with the articulation of her feelings; she speaks of the common people from the perspective and experiences of the common people, eventually realizing that the writing of their stories will be a central act, what Margaret E. Tucker calls 'the movement between Elizabeth as inscriber and Elizabeth as that which is inscribed'.[29] This act also redirects lines of power, and shifts Elizabeth from the realm of the abject back into the realm of being a subject (i.e., still subject to the laws of her statelessness, but also a human being who partakes of community life). Tucker points out the importance of Elizabeth's notebook: 'The notebook that Elizabeth keeps on the farming methods is her first writing in the novel. Not only is the actual garden work a source of healing for Elizabeth, but it leads to language and the power of the written word.'[30] Initially, Elizabeth had started to fill her notebook with knowledge passed on to her by Small-Boy, but the interruption by Camilla is also a violent rewriting of her notes: 'She [Camilla] had a way of grasping the notebook out of Elizabeth's hands and scribbling her own notes, with sketches' (76). Tucker argues that this reveals the way in which 'Elizabeth's writing at this point is subject to erasure.'[31] With her denial of Camilla's racism, and her continual working-through of the triangular relationship, Elizabeth's positive experiences take on more and more autonomy and productivity. Thus, the American farm volunteer called Tom gives the notes a status that Camilla would deny them as a mode of indigenous writing. The notes are also transformed and transformative: 'Elizabeth later describes "her version of agriculture" as "poetic and fanciful . . ."' (112–13). The notebook travels from silence to meaning to poetry, echoing Elizabeth's own movement.'[32]

Part two of the novel opens with Dan, the second of Elizabeth's spirit projections, and the contradictions of his character – both the embodiment of wealth, but also the charismatic leader who appeals to mystics: 'One half of him seemed to come shooting in like a meteor from the furthest end of the universe, the other rose slowly from the depths of the earth in the shape of an atomic bomb of red fire; the fire was not a cohesive flame, but broken up into particles of fine red dust' (104). The biblical allusion to a man being created from dust is countered with the apocalyptic imagery of radioactive fallout after the explosion of an atomic bomb. Dan's charisma is intricately linked with his sadism and abusiveness, and the 'particles' of his character are like the fragmented consciousness that Elizabeth experiences in the first part of the novel. Elizabeth's sexualized response to Dan is received by him as if he had 'triumphantly acquired Pavlov's dog' (106), in other words, he expected a certain emotional and sensual response, and having achieved this, thinks of Elizabeth as being entirely in his control. As the narrator says: 'He'd flung a hook right into her pain- and feeling-centre. This he was to use as he pleased: "Now cry, now laugh, now feel jealous." And he adjusted the button to suit his needs' (117). Dan re-creates Elizabeth, and his myriad lovers, as machinic assemblages, designed and built for nothing but coupling and uncoupling, to use Deleuze and Guattari's terms.[33] First Elizabeth's body is rebuilt as 'a network, a complicated communication centre' (126); then Dan's lover 'Miss Sewing-Machine' is brought onto the scene: 'She was a specialist in sex. A symbol went hand in hand with her, a small sewing-machine with a handle' (127). Elizabeth's nightmare is to be inflicted with Dan's sadistic exhibitionism, but she also experiences a horror of all forms of sexuality, including homosexuality. Eventually she becomes what Deleuze and Guattari, drawing upon Antonin Artaud, call 'a body without organs'; she describes herself as 'simply having a mouth and an alimentary tract' (138). As a body without organs she comes into conflict with the role of the desiring-machines: 'Every coupling of machines, every production of a machine, every sound of a machine running, becomes unbearable to the body without organs.'[34] Elizabeth experiences the desiring-machines 'as an over-all persecution apparatus'.[35] She must find a way of countering the desiring-machines as constructed by Dan, and this is why she invests in her relationship with him: '. . . the body without organs invests a counterinside or a counteroutside, in the form of a persecuting organ or some exterior agent of persecution.'[36] In a synecdochic reduction, Dan is precisely that 'persecuting organ'. But again, in parallel with this experience, language and writing assume an important role. Tom, the American farm volunteer, not only uses Elizabeth's notebook, but he loses an argument concerning spelling with Elizabeth's son. Tom has noticed that 'Shorty' has spelt 'evaporation' incorrectly in his notebook, spelling it '*i*vaporation' (125). After Elizabeth's son refuses to concede his ground, Tom decides to visit the schoolteacher the next day. What he discovers is that all of her words are both 'incorrectly' and 'correctly' spelt: she is using phonetics to teach the children English. Elizabeth laughs when she hears this and says: 'Wherever English travels, it's adapted. That's Setswana English' (126). Elizabeth may soon be reduced, via her breakdown, to a body without organs, but she is gaining in linguistic power. Her ability in the garden is matched by her ability to 'grow' a new literature, one which will also powerfully rework the English language from an African perspective, adapted to her local, personal and community needs.

THE IMPACT OF *A QUESTION OF POWER*

An early review by Roberta Rubenstein of *A Question of Power* recognized Bessie Head's achievement, arguing that the novel 'succeeds as an intense, even mythic, dramatization of the mind's struggle for autonomy and as a symbolic protest against the political realities of South Africa'.[37] The reception and critical engagement with Head's novel has been varied and sustained, although some critics have argued, with perhaps some justification, that *A Question of Power* often exceeds the critical capacity of those attempting to engage with its complex, multifaceted nature (for example, my reading only touches lightly upon some of the key relationships and experiences explored in the text).[38] Angelo Fick argues that Head 'has inspired (and has also been inspired by) a veritable industry of scholarship that has ranged from deeply problematic and banal work . . . to . . . exceptionally perceptive and engaging analyses'.[39] The question of focus is important here. What may be banal for one critic may simply be a reading that takes place in a different critical capacity, and with different goals. For example, the gender politics of *A Question of Power* intersect powerfully and at times problematically with a range of racial stereotypes, in part drawn from apartheid South Africa (people of mixed-race and Asian origin receiving the most derogatory treatment – and description – in the novel). Sope Maithufi has been critical of this treatment, arguing that Head, 'like Fanon . . . ends up confusing the biological essence of the black race with the underpinnings of [its] potential political ideologies'.[40] Maithufi expands upon this statement, with an autobiographical observation in passing, by noting:

As in South Africa, the only dominant anti-white colonial front is militant black nationalism, one which, like Fanon's opinion about 'the black man', unwittingly confirms colonial domination by using blackness in its denotation of biological essence as a conceptual schema for liberation. In the setting of this novel, this premise provides for the creation of female inferiority in the same way that apartheid created black diversity.[41]

While critical consensus has not been reached concerning the theme of gender and race articulated in conjunction with questions concerning 'insanity' or 'madness' in *A Question of Power*, there is some agreement that the novel 'is one of the most intense examinations of this theme',[42] with Adetokunbo Pearse arguing that '[n]o work in the corpus of African literature dealing with the theme of madness . . . captures the complexity and intensity of the insane mind as does Bessie Head's *A Question of Power*.'[43] More recent assessments of Head's impact have remarked on the ways in which her writing has influenced theoretical developments. As Maxine Sample puts it, Head's 'fictional and autobiographical writings of more than fifteen years, shaped by her experience of exile from South African apartheid, offer much to scholars in the areas of postcolonial literatures, cultural studies, and feminism'.[44] This is not to suggest some kind of textual seam to be mined, more a complex space of intellectual and political engagement that can help elucidate theoretical ideas. For example, in engaging in a feminist reading of Head, Margaret E. Tucker's use of Cixous is not unidirectional, as Natasha C. Vaubel explains:

. . . Tucker does not so much use Helene Cixous' theory to explicate Head's creative writing as vice versa. . . . Cobham points to Head's 'interlocution with Cixous' and suggests that 'African women writers . . . occupy within their cultures the intellectual space that in the West has become the province of critics and theoreticians. That is, they use their creative writing to participate in a discourse replete with political, sociological, and theoretical aspirations – as well as didactic overtones – that in Western cultures would differentiate the work of the critic from the artist.' She calls for a reassessing of 'the hierarchical nature of the relationship between the two genres (of Western critical theories and African literatures) . . .'.[45]

It is my contention that, as with the other novelists studied in this book, Head's work does lead to precisely such a powerful and at times profound 'reassessment'.

6 Recoding Narrative

Margaret Atwood's *Surfacing*

A 'distinct feminist voice' has long been heard in Margaret Atwood's novel, *Surfacing* (1972).[1] It is a voice which articulates issues of gender, subjectivity, madness, nationality, ecology and narrative power. Often read in conjunction with Atwood's work of literary theory, *Survival*,[2] which was published in the same year, it is possible in retrospect to see how *Surfacing* created a schema through which key feminist and other critical debates in Canada could take place. M. Prabhakar regards this schema as a 'blue-print of revolt' which in effect facilitates a quest for freedom and autonomy.[3] Yet it is important not to perceive the novel as therefore formulaic; in its critique of gender relations from a feminist perspective, the novel also performs a deeper destabilizing critique, as Erinç Özdemir argues: '. . . the novel valorizes femininity against masculinity, while at the same time it paradoxically dramatizes a desire to destroy all dichotomies and dualistic thinking.'[4] The tension between these two movements can be seen in the historical range of the novel's reception: early feminist readings tended to focus on the valorization of femininity, whereas more contemporary theorists perceive a more dynamic attack upon binary concepts and structures. Regardless of the critical approach taken, most readers are aware of the importance of language in the novel, especially as a tool of oppression and possible resistance to, or subversion of, patriarchal power structures. As Özdemir further argues:

Writing, literary and otherwise . . . [is] a subversive tool for women in trying to create a space for a feminine, 'heterogeneous *difference*' outside the static closure of the binary oppositions that underlie patriarchal ideology. . . . Significantly, Atwood has her heroine in *Surfacing* say, 'It was the language again. I couldn't use it because it wasn't mine' (100). She is depicted as enacting a painful but determined search for another language, one that would allow non-destructive relationships with others and nature. Such a language would preclude the reductive and alienating relationships of domination and subordination reflected by the subject–object split that characterizes the syntax of our current language.[5]

The quest within the novel – where the protagonist is attempting to find her missing father – is thus first of all an attempt to gain a self-reflexive knowledge of the power relations that define the protagonist's identity, an identity which will in turn be rejected or shed like a dead skin. Given that the novel is at first narrated from the perspective of the identity which is eventually rejected, there is not only a thematic shift in the novel, but a narrational shift; the earlier 'version' or subjectivity of the narrator-protagonist is later regarded as 'unreliable'. An ironic tension is created by the narrator-protagonist's journey (into nature and self-identity), as Linda Hutcheon observes: 'This trip into nature, into the literal and symbolic landscape . . . is the voyage of a woman and an artist; it is her attempt to find her self (moral and psychological), her past (personal and gendered), and her identity (private and national).'[6] One of the problems in regarding the novel as a schema is that readings can appear too distant (applying a theoretical straitjacket to the text) or too close (simply following one interpretive thread). Is there a way of reading Atwood's novel which balances the two approaches? One possibility is to maintain an awareness of narrative strategies and structure, as well as having a theoretical focus. In what follows I propose that Atwood's 'unreliable narrator' functions in myriad ways, but, overall, she offers a challenge to more traditional ways of reading, and writing, fictional texts.

READING *SURFACING*

Since its initial publication, *Surfacing* has been an immensely *popular* book, both with critics and with general readers. Part of this popularity stems from the fact that it is a novel that successfully plays games with the reader, undermining, tricking, even teasing the reader with the novel's 'faulty' or 'unreliable narration'. The notion of an 'unreliable narrator' is *de rigueur* within postmodernism; indeed 'unreliability' could be thought of as the defining feature of a postmodern narrator, simultaneously deconstructing the possibility of a *reliable* one.[7] Unreliability can be equated with what is known as the linguistic turn, whereby any statement is perceived as being merely an interpretation within an infinite range of different interpretations. Put differently, any statement is merely perceived as a construct within an infinite range of different constructs: there can be no 'reliability' if there is no solid space of actuality and singularity. Atwood's narrator-protagonist is, crudely speaking and literally, *unreliable*; however, in terms of a general reader-response, the narrator is received and interpreted in a definable sequence: first she is reliable; then she clearly becomes seen as unreliable; then clearly she is reliable again. This sequence can be articulated another way: the reader doesn't realize at first (i.e., in a first reading) that the narrator is lying; then the reader realizes something is amiss, that certain statements don't make sense, or contradict one another, and so on; then the reader learns, *through the narrator*, the 'truth' about her past. For example, the following examples shift from the first to the third positions in such a sequence:

We begin to climb and my husband catches up with me again, making one of the brief appearances, framed memories he specializes in: crystal clear image enclosed by a blank wall. He's writing his own initials on a fence, graceful scrolls to show me how, lettering was one of the things he taught. There are other initials on the fence but he's making his bigger, leaving his mark. I can't identify the date or place, it was a city, before we were married. . . .

. . .

I turned the ring on my left-hand finger, souvenir: he gave it to me, plain gold, he said he didn't like ostentation, it got us into the motels easier, opener of doors; in the intervening time I wore it on a chain around my neck.[8]

Read purely in isolation, each set of statements carries as such its own normative values. The first memory sequence is a 'crystal clear image' even though, according to the grammatical reading, such an image is created by the narrator's 'husband' not the narrator, and the image cannot be spatially or temporally located. The second set of statements shifts from the mark-making of the first to the symbolic powers of the wedding ring, yet, in explaining those powers, the narrator is also undermining her status as a married woman: she is revealing her marital status to be a performance or a lie. The question of normativity is central to notions of reliability/unreliability, but is not always straightforward. Shlomith Rimmon-Kenan takes a common-sense approach to the entire subject, stating that a 'reliable narrator is one whose rendering of the story and commentary on it the reader is supposed to take as an authoritative account of the fictional truth. An unreliable narrator . . . is one whose rendering of the story and/or commentary on it the reader has reasons to suspect.'[9] Of course, Rimmon-Kenan is aware that things are not always this simple: reliability has to be defined through a process of negation, because the unreliable narrator is easier to define, and therefore the reliable narrator is what the unreliable narrator is not. Rimmon-Kenan suggests that there are 'sources' of unreliability, the main ones being 'the narrator's limited knowledge, his [*sic*] personal involvement, and his problematic value-schema'.[10] In extreme opposition to these sources we find the most reliable type to be a 'covert extradiegetic narrator, especially when he is also heterodiegetic'[11] – in other words, a narrator outside of the story-world, who doesn't make personal, value-laden comments about the story-world. Such an approach as Rimmon-Kenan takes, while open to the ambiguities and exceptions to the rule, does not really get to the heart of the shift from the reliable/unreliable binary opposition to that of postmodernism, where unreliability not only rules, but is dissolved in the process (*all narrators are necessarily unreliable*). Unexpectedly, given the dominance of contemporary theory, it is Wayne C. Booth who can tell us more about the concept of 'unreliability' in his early work *The Rhetoric of Fiction*.

Booth, in a chapter on 'Confusion of Distance', refers to an analogous situation to that of Atwood's *Surfacing*: James's *The Turn of the Screw*. Both narratives have unnamed narrators, but *The Turn of the Screw* does not 'resolve' the status of the narrator's statements, whereas *Surfacing* does. Booth runs through the standard arguments for and against the reliability of the narrator in *The Turn of the Screw*, i.e., those arguments that attempt to analyse the psychic 'deficiencies' of the narrator, and those that take her judgements at face value; the resulting 'unintentional ambiguity of effect' found in such modern novels is seen as endlessly proliferating.[12] An examination of 'confusions of distance' created in earlier eighteenth-century fiction enables Booth to prepare the way for his analysis of modern fiction. He argues that there are a number of causes that problematize the question of distance, these are: 'Lack of adequate warning that irony is at work'; 'Extreme complexity, subtlety, or privacy of the norms to be inferred'; and 'Vivid psychological realism'.[13] In relation to *Surfacing*, the latter cause is of most interest, because it appears from this perspective to diminish the capacity for sound judgement in the reader, and it is the one that Booth argues creates sympathy for protagonists who may not morally deserve it: 'The deep plunges of modern inside views, the various streams-of-consciousness that attempt to give the reader an effect of living thought and sensation, are capable of blinding us to the possibility of our making judgements not shared by the narrator or reflector himself.'[14] The pre-eminent form for such a 'deep plunge', according to Booth, is autobiography: '. . . let us finally bind the reader so tightly to the consciousness of the ambiguously misguided protagonist that nothing will interfere with his [*sic*] delight in inferring the precise though varying degrees of distance that operate from point to point throughout the book.'[15] Resisting the relativism of infinite co-present interpretations of any one text, with especial reference to Joyce's work, Booth is reminding the critic that certain 'factual' bases must exist in a text for judgements to be grounded. While this appears immensely outmoded after postmodernism, it is not outmoded in relation to a general theory of functional perception:

> When the novelist chooses to deliver his facts and summaries as though from the mind of one of his characters, he is in danger of surrendering precisely 'that liberty of transcending the limits of the immediate scene' – particularly the limits of that character he has chosen as his mouthpiece. . . . it is enough to say that a fact, when it has been given to us by the author or his unequivocal spokesman, is a very different thing from the same 'fact' when given to us by a fallible character in the story. When a character speaks realistically, within the drama, the convention of absolute reliability has been destroyed, and while the gains for some fictional purposes are undeniable, the costs are undeniable too.[16]

Put simply, Booth is saying that in the above situation we no longer have the capacity to distinguish between ironic or factual narrative; to move beyond these categories, we no longer know whether any statement made by the restricted narrator is true or false because it is necessarily coloured by that narrator's perspective. Of course the ultimate position taken is that all statements can be read ironically and that all statements lose factuality; the suspicion of 'grand narratives' is another way of putting this. Such a leap, from the particular to the general, may miss the point that it is the mechanism for making a judgement that has been degraded. From a post-colonial and postmodernist perspective, such a 'degradation' is a liberation; as Booth puts it, 'The convincing texture of the whole, the impression of life as experienced by an observer, is in itself surely what the true artist seeks.'[17] In other words, the 'partiality' of the perspective is also equal to the entire inner experience of that perspective, and this subjectivity is now the aim, rather than prior notions of objectivity. But still, Booth points out that critical debate continues to be generated by indeterminate narrative structures and mechanisms of judgement, whereas if they were to be simply celebrated (the celebration of 'play'), debate would presumably come to an end. In attempting a genetic explanation of unreliable narrators, via their authorial, archival traces, Booth suggests that the 'inconscient' narratorial agent ultimately overtakes artistic intention and common sense. Ambiguities are generated and then let out of authorial control.

This above analysis appears to be the complete opposite to the way in which Atwood's *Surfacing* is constructed: ambiguities are carefully managed throughout the text, and are deliberately placed, interwoven and eventually critiqued by the narrator. As Thieme notes:

> The reader has to proceed a considerable way into the narrative before s/he is able to gauge the nature of this consciousness and assess the extent of its reliability. The mode of narration is interior monologue. The protagonist relates events and describes her reactions in the present tense, but frequently includes episodes from her past life after the manner of the stream-of-consciousness novel. The ordering and inclusion of these flashbacks is determined by an associative logic and what the reader learns about her is very piecemeal. But from very early on there are details which raise doubts as to her reliability. Thus she speaks of her brother having drowned, but we later discover that he did not really do so.[18]

Ironically, there is a paradoxical reversal here: Booth is attempting to ascertain distance between the author's artistic vision and the unreliable narrator's problematic handling of that vision; within postmodernism, the 'author' is decentred and reduced to having the same status as any other subjective character or narrator. Yet, and this is crucial, Atwood is praised for her authorial control of the unreliable–reliable narrator, at a time when intentionalism fundamentally has no meaning, i.e., the author's artistic vision is perceived as being as subjective as the unreliable narrator's artistic, moral, psychological, etc., vision. Booth worries about loss of authorial control, whereas contemporary critics celebrate authorial control during a period when the death of the author has already supposedly occurred. Finally, for Booth, it is not so much ambiguity and indeterminacy that are problematic, it is that the mechanisms for making judgements have themselves been blunted as such by an expectation that ambiguity and indeterminacy are all that one can expect to read or ever find within a text. In contrast to *The Rhetoric of Fiction*, Andrew Gibson, for example, ponders the development of a postmodern ethics in his *Postmodernity, Ethics and the Novel*. One of the essential differences between the two eras of narrative theory represented by these two books is that of postmodernism's problematization of 'the mimetic premise'.[19] As Gibson argues: 'Of all the unexamined assumptions on the basis of which a traditional ethical criticism of fiction proceeded, one of the most crucial was the assumption that, in fiction, ethics and representation are inseparable. Such an assumption makes it impossible for a novel to have an ethical dimension outside its mimetic project.'[20] It is precisely at the limits of representation, the boundary-blurring moments, the aporetics of a text, and through the text's exploration of the 'unrepresentable' that a postmodern ethics emerges: that is to say, once the ethical project is redefined, then Booth's worries can in the main be set aside. In *Surfacing*, the issue of *who* controls representation is essential to the novel's ethics: mark-making, map-making, linguistic and filmic semiotics, symbols and hallucinatory signs all compete for control of the text itself; the novel is suspended as such between competing modes of representation, where the various language systems form another constellation. But this is not a purely relative network, rather, the constellation provides the tools for perception, via aesthetic and ideological modes. Crucially, the issue of reliability/unreliability is dependent upon the notion of experience, and how this in turn affects mechanisms of judgement and perception.

Different types of experience are brought together in *Surfacing*, such as those of childhood, adulthood, adultery, abortion, problematic relationships, neuroses, fantasies, feminism, fascism, and so on. Each type of experience can be explored via competing critical models, i.e., those which it is argued have the *capacity* to explore/explain the experience's effects to the full. But thinking about *all* of the experiences as bundled explosively together, the novel registers as being an exploration of the concept of experience itself. The narrator, far from being overtly unreliable, meditates upon her selectivity concerning the experiences she will share: 'I have to keep myself from telling that story' (14). At the level of perception, she theorizes that all of her experiences existed as a displacement of other experiences. Early on in the novel, she thinks of her childhood as a time of peace, for example, as well as being a displacement of what was happening in the world: '. . . I had a good childhood; it was in the middle of the war, flecked grey newsreels I never saw, bombs and concentration camps, the leaders roaring at the crowds from inside their uniforms, pain and useless death, flags rippling in time to the anthems' (18). The narrator realizes not only that later, retrospectively applied knowledge colours her notion of the past, but that the immediate experience itself is always already a negation of the ongoing catastrophe of humanity's pain and self-destruction. Experience is not something composed of immediate, chronologically progressive sense-perceptions; rather, it is multi-temporal. Shuli Barzilai explores this: 'A structural analogy may . . . be drawn between the assumptive pronouns of *Surfacing* and the double or multiple images forming one photoplate. In terms of the road unwillingly taken, they represent points of intersection where someone or something in the present meets with someone or something previously encountered.'[21] My suggestion is that this process occurs as a constitutive, not unusual or exceptional, process in the novel. Barzilai argues that here 'temporality is canceled out so that individuals inhabiting the zones of then and now might be convened.'[22] Another way of putting this cancelling out is that chronological progression is 'under erasure' in the deconstructive sense, where the notion is both held in place and temporarily crossed-out or suspended to examine the further complexities of a concept or a process. In *Surfacing* examples of temporality being under erasure, thus revealing the necessary multi-temporal aspect of experience, occur constantly (they may in fact simply make up the fabric of the novel itself): for example, in chapter two:

But Madame doesn't mention it, she lifts another cube of sugar from the tray by her side and he intrudes, across from me, a coffee shop, not city but roadside, on the way to or from somewhere, some goal or encounter. He peels the advertisement paper from the sugar and lets one square fall into the cup, I'm talking and his mouth turns indulgent, it must have been before the child. He smiles and I smile too, thinking of the slice of cucumber pickle that was stuck to the top of his club sandwich. A round historical plaque, on a supermarket wall or in a parking lot, marking the site where a building once stood in which an event of little importance once took place, ridiculous. (23–4)

The narrative present – sipping tea with some old family friends – is conjoined with a strong memory. In narrative theory, this could be thought of as a flashback, or analepsis, except that the narrator uses the word 'intrudes', suggesting that the present is being uncontrollably muddied with the past. Again, from a traditional critical perspective, this passage is presented via an unreliable narrator: she is talking about an event that may or may not have happened (and a child who was aborted), although the event itself is not singular or stable: it is presented as a montage. The event happened either on the way to or from 'something', with the reader's retrospective knowledge suggesting that the 'something' is a sexual liaison or affair. The description of the two people suggests that they are talking at odds, and that what is elided is as important as what might have been said. In relation to the notion of a multi-temporality, however, the central image of the passage is that of the 'round historical plaque' which commemorates a site and an 'event of little importance'. The image of the plaque has been segued to that of the 'slice of cucumber pickle'; in other words, it is not entirely clear if the plaque's commemoration is 'this' event (the illicit meeting). A plaque is an object overloaded with significance and imperatives: it commands that we are mindful of something, usually a person or an historical event; we are being commanded to remember that person or event, to 'intrude' the present with the past, for a range of reasons, from the banal to the extremely important. The narrator remembers that her peaceful childhood was adjacent to the invisible (from her perspective) catastrophe of the war and the Holocaust; she retrospectively commemorates those who suffered alongside her peaceful existence. But in the passage under scrutiny, the commemoration is unwanted, it is a nuisance, and an event that she feels is no longer of any significance anyway: why keep harking back to the past? In this passage, the past is itself problematically conveyed; experiences are selectively shared or fantasized or simply distorted for a while beyond all recognition. The commemoration thus becomes a reminder that the past has constantly to be revisited if we are to make sense of the present, because versions or interpretations of the past will compete or vie with one another for pre-eminence. The narrator performs triage on her memories: 'He puts his hand on mine, he tries that a lot but he's easy to get rid of, easier and easier. I don't have time for him, I switch problems' (24). But the switching, to the narrative present, is not a simple abandonment of the past for the present; the switching of 'problems' means that the childhood memories are now being reinvestigated: 'There used to be a barometer on the porch wall . . .', or, 'When it was first explained to me . . .' (24).

Another way of thinking through this multi-temporality is in relation to Walter Benjamin's 'differentia of time', which Andrew Benjamin suggests 'could be temporal montage, the copresence of different times'.[23] This phrase relates in the case of *Surfacing* to the way in which different times 'intrude' upon the narrative present (or, put differently, construct the narrative present): 'It will awaken a possibility in which the present as temporal montage will reorient itself in relation to the given and thus to that which is given to it.'[24] Gérard Genette, no doubt, would think of *Surfacing*'s differentia of time as sabotage,[25] although at a general level the novel conforms to an historically embedded pattern: 'We know that this beginning *in medias res*, followed by an expository return to an earlier period of time, will become one of the formal topoi of epic, and we also know how faithfully the style of novelistic narration follows in this respect the style of its remote ancestor.'[26] Atwood is pushing at the boundaries of the novel's form with *Surfacing* and her writing in the novel is primarily imagistic. The problem with traditional narrative theory is that it reveals *anachronisms* (jumps in time) where Atwood constructs *temporal montages*; in other words, narrative theory reveals two dimensions while Atwood works with three dimensions at the very least.

Atwood's widening of the concept of a narrator's acceptably explored experiences, undermining the theories of narrative that label the narrator unreliable in the first place, is interpreted in general by critics as a form of *manifesto writing*. That is to say, *Surfacing* becomes not a novel but an implicit or explicit manifesto for eco-warriors, feminists, nationalists, psychoanalytic critics, and so on. Such ideological readings are themselves temporally located, giving the novel an air of being both out-of-date (e.g., outmoded 'seventies' feminism) and of the utmost relevance (e.g., still relevant to contemporary debates about feminism, nationalism, and so on). Such a paradoxical and contradictory formulation is related to the mode of the manifesto itself, and the question becomes: is *Surfacing* a manifesto, or does

Surfacing explore the manifesto mode as being indicative of transformed, previously unreflective, experience? In other words, by defining the narrator's existence as being self-reflexive, rather than unreliable, power is embedded and embodied by her analyses and choices. Manifestoes themselves make up a discursive formation, to use Foucault's terminology (from his *Archaeology of Knowledge*),[27] made up of particular statements; Mary Ann Caws describes some typical statements:

At its most endearing, a manifesto has a madness about it. It is peculiar and angry, quirky, or downright crazed. Always opposed to something, particular or general. . . .

The manifesto proclamation itself marks a moment, whose trace it leaves as a post-event commemoration. Often the event is exactly its own announcement and nothing more, in this Modernist/Postmodernist genre.
. . .

Generally posing some 'we,' explicit or implicit, against some other 'they,' with the terms constructed in a deliberate dichotomy, the manifesto can be set up like a battlefield. It can start out as a credo, but then it wants to make a persuasive move from the 'I believe' of the speaker toward the 'you' of the listener or reader, who should be sufficiently convinced to join in.[28]

There are many instances of the oppositional 'they' in *Surfacing*, from the remembered family, the hunters in the countryside, to the group of friends the narrator is travelling with; various other people become constituted by the 'they': '. . . they must have missed something, I feel it will be different if I look myself' (24). The first-person singular of the novel constantly reasserts itself even through the manifesto moments where some oppositional grouping (say, 'Americans') creates a unified counter-grouping (such as 'Canada') to which the narrator presumably can feel a momentary sense of belonging. The 'battlefield' within the novel is an open-ended chiasmus or crossing between the 'I' and the 'they/we' which replicates to some degree the typical battles within ideological groups who produce manifestoes; in other words, between the charismatic leader and the other members of the group. Continuing with the above extract from Caws, the manifesto mode is considered insane in relation to the normative discourses of society; in *Surfacing*, the narrator is not just dealing with the psychological impact of her abortion, she is dealing with the ongoing taboo of the act of abortion in the first place.[29] Even given a progressive society and debates over women's power to control their own bodies, abortion is an act where discursive norms have not been produced, however, and this complicates the manifesto mode. The event-like status of the manifesto moment is one of complex temporality, relating to the above discussion of the differentia. The manifesto must separate itself spatially and temporally from normative notions of aesthetics, discourse, history, society and so on; it creates its own spatial and temporal zone that is shocking to those who feel that the world they inhabit is the natural one. Suddenly to produce a radically different way of conceiving not only ideas, but events and time, is disturbing and powerful, even if such an alternative perspective ultimately remains iso-lated. Caws thinks of the 'nowness' of the manifesto as essentially modern-ist: 'The manifesto moment positions itself between what has been done and what will be done, between the accomplished and the potential, in a radical and energizing division.'[30] This positioning is one of utmost serious-ness, whereas a purely postmodern discourse would undermine itself through irony and parody. Atwood's *Surfacing* is thus situated dialogically between modernism and postmodernism.

THE IMPACT OF *SURFACING*

In an insightful survey and analysis of Atwood's impact on teaching (in the United States, Canada and Europe), Caroline Rosenthal concludes that Atwood's work 'raises and intersects many different issues: Canadian, feminist, anthropological, and cultural studies concerns as well as postco-lonialist criticism'.[31] In part, these concerns with her work as an act of ongoing creativity and productivity can also be seen to emerge from *Surfac-ing* itself. As Alice M. Palumbo puts it: 'The manners in which this novel has been analyzed by critics (as ghost story, family story, anatomy of a breakdown [etc.]) all highlight the layering of histories and cultures in the novel.'[32] As a layered text, or a *palimpsest*, the novel has had a strangely doubled existence: continually reread for its key themes (especially that of a feminist manifesto), the novel has also undergone a more sophisticated 'archaeological dig' as critics have uncovered its less obvious layers. Simul-taneously, the novel is often doubled, twinned or paired with Atwood's *Survival*, leading some critics to assert not so much that the novel is a blue-print of revolt, as suggested above, but that it is actually a blueprint 'for escaping the nightmare' of the 'Basic Victim Positions' described in *Sur-vival*.[33] One constant during the years since the publication of *Surfacing* has been the way in which the novel generates a sociological and cultural response: that is to say, critics have used the novel to trigger further explo-ration of Canadian society and culture, especially with its tensions and relationships with its immediate neighbour America. In other words, critics constantly utilize *Surfacing* to gain a better understanding of Canada's recent past and the present. For example, in mapping the similarities between the characters called 'Joe' – in *The Edible Woman* and in *Surfacing* – Henry C. Phelps concludes that the 'explicit link' between these two novels created by 'Joe' originates in the ways in which both novels 'develop a remarkably insightful portrait of that legendary decade, the Sixties'.[34] The symbolic transformation of 'Joe' appears to Phelps 'a deliberately devastating in-dictment of the decade', which is given a more general signification in *Surfacing*:

The pervasive sense in the . . . novel of wasted opportunities, deepening bitterness, isolation, and empty – even aborted – lives casts a consciously dark shadow over the era of so-called freedom and liberation. Atwood's skillful embodiment in a single character of the perniciousness of these changes both displays an unexpected facility for implied social commentary and offers a new perspective for examining her already intriguing narratives.'[35]

Early responses to Atwood's novel often shared another notion: that it would *endure*. Only five years after its publication, Bruce King argued that *Surfacing* was 'likely to last beyond the topicality of its themes'.[36] Responding thematically, but also exploring briefly some interesting comparisons with Atwood's poetry, King also maps the novel schematically, but with focus on Canadian literary criticism: 'Margaret Atwood has made her narrator's sensibility express many of the well known topics of Canadian literary criticism: a land of solitude, the lost garden, the sacrificial figure and even what Atwood once described as a tendency towards "paranoid schizophrenia". The novel is a representation of such themes and an attempt to go further.'[37] Importantly, this recognition of Atwood's fulfilling of the literary-critical role mapped out in *Survival* – and, even more importantly, going beyond that role – reveals the 'internationalizing' of Canadian literature and criticism, for which Atwood was partly responsible. It is worth returning to Rosenthal's survey to explore the full extent and the implications of this impact:

In a 1997 *Globe & Mail* SURVEY [*sic*] titled 'The Takeout Window of Canadian Nationalism,' Atwood is listed among the ten most famous and internationally known Canadians. . . . Although Wayne Gretzky leads the inventory and Atwood ranks only after Céline Dion and Anne Murray, she is significantly the only English-Canadian author who is listed at all. Even though her prominence in the countries under consideration [in Rosenthal's article] varies – Atwood is listed second last in Canada while in the US she ranks sixth, the UK seventh, and in Germany she is the fourth best known Canadian – these statistics confirm what I had guessed at before I started research for this article, namely that internationally Margaret Atwood is better known than any other English-Canadian author.[38]

The 'cultlike status'[39] of Atwood explored briefly by Rosenthal in her conclusion, especially in the form of official and unofficial websites, is reflected even more thoroughly in the book collection in which Rosenthal's essay is published, where many pages of essays, photographs, cartoons and bibliographical materials compete to delineate Atwood as icon.[40] This iconic status is given definition in the Atwood entry in the monumental *Encyclopedia of Literature in Canada*, where she is described as: 'Poet, novelist, children's writer, cartoonist, and cultural commentator.'[41] Additionally, in terms of Atwood as icon, Sharon Hengen and William H. New note that 'Atwood's name became synonymous with the cultural flowering that took place in Canada during the last 25 years of the 20th century.'[42] The comments in the *Bloomsbury Guide to Women's Literature* reveal the most sustained contributions and interventions that Atwood has made within feminism; after calling Atwood 'Canada's most important contemporary writer, without peer in range and international stature', the entry goes on to note that the 'influence of Atwood's work on contemporary writing by women is indisputable. She articulates the various experiences of women and of girls in powerfully moving ways that function also as acerbic and telling social criticism.'[43] A key aspect of such experiences is women's mediation via systems of oppressive and commodifying representation, for example the various *visual technologies* of subjection-through-representation. As such, Atwood is renowned for her 'resistance to representation',[44] and her exploration of power relations reveals the ways in which such technologies are both the tools and the very medium of the inscription and reproduction of patriarchal systems of being and thought. The presencing of women via visual technologies is also a mode of exclusion, and this is embodied most powerfully in *Surfacing* in the character of Anna. According to Özdemir, '. . . her soul is trapped in the mirror where she rehearses ready-made images of female beauty, none of which is herself: "a seamed and folded imitation of a magazine picture that is itself an imitation of a woman who is also an imitation, the original nowhere." '[45] This labyrinthine mirroring of subjectivity is not something separate from the medium; rather, it is via the medium that subjectivity is produced. The stress in *Surfacing* on the need for a new language is also a desire for a new medium of representation, a process that has fascinated feminist literary and cultural critics who are working primarily with the new French and North American feminist theorists. Thus the early reception to the novel in terms of the 'grail motifs' (i.e., the quest schema) is recoded from a feminist perspective by a critic such as Sue Thomas: 'These motifs, reconceived in substantially feminist terms, provide a most illuminating mythological context for the central mother/daughter relationship and the narrator's senses of maternal inadequacy and guilt.'[46] As *Surfacing* continues to be reread by a new wave of feminist and other critics, the novel continues to offer a schema that leads to further exploration of the relations between subjects and society, language and power, and the technologies of exploitation and representation.

7 The Rushdie Affair

Salman Rushdie's *The Satanic Verses*

The furore that erupted in the wake of the *fatwa* (death sentence) following the publication of Salman Rushdie's *The Satanic Verses* (1988) brought the postcolonial novel into the public consciousness in a way that no other literary text had ever previously achieved. The issues that generated this furore are immensely complex (although they can be broken down into their constituent parts), and led at a number of levels to a sustained re-examination of reading practices, and the relationships between multiple secular and religious responses to literary texts (or, perhaps more accurately, the *gulf* between multiple secular and sacred responses). Any survey, however, of the 'Rushdie Affair', as it was soon known, risks reducing or stereotyping the participants. While it would be naïve to expect a critic *not* to take a particular angle, this chapter will attempt to present multiple perspectives on the debates and the novel, regarding overall the publication of the novel as an historical event, whereby a literary text became the focal point for expressing cultural and ideological differences. To reduce the multiple perspectives to two sides – for example, a homogeneous secularism versus a homogenous Islam, or a singular 'aesthetic' versus a singular 'religious' reading – is already far too simplistic. Instead of reproducing binary stereotypes, this chapter will attempt to survey the Rushdie Affair using the concept of the critical constellation: that is, a number of competing and even contradictory perspectives on the novel may be taken by one individual, creating diverse patterns or interpretive frameworks of reader-response. For example, taking an experiential approach, Pnina Werbner notes:

When Muslims I know read *The Satanic Verses* they are deeply offended not by the rational questioning of the Qur'an's divine source – they are used to such sceptical critiques – but by the juxtaposed contiguity of profane language and profane acts or persons with the image of the Prophet and his companions and wives. The book is perceived as a single and undivided physical space.[1]

In other words, the offensiveness is not simply caused by a religious or moral response, it is also an 'aesthetic' one:

The offence is a gut feeling of shock. All the Muslims with whom I have discussed the book feel certain that Rushdie as a Muslim, albeit a lapsed one, intended this

offence. The aesthetic canons they deploy make this conclusion logical and inescapable. What they find difficult to comprehend is the West's incomprehension.
Instead, they believe that a West which praises the book does so because it shares
the author's desire to offend and ridicule them and their faith. This explains the
religious Muslim intellectual response. . . . It also explains why even the moder-
ately religious responded so violently. Their response was one of aesthetic 'disgust'
and shock, a response rooted in the imagination, intuitive and emotional rather
than self-interested, analytical or jurisprudential.[2]

It is important to think more closely about this quotation, to note and mark
its points of resistance to stereotyping. What Werbner is foregrounding is
the ways in which a range of Muslim readers *do not* reproduce the stereotype
produced and recycled by some western critics: the stereotype that says
'Muslim readers respond politically or religiously to *The Satanic Verses*, but
they have no aesthetic understanding (and thus miss the fact that the novel
is fictional, self-parodic, etc.).'[3] Instead of this stereotyping, Werbner shows
how in her sample of Muslim readers, the reader-responses involve an
'imaginative' theory of reading, one which binds personal intuition and
emotion with other analytical processes. The crude western journalistic
answer to Muslim readers – which can be reduced to the formula or statement: 'it's just a novel' – shows how there is a concomitant lack of awareness
of the postcolonial novel as a vehicle for ideological and political resistance
and change. In other words, if *The Satanic Verses* is 'just a novel', some kind
of hermetically sealed purely self-referential device, then, bizarrely, that
means that it can have no impact upon ideas and processes of being in the
world. However, if Rushdie's novel is 'a novel that performs a subtle and
sophisticated critique of Islam, *for its own good* (i.e., a more liberal[4] notion
of Islam)' (another circulated statement), then suddenly the novel *does*
engage with the ideology and being-in-the-world; in which case, Muslim
responses that were previously discounted by western readers should surely
now be engaged with, even listened to and respected. As Alex Knönagel
puts it: 'One would be mistaken . . . in downplaying the religious component in a novel that not only carries a religious reference in its title but
abounds with Islamic references and connotations. In its very structure, the
novel raises issues that are of cardinal importance from the point of view
of Islamic ethics and aesthetics.'[5] The conjunction of 'ethics and aesthetics'
is key. As Knönagel further argues: 'A comprehensive study of *The Satanic
Verses* shows that the novel presents in its text the description of a world
in which most values presented by and promoted in the Qur'an are inverted.
In fact, the whole novel can be read as an inversion of the qur'anic text.'[6]
This 'inversion' is merely one manifestation, albeit the most controversial,
of Rushdie's methodology. As Stephen Baker puts it, this methodology is
one which 'is based on endless conflict and revision, particularly in its
engagement with cultural, literary and socio-political history'.[7] In the
reading of the novel that follows, two main sections of the book are examined: first, the Jahilia ('Mahound') and 'Return to Jahilia' chapters, which

lie at the heart of *The Satanic Verses* controversy; second, section five of the novel, 'A City Visible but Unseen', which is a powerful parody of immigrant London, and is generally considered the most 'accessible' part of the novel for secular readers. Because of the complex interplay of critical and other reactions to the novel, the following section is mediated more obviously by selected critics, and thus it is also a reading of 'the readers'.

READING (THE READERS OF) *THE SATANIC VERSES*

As with Rushdie's previous novels, *The Satanic Verses* contains a labyrinthine world of multiple locations and characters, in which radically different modes of writing – 'political satire. and religious fable; realism and fantasy – are combined.'[8] One way of grouping the many characters is around the central figure of the Prophet, in tension with three clusters of paired characters: Chamcha and Salman the Persian; Gibreel and Baal; the Imam and Ayesha.[9] Werbner notes that '[f]our of the characters are counter-selves of Rushdie himself, and all four are partially or entirely flawed morally, negative figures who implicitly seem to lampoon and ridicule the author for his unprepossessing appearance, his cowardice in the face of adversity, his betrayal or jealousy of women, his skepticism, his arrogance, and his vindictiveness.'[10] Werbner also utilizes the concept of the Bakhtinian 'chronotope' to examine time and space in the novel, the latter being a useful literary-critical concept for thinking through the relations between a novel and its cultural and historical contexts. As Sue Vice summarizes:

The chronotope operates on three levels: first, as the means by which a text represents history; second, as the relation between images of time and space in the novel, out of which any representation of history must be constructed; and third, as a way of discussing the formal properties of the text itself, its plot, narrator, and relation to other texts.[11]

The novel's two 'split' settings thus function as chronotopes; these settings are London and India/Iran and Mecca and Madina, where the first chronotope represents diaspora and home, the second, home and diaspora.[12] Werbner explains the structural relations between chronotopes:

The two chronotopes both mirror and comment upon each other. This is underlined by a further pair of women, one in each chronotope: Hind, the powerful wife of the ruler of Jahilia, the city of sin and ignorance before its purification by the Prophet and his followers, and Margaret Thatcher, Maggie the Bitch, Mrs. Torture, in the crumbling London of corruption and racism, trying to fight the tide of history and recreate Britain's imperial glory. A third woman, Ayesha, Empress of Desh, counter-person of the Shah of Iran, parallels the other two women in attempting to reverse the tide of history by returning to a Zoroastrian calendar.

The book, in other words, is a structuralist's dream, and the actions in both chronotopes parallel each other, and throw light on the meanings implied by the events and actions each chronotope contains.[13]

Turning to the controversial 'Jahilia' chapters, the reader can begin to unpack the problematic of the text from an Islamic perspective, starting with the names themselves. The chapters utilize colonialist, derogatory names: for example, 'Mahound' being an archaic way of referring to the prophet Mohammed (derived from the sixteenth-century French *Mahun*) and 'Jahilia, the Arabic word for "barbarism"', being used by Rushdie with reference to Mecca.[14] From an Islamic perspective, there are an additional three essentially troubling components of these chapters: the narrative of the so-called 'satanic verses' themselves; the notion that the Qur'an is written by a human being, i.e., it is not received revelation; and the naming of the Jahilia brothel 'The Curtain' (*Hijab*), while its inmates bear the names of Muhammad's wives. These components of the novel create an insulting constellation, according to Aamir Mufti: 'While the first two sequences put in question the infallibility of the revelation – in the first case by problematizing the mode of transmission of the word of God, and in the second by suggesting the addition and emendation of passages by a human – the last personalizes the offence by playing irreverently with figures held in deep reverence by believers.'[15] One section of these chapters will be quoted, before proceeding to discussion about the text, its form and content, and the ways in which similarly isolated fragments of the novel have generated such intense debate. The fairly lengthy quotation is from 'Return to Jahilia' and it is narrated as a dream:

And Gibreel dreamed this:
    . . . Mahound had no time for scruples, Salman told Baal, no qualms about ends and means. The faithful lived by lawlessness, but in those years Mahound – or should one say the Archangel Gabreel? – should one say Al-Lah? – became obsessed by law. Amid the palm-trees of the oasis Gibreel appeared to the Prophet and found himself spouting rules, rules, until the faithful could scarcely bear the prospect of any more revelation, Salman said, rules about every damn thing, if a man farts let him turn his face to the wind, a rule about which hand to use for the purpose of cleaning one's behind. It was as if no aspect of human existence was to be left unregulated, free. . . . Salman the Persian got to wondering what manner of God this was that sounded so much like a businessman. This was when he had the idea that destroyed his faith, because he recalled that of course Mahound himself had been a businessman, and a damned successful one at that, a person to whom organization and rules came naturally, so how excessively convenient it was that he should have come up such a very businesslike archangel, who handed down the management decisions of the highly corporate, if non-corporeal, God.[16]

The dream-sequence or passage follows a logic of contamination: the action of dreaming itself suspends the reality of revelation, then those obsessed by 'the law' become virtually interchangeable – i.e., Mahound/the Archangel Gibreel/Al-Lah – and then the outpouring of 'rules' becomes a way of demeaning the act of revelation because the 'rules' are seen as simply an inconvenience or an imposition. The 'rules' are then ridiculed, and lead to Salman's comparison of God and Mahound with a businessman; the logic of contamination is thus continued, whereby the divine, via comparison, can be reduced to human status. Thus the transcription of the 'recitation', or 'Al-Qur'an', becomes in the novel one more human ruse, instead of a recording of a text outside of any human chronotope. Another way of formulating this extract is via the portrayal of Mahound's caprice;[17] in other words, when the people are in dispute with Mahound, he can 'conveniently' be supported by his capricious generation of 'law': 'It would have been different, Salman complained to Baal, if Mahound took up his positions after receiving the revelation from Gibreel; but no, he just laid down the law and the angel would confirm it afterwards' (364–5).

The above reading, however, could be attacked for taking a section of the novel and treating it as a synecdoche, that is, as a part that stands in for the whole. Apart from the fact that literary critics usually quote selections from texts as part of larger discussions, it is precisely this fragmentary approach to the novel that generated much of the counter-Muslim criticism. That is to say, Muslim readers were often deemed by westerners to have misread the novel because they were not considering its *total* writing strategies (e.g., if a section is part of a larger parody, then it should *not* be read as offensive, and so on). Taking a position that bridges both of these perspectives (i.e., for *and* against reading the novel through selections), Mufti argues that a new conception of postcolonial reception is required:

A reconceptualization of reception appropriate to the realities of the postcolonial 'global ecumene' . . . must account for forms of mass 'consumption' other than 'reading' in the narrower sense of that word. Extracts published in the print media, in English and in translation, commentary in print, on the airwaves, and from the pulpit, fantasticated representation in the popular cinema, rumours and hearsay, such are the means by which the novel has achieved circulation in the Islamic world.

It is my argument here that this piecemeal and fitful reception at the popular level is not simply accidental, and that in a sense the novel even *requires* it. First of all, the novel's political project – to intervene in the public political conversation within the Islamic world – required breaking out of the minuscule audience to which the English-language writer in South Asia is traditionally confined. And secondly, the almost obsessive attention given in Rushdie's novels to the dynamics of mass communication – the fantasy-like distortions and fragmentation that events and objects go through in the process of entering the public informational sphere – the insistence in [*The Satanic Verses*] on the 'impurity' of any situation in the contemporary world, and the novel's self-conscious use of pastiche and non-linear narrative, themselves point towards the filtered reception the novel has received.[18]

In other words, the argument is that the global 'reading' public – spanning First and Third Worlds, languages, religions and modes of capitalism, etc.

– no longer consume a novel in its 'totality' or pristine literary form (e.g., a film or television version of a novel may be more widely known than the written text). Rather, the global 'reading' public receive texts, knowledge, entertainment, and so on, precisely in fragmented form. Instead of this being a way of misreading Rushdie's novel, Mufti is arguing that the new 'theory of reading/consumption' is embedded, and explored, in *The Satanic Verses* (or, to put it another way, this is how the novel was written in the first place). Mufti calls this reading (and presumably writing) process 'reception by pastiche',[19] which needs some unpacking here, before returning to the novel.

In many respects, Mufti's pastiche is another word for 'hybridity': '. . . that is, hybridity of form, in this case the juxtaposition and overlapping of realist and fantastic modes, the oscillation between fictional and journalistic language, the parodic rewriting of historical and religious narratives of metropolitan texts, genres, and motifs, [and] the use of the resources of literary as well as popular culture'.[20] Mufti argues that this mode of pastiche in *The Satanic Verses* takes 'a deeply political and critical turn', and that this in itself is facilitated by the novel's ambivalence of form.[21] In other words: 'Pastiche, in this context, is neither a purely formal question, nor merely the textual correlate of a hybrid "external reality." Pastiche and its ambivalence of form are here the very conditions that enable the literary text to enter the political sphere.'[22] To put this yet another way, the questions concerning *The Satanic Verses* in relation to fiction/the real are recast by the novel precisely via its 'ambivalence of form', and it is the ongoing state of 'ambivalence' that allows the text to intervene in the political. Rather than drawing upon Fredric Jameson's infamous work on parody and pastiche, Mufti is basing his reading on Jean Franco, where 'pastiche is also a corollary of the decline of the "high" narrative of the (postcolonial) *nation's* cultural originality.'[23] Mufti argues that there is a blending of parody and pastiche in Rushdie's writing: '. . . pastiche is hybridity or melange, but it is also imitation and citation. It is not merely the seemingly random juxtaposition of different discourses; it is also a representation of something that went before. More specifically, it ironically enunciates the signs of the colonizer in order to subvert their meanings.'[24] One of the problems with this definition is that if the religious response to, say, the irony in *The Satanic Verses* is to ignore it, or not even perceive it in the first place, then presumably the opposite reading is possible: that the 'ironic' statement is not read by secular readers in its unspoken form. To make sense of the latter, irony works by saying one thing, but meaning another. If the ironic statement here is that 'the revelation of the Qu'ran was in fact human in process', then the actual meaning is the opposite, that 'the Qu'ran was received from God'. But a secular reading may stick with the first *level* of irony, just as ignoring the statement's ironic status also sticks at this level. In other words, both 'misreadings' end up at the same place. From a postcolonial perspective, to adopt and enunciate 'the signs of the colonizer in order to subvert their meanings' thus becomes a dangerous task, because the ideology of colonialism may simply be reinscribed, or un-ironically repeated, even if this was never the intention of the author:

As many of its Islamic critics have pointed out, the Jahilia chapters employ motifs, imagery, emphases, and phrasing – ranging from the use of the medieval derogatory 'Mahound' to a fascination with the sex life of the Prophet – that have a well-known pedigree in the discourses of orientalism. . . .

But in fact the repetition here goes beyond the mere inversion of an orientalist hierarchy. For by simply *accepting* the colonizer's words, even if with the intention of standing them on their head, that is, by inserting the polluting colonial sign within the space of the authentic and divine, the novel enacts another, *formal* transgression within the discursive field of contemporary 'Islam,' throwing into question the assumption of purity vis-à-vis colonial-metropolitan culture upon which the former is based.[25]

For secular readers, the 'formal transgression' of the pure/impure binary opposition is a mode of rejecting orientalist discourse[26] and monotheistic (one God) religious authority. Thus Mufti is arguing that the insertion of 'the polluting colonial sign within the space of the authentic and the divine' is a doubled gesture: *simultaneously* performing a critique of colonialism and monotheism. As mentioned at the start of the chapter, different critical constellations will be brought into tension here, and it is useful briefly to examine this notion of a doubled gesture in relation to another section of the novel: 'A City Visible but Unseen'.

Rushdie's description of a nightmarish urban space – which is also a vision of a dystopian London – is focused on the migrant cultures that live out their 'indeterminate' identities of belonging and not-belonging through their ongoing redefinition of the situations that they have found themselves in; in the words of Muhammad Sufyan, the landlord of the Shaandaar Cafe: '. . . not so much an immig as an emig runt' (243). Sufyan's wife, Hind, is the real power behind the-throne in their diasporic life; she has created their success through her cooking skills, learned in their early days of marriage together: 'In those days she had admired his pluralistic openness of mind, and struggled, in her kitchen, towards a parallel eclecticism, learning to cook the dosas and uttapams of South India as well as the soft meatballs of Kashmir. Gradually her espousal of the cause of gastronomic pluralism grew into a grand passion' (245–6). Sufyan's political activities, which he keeps secret from his wife (ironically, she thinks that he is visiting prostitutes while he is out at meeting), lead to their sudden and rapid move to England, where all of his school-teacher's knowledge counts for nothing, while her cooking in the meantime becomes their saviour. In the role-reversal that ensues, however, Hind discovers her position of power to be empty, where '[e]verything she valued had been upset by change; had in this process of translation, been lost' (249). What is it that she values? The list includes: language, familiar surroundings, customs, social position, and

security. These things have either been lost entirely, or radically transformed; the process in the novel which describes this transformation is
'translation'. As Homi Bhabha argues:

. . . caught in-between a 'nativist', even nationalist, atavism [reversion] and a postcolonial metropolitan assimilation, the subject of cultural difference becomes a
problem that Walter Benjamin has described as the irresolution, or liminality, of
'translation', the *element of resistance* in the process of transformation, 'that element
in a translation that does not lend itself to translation'. This space of the translation
of cultural difference *at the interstices* is infused with that Benjaminian temporality
of the present which makes graphic a moment of transition, not merely the
continuum of history. . . . The migrant culture of the 'in-between', the minority
position, dramatizes the activity of culture's untranslatability; and in so doing,
it moves the question of culture's appropriation beyond the assimilationist's
dream.[27]

Bhabha argues that each time the immigrant culture undergoes an attempted
'translation', the *untranslatable* element or cultural marker of existence and
identity remains beyond assimilation, or beyond the fantasy of complete
reproduction. In other words, the 'appropriation' of culture always breaks
down as the appropriative gesture moves towards becoming 'an encounter
with the ambivalent process of splitting and hybridity that marks the identification with culture's difference'.[28]

  In *The Satanic Verses*, Sufyan and Hind's daughters embody the ongoing
'in-between' hybrid production and simultaneous disruption of identity.
When the house is visited by Saladin Chamcha, one of the novel's main
protagonists, they are described as

two teenage girls, one spike-haired, the other pony-tailed, and both relishing the
opportunity to demonstrate their skills . . . in the martial arts. . . . Sufyan's daughters, Mishal (seventeen) and fifteen-year-old Anahita, leapt from their bedroom
in fighting gear, Bruce Lee pajamas worn loosely over T-shirts bearing the image
of the new Madonna; – caught sight of unhappy Saladin; – and shook their heads
in wide-eyed delight. (244–5)

The girls are literally 'dressed to kill' with the symbolic wearing of 'Bruce
Lee' martial arts outfits over the iconic image of pop-star Madonna. Sub-
verting their mother's preferred notion of them as subservient girls-in-
waiting-for-(an arranged)-marriage, they instead represent a newfound
autonomy and the breakdown of traditional gender values. Instead of a
'mimicry' of the authority figures in her life, the younger sister 'mimics'
(initially) the elder's rejection of expected decorum. As Chamcha looks
disapprovingly at the icons on the girls' clothes, Mishal reads his mind
('Scraphead Youths' Criminal Idols'), 'and then, laughing at his disapproval,
translated it into yellowpress headlines, while arranging her long, and,
Chamcha realized, astonishing body into similarly exaggerated cheesecake
postures. . . . Her younger sister, not to be outdone, attempted to copy
Mishal's pose, with less effective results' (263). But as much as they reject

their parents' homeland, they still do not appear to have effaced their newly produced immigrant identities; the girls' rejection of an immigrant identity dovetails with Chamcha's own rejection of his ethnicity (he has had an extreme Anglophile upbringing), although he fails to realize this: '. . . he tried to explain that he thought of himself, nowadays, as, well, British' (258–9). The girls react with a parody of their parents: '"What about us?" Anahita wanted to know. "What do you think we are?" – And Mishal confided: "Bangladesh in't nothing to me. Just some place Dad and Mum keep banging on about"' (259). Anahita supplements Mishal's statement with her name for Bangladesh: 'Bungleditch', but Chamcha, in another moment lacking self-awareness, thinks: 'But they weren't British, he wanted to tell them: not *really*, not in any way he could recognize' (259). Crucially, this statement is followed by a summary of Chamcha's own undecidable space of existence, as the certainties in his life slip away. Dominic Head argues that in this mode of writing, Rushdie should be viewed as 'the chronicler of the unfettered migrant sensibility, that version of postcolonialism that unhooks historical tradition from place, and that creates new, self-conscious kinds of identity from a fragmentary vision'.[29] This highly creative 'sensibility' is one that goes beyond binary thinking and the straightforward 'clash of cultures' thesis that often lies behind oppositional readings of the novel. As Bhabha puts it:

The conflict of cultures and community around *The Satanic Verses* has been mainly represented in spatial terms and binary geopolitical polarities – Islamic fundamentalists vs. Western literary modernists, the quarrel of the ancient (ascriptive) migrants and modern (ironic) metropolitans. This obscures the anxiety of the irresolvable, borderline culture of hybridity that articulates its problems of identification and its diasporic aesthetic in an uncanny, disjunctive temporality that is, at once, the *time* of cultural displacement, and the *space* of the 'untranslatable'.[30]

The intense existential angst of the novel's dystopian vision of contemporary London articulates this uncanny intersection of migrant, diasporic time and space, made even more unbearable by the cold and penetrating dampness of slush:

Water began to drip steadily through the dormer window. Outside, in the treacherous city, a thaw had come, giving the streets the unreliable consistency of wet cardboard. Slow masses of whiteness slid from sloping, grey-slate roofs. The footprints of delivery vans corrugated the slush. First light; and the dawn chorus began, chattering of road-drills, chirrup of burglar alarms, trumpeting of wheeled creatures clashing at corners, the deep whirr of a large olive-green garbage eater, screaming radio-voices from a wooden painter's cradle clinging to the upper storey of a Free House, roar of the great wakening juggernauts rushing awesomely down this long but narrow pathway. From beneath the earth came tremors denoting the passage of huge subterranean worms that devoured and regurgitated human beings, and from the skies the thrum of choppers and the screech of higher, gleaming birds. (254)

In this hellish urban space, the rhythms of the working day override the natural rhythms of the seasons: the snows may just be melting, but contractors are painting the outside of a pub, the street-cleaners are removing the debris of the previous day's business in preparation for the next, and the commuters are already travelling in their subterranean, gloomy world, while 'juggernauts' pollute above-ground with their noise and smell. The demands of market capitalism override any 'organic' or more community-based existence, and this both displaces the past lifestyles of diverse immigrant groups, and provides the potential for gaining the cold hard cash needed to reinvent themselves and their fortunes. The problem for Chamcha is the fickleness of the market, and its racist effacement of ethnicity, which also ties in with the representation of institutionalized racism in Britain. Head argues that Rushdie's 'treatment of this topic can be put in the context of the riots of 1981 (especially in Brixton), insofar as these were a response to Thatcher's British Nationality Bill'.[31] The latter Bill was a powerful intervention in the redefinition of identity, which conflicted with, and disrupted, new groups of immigrants who had made a vital contribution to their new homeland:

Rushdie was particularly outraged by the British Nationality Act of 1981, which, building on earlier legislation, sought further to erode the automatic right of British citizenship for people of the former colonies: to be British one had to prove one's descent from an ancestor born in Britain (being born in Britain oneself was now insufficient). This attempt to shore up a national identity (for this was really about Englishness) on the basis of biology flew in the face of the migrant hybridity that the end of Empire brought with it.[32]

What is perhaps most 'uncanny' about the portrayal of London in the light of the Conservatives' attempts at excluding vast swathes of former colonized peoples is the ways in which Thatcher's Britain unleashed a new wave of extremist thought and behaviour on behalf of a society that would later deny its *own* 'fundamentalisms'. An example of the latter in the novel is the character Hal Valance, the epitome of the Thatcherite new 'classless' class, with his mantra of '*Follow the money*' (265).[33] Valance expresses amazement at the Thatcherite project in 1980s Britain, the invention of 'a whole goddamn new middle class in this country' (270). As he says to Chamcha, Thatcher wants 'new' people, 'without background, and without history. Hungry people. People who really *want*, and who know that with her, they can bloody well *get*' (270). Valance is himself an expression of this newness, but one which is parodied for its vacuity and excess; even his name is a joke at the expense of the new Thatcherite middle class, a 'valance' being a piece of soft-furnishing or fabric that covers unwanted structural detail in a house, this being the favourite mode of interior decoration in 1980s Britain. For example, the privatization of public housing in Britain was matched by the sudden appearance of ghastly floral valances that adorned and transformed every humble dwelling into a postmodern fantasy of gracious living.

While this surface dressing reached its apogee in the homes of 'Essex' man and woman, much parodied at the time, it also represented a desire to belong to another *indeterminate* class through an expression of new-found wealth. In the novel, Hal Valance has made his money from one of the great engines of Thatcherism: advertising. He subsequently becomes his own most fantastic 'self-created image' smoking 'absurd, caricature cigars', wearing and flying the Union Jack flag while associating with Thatcher, or 'Mrs Torture' (266). Valance is '[t]he personification of philistine triumphalism . . . one of the glories of the age, the creative half of the city's hottest [advertising] agency, the Valance & Lang Partnership' (266). Yet Valance also expresses the great irony at the heart of the Thatcherite vision of 'newness': it is a vision based upon an old-fashioned British racism, or, to put this another way, the people of Great Britain could reinvent themselves under Thatcher, as long as they were white. As Valance says to Chamcha: 'Within the last three months, we re-shot a peanut-butter poster because it researched better without the black kid in the background. We re-recorded a building society jingle because T'Chairman thought the singer sounded black. . . . We were told by a major airline that we couldn't use any blacks in their ads' (267). The Thatcherite project, then, fails to realize its greatest resource: the immigrant communities and peoples who were, and still are, building a genuinely new Britain.

THE IMPACT OF *THE SATANIC VERSES*

Just as different critical constellations can be viewed in the multiple readings of *The Satanic Verses*, so can the reconstruction of the novel's impact be seen from multiple perspectives. Homi Bhabha formulates a three-word sentence to summarize the root cause of the impact of the novel: 'Hybridity is heresy.'[34] If we accept contemporary modes of fragmented reading and multimedia reception, then the initial highly politicized and religious reactions to the novel form a crucial part of the its wider and sustained impact. In India, for example, *The Satanic Verses* quickly received critical attention, leading to its distribution ban by the finance ministry on 5 October 1988.[35] British Muslims also reacted strongly, with calls for the novel's ban, and book-burning events in Bolton and Bradford. But it was the riots in Islamabad, in Pakistan, which revealed the intensity of feelings about the publication of the novel, with scores of demonstrators injured and six people killed.[36] While all of these, and other events with similarly tragic consequences, were a major part of the international responses, it was the issuing in February 1989 of the Ayatollah Khomeini's '*fatwa*' – or legal ruling that Rushdie should be 'sentenced to death' – that triggered a truly global reaction.[37] While there is not space here to go into an extended analysis of the immense flood of publications and mainly visual media that followed the *fatwa*, the rest of this chapter will examine some key areas and debates that came out of the Rushdie Affair.

Much of the flood of Rushdie Affair publications cross critical domains, and are generated via a socio–political mode of analysis and writing. A recent example of such an approach, taken by Bridget Fowler, utilizes the theories of Pierre Bourdieu to reassess Rushdie's interventions in 'historical meaning'.[38] A recurrent associated question is how far Rushdie knew what he was doing as he wrote the novel, i.e., how far his awareness of Islamic historical developments coincided with his awareness of the level of critique and/or offensiveness of his own text. Fowler argues that while '[t]here are overpowering textual grounds for concluding that Rushdie had a visionary awareness of the risks that he was running', it must also be added that 'his position *within the literary field* cut him off both from the Indian and Pakistani migrants in Britain and from the masses in the subcontinent. Despite his claim to speak for these publics in a form of secular critical prophecy, Rushdie could not overcome this distance.'[39] Turning then to *The Rushdie File*, a collection of reviews, speeches and newspaper reports, Fowler proceeds to examine reader-responses to the novel in the following categories: 'The Popular Aesthetic'; 'An Islamic Critical Aesthetic'; and 'The Critical Aesthetic of Modernism'.[40] Rather than making snap judgements about readers, Fowler instead analyses the socio–political domains that they either base their perceptions upon or are setting out to defend. Thus, in the Popular Aesthetic, from Bourdieu's perspective, 'basic principles of "vision and division" among the people' are being preserved;[41] within the Islamic Critical Aesthetic, readers are performing a critique, and thus defend the novel from multiple perspectives; and in the Critical Aesthetic of Modernism, Rushdie's novel is said to engage with universal and historical themes.[42] Fowler concludes her analysis of the responses to Rushdie's 'Islamic reformism'[43] with an historical summary of the Islamic novel:

. . . at the heart of [*The Satanic Verses*] is a secular and 'objectivist' analysis which is particularly disturbing because of the multiplicity of stories it tells and perspectives it bears. The birth of the Islamic novel is itself relatively recent: in the regional Indian languages, not until the very late 19th century. . . . Marx says of the modern painter that he had to create his own consumers. Rushdie's act as a heroic modernist – alongside other secular novelists, such as Sadaawi and Mahfouz – was to create his own dissident writing and this to help invent the autonomous artist for a Muslim public.[44]

The overriding question for sociological analysis must surely be 'where does this "dissident" writing emerge from?' The Latin etymology of the word 'dissident' – to be distant from – is a clue here: it can apply as much to the relations between a British educated elite, of which Rushdie is a part, and the harsh everyday realities of Muslim migrants in Britain as it does to any other counter-cultural meanings. Rushdie's professed aim to be writing for Muslim readers may not, therefore, ring true when the actual reader is probably one 'whose educational and class habitus is similar to Rushdie's, most typically, the Western, metropolitan reader from the professions'.[45]

This question of audience and readership, long an issue in literary critical studies, has been given fresh impetus by the Rushdie Affair, particularly among critics of the 'postcolonial' approach to literature. The question of hybridity, in other words, can be dangerously abstracted away from the mundane existence(s) of 'migrancy'. *The Satanic Verses* has generated immense volumes of debate concerning this term, which, in Shailja Sharma's estimation 'can be called the reigning trope of the twentieth century'.[46] Adding issues of class to the migrancy debates is a way of once more problematizing and complexifying binary thinking in relation to the Rushdie Affair. As Sharma argues: 'The myth that Rushdie represents, in some unproblematic way, the experience of immigration, or more generally, postcoloniality, is often fostered by First World critics eager to sacrifice ideological differences to easy definitions. This myth hides the fact that Rushdie writes primarily for a metropolitan readership from a relatively secure position within the metropolitan intellectual Left.'[47] Reopening debates about migrancy in relation to Rushdie's writing and socio-historical background can lead to a more informed notion of class operating within Muslim Britain. As Sharma continues:

It seems to me that insofar as the Rushdie affair brought to the fore class tensions that pre-existed in the Asian community in Britain, it served to highlight different aspects of immigrant life and migrancy, differences that had long been suppressed under the debates over racism and minorities, differences that have since been subsumed under readings of *The Satanic Verses* as a novel of migrancy. The uniformity of the immigrant experience, in other words, has been called into question. Whether the opening of these schisms is detrimental to any collective politics is another issue, and far more complex. This division certainly encourages us to conceive of a more nuanced politics of 'minority' representation within diaspora communities in Europe.[48]

In terms of the intertextual sources and literary traditions revealed within *The Satanic Verses*, however, some critics have argued for a class reading based upon Rushdie's affiliations to Muslim secularism, suggesting that to flag up or entirely prioritize the western network of resources that Rushdie draws upon further effaces Muslim culture. For example, as Feroza Jussawalla argues: '. . . seeing *The Satanic Verses* as an exercise in European postmodernity by a hybrid metropolitan intellectual fails to show how deeply rooted it is in Muslim cultural and religious traditions.'[49] Rufus Cook's analysis of 'antimimesis' at work in Rushdie's writing would be a prime example of an elision of 'traditions' from Jussawalla's perspective.[50]

The Rushdie Affair has generated a huge amount of criticism that debates and explores the relationships between texts and 'reality', however the latter is to be defined. That is to say, competing definitions of 'the literary' generated by publication of *The Satanic Verses* have also depended upon, and predicated, competing definitions of 'the real'. Sabina and Simona Sawhney suggest that it was *The Satanic Verses* and the storm around it that provoked more discussions, in more countries, about the status of the literary than perhaps any other work of our time. . . . The polemical debates that ensued over *The Satanic Verses* forced many people – readers and writers of all kinds – to reflect seriously about the effects and scope of literature, its responsibility and freedom.[51]

In an earlier article, Simona Sawhney examines the novel's exploration of 'sacred space', introducing the useful word 'antinomies' into the discussion of the time and space of textual production ('childhood and adulthood, colonialism and Postcolonialism, faith and scepticism, India and England, the epic and the novel . . .'), suggesting that rather than regarding these as being sequentially presented by Rushdie, they are instead constantly 'informing and transforming one another . . . inhabiting one another'.[52] This constant crossing or chiasmus has generated an awareness that within hybridity the language-games[53] or western concepts of postcolonialism may irresolvably come into conflict with the proper names of sacred text.

8 The Optical Unconscious
Arundhati Roy's *The God of Small Things*

Just under a decade after the publication of Rushdie's *The Satanic Verses*, another immensely creative and in many ways controversial novel was published: Arundhati Roy's Booker Prize-winning *The God of Small Things* (1997). Published in the fiftieth year of India's independence,[1] *The God of Small Things* performs a critique of the Indian caste system and of patriarchal values within marriage and society, transgresses conservative codes of caste and 'good taste' in its depiction of intimate human relationships, and creates a new poetic prose that deconstructs the dominance of English grammar and opens a new chapter in magical realism. Beginning this chapter with a reference to Rushdie is not an arbitrary gesture: Roy's adoption of a hybrid form of writing creates links with Rushdie's work, as many critics have noted. Jean-Pierre Durix argues that, '[b]esides echoing the preoccupations of characters in V.S. Naipaul's novels, Arundhati Roy is also rooted in the post-colonial literary tradition of Gabriel García Márquez and Salman Rushdie.'[2] Marta Dvorak links *The God of Small Things* with Rushdie's first novel *Grimus* (1975), 'in which the author, well before *Midnight's Children*, already made abundant use of devices to which Roy subsequently resorted so heavily, namely compound neologisms, extravagant capitalization, sentence fragments and excessive paragraph breaks, intrusive parenthesis, copious metaphoric transference, Joycean seriation and graphic juxtaposition, and heterosemiotic intertextuality.'[3] Intertextual linkages are noticeable at the level of style and form, for example, with Roy's extensive – or 'extravagant' – use of capitalization for effect: 'Other Indian writers before Arundhati Roy – particularly G.V. Desani with his novel *All about H. Hatterr* [1948], which had such an influence on Salman Rushdie – have used obtrusive capitalization in order to mock the pomposity of sages or would-be sages.'[4] At the level of content, intertextuality is also noticeable, as Alex Tickell has suggested:

The pickle advertisements [in *The God of Small Things*] immediately makes one think of Salman Rushdie's 'chutnified' histories in that other Booker Prize-winning text, *Midnight's Children*, but in its combination of linguistic flexibility, telepathic child-protagonists, and Western form welded to mythical-popular content (the kathakali dancer turned chutney-logo), Roy's novel also recalls the related mythic-realism of Vikram Chandra's *Red Earth and Pouring Rain* and the dialogic interminglings of Amitav Ghosh's early novel *The Circle of Reason.*[5]

Such intertextual linkages reveal how Roy works within a strong tradition of Indian writing in English, while developing a unique style (and humour) of her own; however, her writing also spans a number of critical and creative domains, leading critics to debate how far she fits a western 'cosmopolitan' model of writing, divorced in many ways from indigenous cares and concerns, and how far she is developing an autonomous mode of Indian writing that has detached itself from 'colonial' or postcolonial concerns. Tickell warns readers to think about the meaning behind the act of making intertextual linkages and comparisons:

> As we make these critical comparisons we should remember . . . that the dominance of the culturally hybrid Indian novel in Europe and North America after the publication of Rushdie's *Midnight's Children* in 1981 has coincided, as Arnab Chakladar has noted, 'both with the interests of the burgeoning field of postcolonial studies . . . and with [a] resurgence of interest in the British Raj in the culture at large.' This correspondence between commercial and academic spheres (as an indication of the market value of postcolonial texts as 'cultural capital') has already been recognized by a number of influential postcolonial theorists.[6]

However, it is also crucial in relation to 'market value' to think about the ways in which Roy's writing has been successful within a global market that reflects India's international connections, migratory patterns and role. In other words, global success does not have to be attributed to the rise of postcolonial studies, even if the latter has led to a increased interest in nonwestern authors. The phrase 'cultural capital' can be reassigned and recoded as 'Indian cultural capital', whereby Roy's indigenous roots are more important than any other factor. Roy's writing can be thought of, in this latter sense, as a 're-translation'[7] whereby the everyday contradictions or reality of local Indian life, impacted heavily by globalization (be it the construction of a massively disruptive World Bank-funded dam, or the introduction of cable television to remote, rural impoverished communities) feeds into her creative voice.

READING *THE GOD OF SMALL THINGS*

The reader is plunged into *The God of Small Things* as if into a river: the monsoon breaks in Ayemenem and turns the countryside into 'an immodest green': 'Boundaries blur as tapioca fences take root and bloom. Brick walls turn mossgreen. Pepper vines snake up electric poles.'[8] The lush language of the opening page does not prepare the reader for the linguistic disruption that is to come, although the genealogical confusion of family history is a foreshadowing of narrative and language disorder that will follow. The protagonists of the novel are almost immediately introduced; Rahel has returned to Ayemenem to see her twin brother Estha: 'They were two-egg

twins. "Dizygotic" doctors called them. Born from separate but simultaneously fertilized eggs. Estha – Esthappen – was the older by eighteen
minutes' (4). While the twins used to have one mind, joint identities that
they think of as 'Me' (4), they are now thought of by Rahel in the third
person as 'Them' or 'They': the 'small things' (5) of their shared, childish
perspectives have been replaced by their separate identities. It is at this
moment in the novel that the writing takes on a new patterning:

Their lives have a size and a shape now. Estha has his and Rahel hers.

Edges, Borders, Boundaries, Brinks and Limits have appeared like a team of
trolls on their separate horizons. Short creatures with long shadows, patrolling the
Blurry End. Gentle half-moons have gathered under their eyes and they are as old
as [their mother] Ammu was when she died. Thirty-one.

Not old.

Not young.

But a viable die–able age. (5)

The breaking down of the sentences and the paragraph into discrete, isolated units creates a pattern on the page that is closer to poetry than prose;
other unusual features include the capitalization, mentioned above, with
the list of words: Edges, Borders, Boundaries, Brinks and Limits. One way
to start interpreting Roy's 'stylistic acrobatics'[9] is via focalization, i.e., the
narrative is being written from the twins' perspective or point of view.
Christine Vogt-William adopts this approach, noting that '[w]hen the narrative perspective draws nearer the twins' viewpoint, the text contains
numerous instances where words and whole phrases have capitals. This is
a signal to the reader that he has gained access to the children's minds,
making apparent the often incomprehensible and threatening adult world.'[10]
The breaking up of text into fragments or incomplete sentences also has
the effect of slowing the reader down, forcing him or her to pay attention
to language use, and to think about the ways in which the normal English
language is 'made strange' or defamiliarized. But what is most 'strange'
about the passage quoted above is that we are given a child's focalization
through the eyes of two adults, suggesting that the twins may have physi-
cally aged, but they have possibly not completely grown up. Later we will
discover that they have both experienced great trauma, and have dealt with
it in different ways; the trauma is the block that holds them back from
perceiving the world in more usual adult ways. The source of the trauma
is hinted at in the passage which describes Estha and Rahel's cousin Sophie
Mol's funeral; in this passage we see some of the family huddled together:
'Margaret Kochamma, Chacko, Baby Kochamma [Navomi Ipe's nick-
name], and next to her, her sister-in-law, Mammachi – Estha and Rahel's
(and Sophie Mol's) grandmother' (7). Events, on first reading, then become
more confused: still being narrated from the twins' perspective, Sophie
Mol appears to have been buried alive at her funeral, and a mysterious visit
to the police station leads to an ambiguous exchange between their mother

and the Station House Officer, who treats their mother, Ammu, abusively. What the reader will later learn is that the twins are blamed for the drowning of Sophie Mol, and, even more painfully, they have witnessed the brutal, and ultimately fatal, beating of Velutha – their mother's lover – at the hands of the police, a beating that leads to his death. The constant physical *returning* that takes place in the first chapter will be matched, and then surpassed, by the intricate network of remembering, of returning to the past through memories and dreams, throughout the entire novel. For Estha, Rahel's return opens an almost overpowering floodgate: 'The world, locked out for years, suddenly flooded in, and now Estha couldn't hear himself for the noise' (16). Rahel's return is not just a return to their mutual telepathy, it is also a return to past trauma, a way of recovering lost life, time and identity.

Memory in *The God of Small Things* is given architectonic form, with the two main houses in which much of the novel takes place: Ayemenem and the History House. Chapter Eight, ironically entitled 'Welcome Home, Our Sophie Mol', opens with a description of Ayemenem:

It was a grand old house, the Ayemenem House, but aloof-looking. As though it had little to do with the people who lived in it. Like an old man with rheumy eyes watching children play, seeing only transience in their shrill elation and their wholehearted commitment to life.

The steep tiled roof had grown dark and mossy with age and rain. The trian-gular wooden frames fitted into the gables were intricately carved, the light that slanted through them and fell in patterns on the floor was full of secrets. Wolves. Flowers. Iguanas. Changing shape as the sun moved through the sky. Dying punctually, at dusk. (157)

The family house, which hides if not shelters the events of their past, is also flooded with the light of secrets, the patterns that bring the natural world into the artificial hierarchy of patriarchy and a family that lives according to the cultural laws of caste. From Rahel's returning perspective, the house looks empty: 'The doors and windows were locked. The front verandah bare. Unfurnished' (4). In reality, the house is still lived in, only it has been divided and muted by events. Ayemenem House can be thought of as being 'a metonymy of . . . traditional patriarchy',[11] or even, as Cynthia Carey sees it, as a character: 'Much of the action of the plot will be prepared or acted out in this family home, which, on the outside, appears unchang-ing and represents the "dignity" of ancestry and archaic traditions and functions to glorify and immortalize the past.'[12] Not only will much of the action take place in the house, but the house itself presents a schema of society: 'We read . . . that Paravans were not allowed in by Pappachi [Estha and Rahel's grand father]. The house represents the strict observation and exclusiveness of hierarchies, of class and caste, of boundaries and affiliations.'[13] In the second chapter, 'Pappachi's Moth', the metaphor of the classification system is given an ironic twist with its application to human society:

Pappachi would not allow Paravans into the house. Nobody would. They were not allowed to touch anything that Touchables touched. Caste Hindus and Caste Christians. Mammachi told Estha and Rahel that she could remember a time, in her girlhood, when Paravans were expected to crawl backwards with a broom, sweeping away their footprints so that Brahmins or Syrian Christians would not defile themselves by accidentally stepping into a Paravan's footprint. In Mammachi's time, Paravans, like other Untouchables, were not allowed to walk on public roads, not allowed to cover their upper bodies, not allowed to carry umbrellas. They had to put their hand over their mouths when they spoke, to divert their polluted breath away from those whom they addressed.

When the British came to Malabar, a number of Paravans, Pelayas and Pulayas . . . converted to Christianity and joined the Anglican Church to escape the scourge of Untouchability. . . . It didn't take them long to realize that they had jumped from the frying pan into the fire. They were made to have separate churches, with separate services, and separate priests. (71)

The state of 'Untouchability' is thus one that is carried with the Paravans and others as a sign that transcends all other affiliations: a sign that permits their endless persecution and doesn't make the invisible visible, as planned when they convert to Christianity, but makes them doubly invisible: 'After Independence they [the Untouchables] found they were not entitled to any government benefits like job reservations or bank loans at low interest rates, because officially, on paper, they were Christians, and therefore casteless. It was a little like having to sweep away your footprints without a broom. Or worse, not being *allowed* to leave footprints at all' (71). The Touchables thus distinguish themselves through an act of differentiation from the Untouchables: they judge the Untouchables to be absolutely different and other to themselves. As René Girard has observed, the Greek root word for these actions – κρίνω – also means to condemn, or pass over for judicial punishment; in other words, in this passage on caste, Roy is foreshadowing the need for an Untouchable *scapegoat*, who will be 'touched' later on in the novel, with his brutal beating to death.[14] As Girard says: 'The further one is from normal social status of whatever kind, the greater the risk of persecution.'[15]

While Ayemenem House is a three-dimensional manifestation of social borders and positioning, or the creation of scapegoats (there are other beatings that take place in the house – the ones that Mammachi suffers at the hands of Pappachi), the History House, as Carey notes, is Ayemenem's uncanny double, 'where the trap of colonialism replaces that of family, where the hypocrisy of heritage, history and consumerism are uncovered. The History House is the house of Kari Saipu, an Englishman gone native, and represents the drama of being excluded from "History", or being locked into the official version of it.'[16] Many events take place in the house, and before it is transformed into a hotel called 'Heritage' (120) for tourists who need to be shielded from the poverty that surrounds them, Vellya Paapen, Velutha's father, tells how he saw the 'pedophile ghost' of Kari

Saipu (189–90). Intertextuality is foregrounded in relation to the History House, which is built across the river, on/in the Heart of Darkness – a reference to Conrad's novella which is matched by references to Marxism: 'So there it was then, History and Literature enlisted by commerce. Kurtz and Karl Marx joining palms to greet rich guests as they stepped off the boat' (120).

Roy further complicates the doubling of Ayemenem and the History House with a third key architectural location: Velutha's 'little laterite hut' (75), which Estha and Rahel enter to get assistance repairing the abandoned boat that they have found and claimed. What surprises them most when they step inside the hut is to find discarded objects from their own house: 'Rich things in a poor house. A clock that didn't work, a flowered tin wastepaper basket. Pappachi's old riding boots (brown, with green mold) with the cobbler's trees still in them. Biscuit tins with sumptuous pictures of English castles and ladies with bustles and ringlets' (199). If the History House is the uncanny double of Ayemenem, then Velutha's hut is an even more uncanny collection of 'alien presences'[17] in the Untouchable space; in other words, the introjection of the commodities of wealth and 'touchability' into the abject space of poverty and exclusion. Claiming these discarded commodities is a powerful act of recycling that questions caste barriers. Velutha's father has feared such indeterminate acts all along, as foreshadowing some later more powerful and problematic transgression: 'Vellya Paapen feared for his younger son. He couldn't say what it was that frightened him. It was nothing that he had said. Or done. It was not *what* he said, but the *way* he said it. Not *what* he did, but the *way* he did it' (73). The introjection of Touchable commodities into Untouchable space is also massively disruptive of the architectonics of the entire caste system, which has been 'hailed as the central organizing principle in society in spite of the fact that the Indian state has passed several acts ensuring that the practice of caste discrimination is eliminated'.[18] The introjection also prefigures Ammu's entry into Velutha's world, and the death sentence that this will impose upon him.

Why does Roy create a third location with Velutha's hut, one which disrupts the neat binary oppositions between home and a haunted house, the inside versus the outside? One possibility is that binary oppositions are themselves broken down in the novel. Thus the 'homeliness' of Ayemenem House is shown to be a sham, something that never really existed, especially for its female inhabitants; the homely switches to the unhomely, Freud's *unheimlich* (translated as 'uncanny'). What should be uncanny – the haunted History House – becomes instead a refuge; what should be a refuge – Ayemenem House – becomes a house of correction and a prison house. Anthony Vidler notes that: 'For Freud, "unhomeliness" was more than a simple sense of not belonging; it was the fundamental propensity of the familiar to turn on its owners, suddenly to become defamiliarized, derealized, as if in a dream.'[19] *Defamiliarization*, a concept explored in most detail by the critics who were called the Russian Formalists, is one important definition of the poetic. Roy's language-games are perhaps her best-known literary device, yet she also defamiliarizes the spatiality of her novel, its architectonics, and its social world, as much as she plays with grammar.

Is there a connection between the uncanny houses in Roy's novel and language beyond the processes of defamiliarization? The key element that links spatiality and language in the novel is its 'shock' effects – used elsewhere as a device by modernist artists who argued that 'the uncanny readily offered itself as an instrument of "defamiliarization" or *ostranenie* [making strange]; as if a world estranged and distanced from its own nature could only be recalled to itself by shock, by the effects of things deliberately "made strange".'[20] There are many shocks in *The God of Small Things*, and its publication also generated a series of shocks, with its outspoken critique of caste, as much as its more subtle criticism of the colonial past. But how do such shocks link houses and language? One way of answering this question involves exploring Roy's deconstruction of logocentrism: that is to say, Roy rejects the colonial acquiescence in, and reimposition of, the pure/impure binary, reinforced by colonial thinking, which needed to maintain or preserve 'the "difference" between the colonizers and the colonized'.[21] Binary thinking is generally acknowledged to be a mode of hierarchy: that is to say, the framework of binary oppositions are not neutrally brought into existence; instead, one side of the opposition will forcefully take priority over the other side. Roy's example of the conversion to Christianity actually failing to liberate the Untouchables – i.e., those for whom Christianity should exist and should shelter – reveals the historical complicity with colonialism, which in itself predicates structures of purity/impurity, self/ other, good/evil, and so on. Twentieth-century theorists have attacked this mode of thinking from a number of perspectives, one of these being the 'linguistic turn', the foremost exponent of which was Jacques Derrida. Derrida's deconstruction is a method of revealing that the excluded, downtrodden, abject side of an entire chain of binary oppositions is in fact the very series of values that found systems of thinking and being in the first place. In other words, each of the binaries is shown to be *artificially* held apart by oppressive systems of thought. The dominance of self-present 'pure' speech over endlessly disseminated 'impure' writing is known as 'logocentrism', and it is logocentrism which Roy's novel undermines at almost every stylistic twist and turn. In more general terms, as Marta Dvorak explains, logocentrism underlay the colonialist educational 'civilizing' project in India and elsewhere: '. . . the aesthetic and functional rationales of colonial educational policies in which English was projected as a humanistic, civilising branch of study as well as a language of social and material advancement, the sole path to modernisation'.[22] The problematic of writing back against such a project, in the language of the colonizer, is complex; utilizing English may signal complicity with a colonialist–postcolonialist sensibility (i.e., a repackaging of exoticism in a contemporary format), or it may be a more subversive gesture, depending upon how the language is handled. Roy's training as an architect and her experience in writing screenplays, Dvorak suggests, gives her writing an architectonic and cinematic structure which she develops in *The God of Small Things*: 'Her sudden time shifts, alternating fast forwards and flashbacks, or rapidly edited loops and turns circling yet moving forward have been dubbed cinematic techniques by certain reviewers.'[23] There are diverse ways in which this notion of Roy's writing can be interpreted, but sticking for the moment with the architectonic and the cinematic, Roy creates a literary version of the 'close-up' where she goes beyond the 'naked eye' of logocentrism to an uncanny world of doubling, and the return of the repressed Other. In 'The Work of Art in the Age of Its Technological Reproducibility', Walter Benjamin theorizes an 'optical unconscious' by comparing Freud's ideas with specific film techniques:

On the one hand, film furthers insight into the necessities governing our lives by its use of close-ups, by its accentuation of hidden details in familiar objects, and by its exploration of commonplace milieux through the ingenious guidance of the camera; on the other hand, it manages to assure us of a vast and unsuspected field of action [*Spielraum*]. . . . With the close-up, space expands; with slow motion, movement is extended. And just as enlargement not merely clarifies what we see indistinctly 'in any case,' but brings to light entirely new structures of matter, slow motion not only reveals familiar aspects of movements, but discloses quite unknown aspects within them. . . . Clearly, it is another nature which speaks to the camera as compared to the eye. 'Other' above all in the sense that a space informed by human consciousness gives way to a space informed by the unconscious. . . . This is where the camera comes into play, with all its resources for swooping and rising, disrupting and isolating, stretching or compressing a sequence, enlarging or reducing an object. It is through the camera that we first discover the optical unconscious, just as we discover the instinctual unconscious through psychoanalysis.[24]

Roy's linguistic playfulness is the written version of a close-up and cinematic slow motion; sentences and paragraphs are literally slowed down by their fragmentation, and their disarticulation into otherwise unnoticed constituent parts constitutes a series of close-up shots. Furthermore, such a mode of writing foregrounds the graphic surface of the text, where words form images on the page, and are not merely transparent devices transmitting messages. Marshal McLuhan's phrase 'the medium is the message' is relevant here, and in Roy's case, the medium is the optical unconscious of the twins, and the exploration of the uncanny return of the repressed Other. In other words, those people and memories that have been repressed, excluded from self-present or logocentric consciousness/society, return to haunt and 'contaminate' the artificially 'pure'. In a brilliant, and deeply critical, reading of *The God of Small Things*, Marta Dvorak argues that what I am calling Roy's revealing of the optical unconscious is simply an 'exoticist strategy' which 'satisfies the cosmopolitan desire to know the other, yet in a clever sleight of hand . . . translates the foreign into the familiar'.[25] Instead of defamiliarization, Dvorak argues, Roy is a post-modernist whose writing is driven by 'a dynamics of domestication and familiarisation'.[26] Dvorak analyses Roy's language-games with precision and great insight, but concludes that '[t]he aesthetic purpose of Roy's overall dynamics of saturation remain unclear'.[27] Thinking about the link between the uncanny houses in Roy's novel and her language-games, it becomes apparent that she is utilizing a montage technique (thus the three main houses, not two in simplistic binary opposition), and the fact that montage can further be linked with orality suggests that her revealing of the optical unconscious is relevant to an indigenous *and* an 'allogenous' readership. It is my contention that Roy's dynamics of linguistic saturation are developed to bring into cognition what Benjamin calls the *Spielraum*, the 'vast and unsuspected field of action' where free linguistic play goes beyond normal and normative modes of perception. Furthermore, because of the links between montage and orality, I argue that Roy's *Spielraum* is not merely an arbitrary postmodern trick, but an attempt at dislocating embedded socio-political structures, i.e., the laws of social exchange.[28] To get a sense of how Roy's *Spielraum* is constructed, it is necessary to turn far more closely to her language-games.

Chapter ten of *The God of Small Things*, called 'The River in the Boat', explores the ways in which change can occur in life, in an instant, with profound and lasting results. The writing in this chapter becomes densely poetic, with the graphic surface becoming as important as the message. The finding of the boat by Estha and Rahel triggers an entire sequence of events:

Things can change in a day.

It *was* a boat. A tiny wooden vallom.
The boat that Estha sat on and Rahel found.
The boat that Ammu would use to cross the river. To love by
night the man her children loved by day.
    So old a boat that it had taken root. Almost.
    A gray old boatplant with boatflowers and boatfruit. And underneath,
a boat-shaped patch of withered grass. A scurrying, hurrying boatworld.
    Dark and dry and cool. Unroofed now. And blind.
    White termites on their way to work.
    White ladybirds on their way home.
    White beetles burrowing away from the light.
    White grasshoppers with whitewood violins.
    Sad white music.
    A white wasp. Dead.

    A brittlewhite snakeskin, preserved in darkness, crumbled in the Sun.

    But would it do, that little vallom?
    Was it perhaps too old? Too dead?
    Was Akkara too far away for it? (192–3)

The repetition of the word 'boat' in this passage functions through a process of accumulation and amplification, leading to the compound words of 'boatplant', 'boatflowers' and 'boatfruit'. Juxtaposition of two adjectival participles, used extensively elsewhere in the novel,[29] describes the 'boat-world' underneath, those creatures simultaneously sheltered and exposed by the antiquated skeleton of an abandoned vessel. Repetition of the word 'White' leads to variation on a theme, climaxing with the realization that darkness preserves the objects of the hidden boatworld, whereas light bleaches and destroys it (foreshadowing the coming to light of Ammu's and Velutha's transgressions). Finally, the graphic surface, generated by the disruption of normal prose-paragraph structuring, is concluded with a three-line 'stanza' that asks a series of questions, answered in a type of negative dialectics, since we already know that the boat will be, and has been, used (the latter reflecting the convoluted temporality, or anachronisms, of the novel). The boat has 'almost' taken root, and this signifies that it is still *detached* from the world of total death and decay, that it still has the possibility of returning to its fully functioning life.

The oral syntax of this extract is partly derived from montage methods: 'Montage (as a non-linear practice)' is one of the ways in which 'space becomes linked with orality (the acoustic being the realm of non-linear signification).'[30] Elsewhere, in a different context, Thomas King calls texts that fuse or blend oral and written literatures – here, the non-linear syntax of poetic writing mimicking speech patterns and rhythms – 'interfusional literature'.[31] Roy's *Spielraum* is not simply postmodernist excess; rather, it is a space of writing that juxtaposes law and desire (for freedom): the love laws ('the grammar structuring the interpenetration of global and local power, the regulations governing capitalist distribution, cast, and women'[32]) versus creative transgression. As Janet Thormann notes: 'Before the subject is fully submitted to the laws of language governing phonemes, morphemes, and syntax, what Lacan calls "lalangue" materializes desire in letters, in materialized sounds, sensuous images, and the representations of things. Unconscious jouissance [desire/pleasure] infuses the detached signifiers of lalangue.'[33] Ammu and Velutha's love for one another is a 'residue',[34] something that cannot be subsumed or effaced by the love laws of caste and society; in writing her *Spielraum*, Roy creates language as 'thing' or 'object'[35] which constantly brings back into being the transgressive desire of Ammu and Velutha, the twins, even of Kari Saipu. The fact that the *Spielraum* is also composed of diverse discourses – film, television, romance, soft porn – does not mean that the text somehow commodifies itself (i.e., simply puts itself up for sale to westerners); rather, it functions precisely in those areas within Indian society where transgressive glimpses and opposition to the love laws are found; as with a recent court case dealing with the pornographic use of a cell-phone camera, Indian society has an infinite number of ways of circulating the signifiers of otherwise banished desires.

THE IMPACT OF *THE GOD OF SMALL THINGS*

Roy's novel very quickly gained a cult following around the world, as well as a vociferous group of detractors who were mainly shocked and appalled by the transgressive sexuality of the novel. It comes as no surprise, however, that a novel translated into more than forty languages should attract considerable critical attention. Many critics have noted that Roy's newfound fame arising from publication of *The God of Small Things* has been put to good use with her ongoing political activism and journalism: for example, campaigning against the Sardar Sarovar Dam project and the testing of nuclear weapons in India.[36] Chelva Kanaganayakam noted that: 'Four years after the publication of Arundhati Roy's *The god of small things* the novel still remains something of an icon – a reminder that the efflorescence of Indian writing in English is hardly a short-lived affair.'[37] The myriad critical comparisons with Rushdie's work have led to a more in-depth awareness of Indian writing around the globe; as Kanaganayakam argues:

If it is possible to speak of a second phase of regeneration after the arrival of Salman Rushdie on the literary scene, it is probably Roy's work that inaugurated it. Rushdie's role was to question the pieties and half-truths that masqueraded as expressions of transcendence. Roy's text, which reflects the subversive potential of Rushdie's writing, also explores the possibilities of wholeness by offering a secular myth, derived from, but in opposition to, dominant religious myths. While Rushdie's project is one of deconstruction, Roy's purpose is recuperation, although her tone of bitterness and despair often masks the conviction that secular myths that derive from religious ones have a redemptive power.[38]

The novel, for example, recodes the 'ideal' family away from that of propriety and hierarchy: 'In a novel that repeatedly draws attention to the breakdown of all family structures, the only family that seems to flourish, albeit briefly, is that which includes Velutha, Ammu and the two children Rahel and Estha.'[39] How far such a recoding is actually 'redemptive' is clearly open to debate, but the notion that Roy creates powerful echoes of originary and primal myths is important in terms of the indigenous narratives and structures that pervade *The God of Small Things*. Roy's novel repeatedly foregrounds the ways in which such narratives and structures are represented and made more or less accessible to the western gaze. She explores the commodification of indigenous intertexts, but she also feeds them into her linguistic *Spielraum* so that, regardless of the ways in which they are consumed and appropriated, they still have a profound effect. One such example, raised by Alex Tichell, is the staged-for-tourists performance of the kathakali dancers:

In her representation of kathakali Roy is clearly alive to the way in which folk-stories and aspects of indigenous myth are now over-determined as authentic markers of difference.

. . .

. . . the kathakali performance itself operates as a commentary on the politics of cultural commodification. Like the commercially successful Indian-English novel, the kathakali in Roy's work is caught between two (culturally distinct) constituencies: a reduced indigenous audience at the temple and a more lucrative foreign tourist audience at the Heart of Darkness hotel.
. . .

Hence, in the ethical dilemma of its divergent audiences, Roy uses the kathakali to throw into relief the fact of her own intrinsically marketable position within 'competing regimes of value'. And although not a direct repudiation of the exoticizing tendencies of cosmopolitanism, at the very least this sub-narrative indicates Roy's awareness of the involuntary, assimilative demand which global capital makes in its encounter with local postcolonial cultures.[40]

The kathakali performance is not just that of the tourist event: its performed myths, however truncated in this instance, are interwoven throughout the entire novel, tracing 'the fate of those who had broken taboos'.[41] To read *The God of Small Things* is to traverse an entire architectonic space of writing that cannot be separated into binaries or hierarchies, inside or outside, western or indigenous, global or local. Traversing *The God of Small Things* involves recognizing the full force of the postcolonial novel in English, with its ongoing dialogue between identity and difference.

Conclusion

Ending with Joy Kogawa's *Obasan* and Phyllis Greenwood's *An Interrupted Panorama*

The handful of texts studied in this book all share a number of features: they have impacted significantly upon the ways in which readers think about and study postcolonial literatures; they have led many people to wider networks of reading – opening up entirely new literary canons; they have contributed to the development of what is called 'postcolonial theory' – in other words, the more abstract mode of critical analysis that now exists as a discipline in its own right; and they have changed the ways in which people think about historical, political and social situations. This study ends briefly with the receptions to Joy Kogawa's novel *Obasan* (1981), which is about the internment of the Japanese in Canada during the Second World War, and the modes of forgetting and remembering, silencing and voicing of that event. Expanding my network of reading, inspired by Kogawa's writing, I also conclude with a more experimental text, Vancouver artist Phyllis Greenwood's *An Interrupted Panorama* (1997).

The protagonist of Kogawa's *Obasan*, Naomi Nakane, is in search of her lost mother, and goes through a process of recovering the fragmentary memories of the past through the emotional intensity and practical resources of her politically aware aunt Emily.[1] What is intriguing about the publishing history of *Obasan* is that unlike other texts that cover this subject matter, such as John Okada's *No-No Boy* (1957), Kogawa's novel went on to gain almost immediate recognition and success, winning the *Books in Canada* first novel award the year following its publication. Susan Knutson argues that

> *Obasan* played a significant role in educating the public and the Canadian government about the injustices imposed on Japanese Canadians during and after the Second World War. Kogawa's voice became an authoritative one in the community's campaign for official apology and redress, both of which were achieved in 1988 under the Conservative government of Prime Minister Brian Mulroney. In this way, *Obasan* had a political impact unusual for any work of art.[2]

Other critics have emphasized the diverse ways in which *Obasan* has generated or evoked a mode of 'political consciousness'. Teruyo Ueki ponders the relationship between the text and its impact upon actual redress:

> In her essay on *Obasan*, Carol Fairbanks uses the term "political efficacy" . . . to measure the extent to which characters develop a sense of political involvement.

However, I want to use this term as meaning to what extent the novel evokes a political consciousness among its readers, leading them to active involvement in social reformation. Kogawa's book, in this sense, is a good example of successful "political efficacy," in view of its remarkable contribution to the advancement of the Redress movement in Canada. In my opinion, this "political efficacy" arises from the "literary efficacy" of the novel's paradoxical scheme of revelations in concealment.[3]

Laurie Ricou, from a critical and pedagogical perspective, also meditates upon the political/literary efficacy of this novel, revealing how teaching *Obasan* 'has been unlike any other experience I have had in teaching Canadian literature'.[4] For many students, the novel is particularly unsettling not just because of the harrowing events of Japanese internment, but because of the critique of North American atrocities; more subtly, there is a difference between the American and Canadian speed of redress, with the former officially apologizing and 'settling' far more rapidly than the latter. Ricou notes how in his teaching experiences '*Obasan* reveals legislated racism, a historical and political fact that, especially for students in Vancouver [where Ricou is a professor at UBC], seems staggering news. In no other teaching I do am I so aware of how entrenched and unquestioned is the assumption of Canadian tolerance and generosity.'[5] In America, Japanese property was not 'liquidated' as it was in Canada, and Japanese Americans were allowed to return to their homes after the war; in Canada, a policy of 'dispersal' kept Japanese Canadians scattered throughout the West. Kogawa's family was initially moved from Vancouver to Slocan in British Columbia; after the war they were offered a home in Coaldale, Alberta, or they would have to have returned to Japan. Kogawa did eventually come back to Vancouver in 1956. Where does an awareness of Japanese internment and the injustices performed by the American and Canadian governments take readers? Teruyo Ueki's concept of 'literary efficacy' may be more generally rewritten as an 'aesthetic efficacy' when the vast range of reader-responses are incorporated into *Obasan*'s reception history.

THE PANORAMA RECONFIGURED

Readings of *Obasan* can be thought of as largely tending towards the resolutionary or the revolutionary:[6] the former regarding the impact of the novel as leading to progress in redress, the latter regarding the impact of the novel as one which opens up a space for further political interventions and an assertion of difference. Maintaining the tensions of difference may involve reading *Obasan* as a literary montage;[7] another methodology here, also based upon the visual arts, is that of the 'interrupted panorama'. Phyllis Greenwood, in *An Interrupted Panorama*, rejects the panorama as an aesthetic, conceptual and technological device for the domination of peoples and place, and reconfigures it as a way of attempting to reach an understanding of stories and art-forms through partial glimpses and subjective human knowledge. At this point in the closing pages of this study of the postcolonial novel, it is worth thinking of the more concrete ways in which a powerfully written, high-impact novel such as *Obasan* influences and relates to other creative and critical writers, working through and across myriad genres. In other words, this study concludes by briefly going beyond the novel form. Greenwood's *An Interrupted Panorama* is an important creative and critical exemplar, as noted by Ricou: '[Her] . . . haunting visual/textual response to the Fraser River . . . uses four narratives to organize it: one is Japanese printmaker Hiroshige's *53 Stations on the Tokaido Road*, a means of incorporating both an essential aesthetic, and a history of the removal of Japanese Canadians from their home river in 1942.'[8] Greenwood writes:

The impetus for *An Interrupted Panorama* began some years ago as a response to a specific piece of work by the 19th century Japanese printmaker, Hiroshige. It developed to include an interest in the western phenomenon of panoramic presentations of the same time period. Combining these two art historical references with the history of the Fraser River, and with a subjective and fragmented family history, conflated four parallel stories, so to speak. Each of them is involved with notions of beginnings and endings, but also with the sense of the continuum. Simon Fraser's "discovery" in 1808 of the river named for him marked the destruction of an aboriginal way of life and the beginning of European settlement on the river. Panorama paintings of the early 1800s marked the beginning of western preoccupation with two concepts: the moving image (in scrolled panoramas) and illusory space (in the construction of panorama buildings). Hiroshige's prints, also of the early and middle 1800s, marked the decline of a printmaking tradition and the beginning of mutual influences between Japanese and Western art.[9]

The 'interruptions' are also restorations: of childhood memories, of places that can, and cannot, actually be seen (the river as seen from the 'rest stops' that narrate a history of her father's alcohol intake; the river from viewpoints that are structurally imposed). Greenwood also theorizes the panorama as being a device that reveals technological shifts into an eventual obsession with hyperreality – that is to say, the moving image and illusory space *par excellence* in the twenty-first century. There are other notions of restoration, however: restoration as a fixing of memory surfaces, as in the restoration of a canvas. Vancouver artist/photographer Jeff Wall has also touched upon the panorama in his 1993 back-lit transparency *Restoration*, which examines repair work on Edouard Castres's *Panorama of the French Army Entering Switzerland*, 1881, housed in Lucecne since 1889. Wall also discusses the transitional moment in his own work between technologies of representation: 'A panorama can never really be experienced in representation, in any other medium. I made a 180-degree panorama photograph of a 360-degree picture, and so had to show only half of it. The geometry of that struck me as appropriate. . . . It itself expresses the fact that the panorama is unrepresentable.'[10] Wall's picture is not just about the panorama *per se*, but the people involved in its restoration; yet the 'unrepresentable' nature of the panorama may relate to the ultimate impossibility of *total restoration* of/to the past object or event. Wall comments on the 'failure' of the panorama and a return to its devices in virtual reality: new technologies and old solutions. The 'subjective history' (her words) in Greenwood's project includes the story of Japanese internment and the appropriation of their property and goods. Her grandparents occupied a Japanese farm: 'All the Okabe family's belongings had disappeared by the time my grandparents took over the farm, except for three small vases left in their prayer shrine . . . and a bamboo baby walker.'[11] Greenwood eventually tracked down the Okabe family via the Mission Community Archives and a 1992 exhibition called *Rites of Passage: the History of the Japanese Canadian Community in Mission, B.C.* She writes of meeting Mr Okabe, who was 12 years old when his family home was forcibly evacuated:

I wrote Mr. Okabe a letter explaining my project and met with him at his home to return his family's vases. Mr. Okabe described to me how his family had been given 48 hours to leave in May, 1942 and were allowed to take 40 pounds of belongings. . . . The Japanese from Mission were put on trains to Lethbridge, and then Picture Butte, Alberta, where they were contracted out to work from dawn to dusk on sugar beet farms. Living in terribly cramped conditions, freezing in winter in uninsulated shacks, they were forbidden to speak Japanese by the R.C.M.P., fingerprinted, made to pay seven dollars per month per child for schooling and earned this by endless, repetitive, backbreaking, thinning, hoeing and harvesting ton after ton of beets.[12]

This partial restoration of some precious family property – the vases in the prayer shrine – leads also to a partial restoration of a family narrative, one of hardship and pain. The incorporation of that narrative into the woven texture of Greenwood's *An Interrupted Panorama* is an essential moment, one that ties in with the complex ethnicity of the peoples involved, and displaced, in the exploration and attempted domination of the Fraser River in British Columbia. At this moment in the narrative, two paintings are visible in the continuous black band that runs along the bottom of the four interwoven texts: *Cougar Point* and *Prince George* (Greenwood, oil on linen, 1995–7). The paintings have 'curved notches removed from the corners' which signify 'registration marks on Japanese prints and . . . the "corners" in photographic albums, where we capture and store scenic memories without concern for the future of the landscape'.[13] In Greenwood's work, landscape and memory are inextricably linked, as technological boundaries are questioned and critiqued. As Kogawa writes: 'Our wordlessness was our mutual destruction.'[14] The postcolonial novel in English thus opens up, through diverse and challenging form, words that maintain the 'concern for the future' as well as an interrogation of colonialist narratives of the past.

SUBVERTING BOUNDARIES

One of the recurrent issues that has foregrounded itself in this study is the ways in which postcolonial novels constantly question and subvert bound-aries – for example, through: counter-discourses writing back *and* through the canon (Coetzee, Rhys, Harris, Ngũgĩ); syncretist vision which offers multiple perspectives through narrative fusion (Harris); the inauguration of new ways of perceiving and mapping colonial contact and postcolonial independence (Achebe, Ngũgĩ); complex representations of 'madness' and sexuality (Head); feminist rejection of linear and logical narrative structures (Atwood, Head); secular critique of orthodox religions (Rushdie); immense linguistic and aesthetic creativity (Rushdie, Roy); and the evocation of a 'political consciousness' (Kogawa and all of the above). There are many other ways of reading and analysing the texts under discussion, but fore-grounding the questioning and subversion of boundaries facilitates further reflections on form. As Bart Moore-Gilbert argues:

Postcolonial criticism has not simply enlarged the traditional field of English studies, or refocused attention on neglected aspects or areas within it. It has also, in association with other relatively recent critical discourses as various as feminism and deconstruction, significantly altered the modes of analysis which were domi-nant within the discipline in the period from 1945 to 1980. Most notably, per-haps, it has helped to undermine the traditional conception of disciplinary boundaries.[15]

This study has focused on the subversion of boundaries as a 'textual effect' rather than a 'reading strategy'.[16] As different genres are brought into view, performative versions and developments of the writing strategies explored here reveal the full scope, and power, of postcolonial artistic production. In some ways, to continue with the textual focus – reading and responding to the novels themselves – is now to read against the grain. It may also be thought of as a way of *listening again*: to other voices, other perspectives outside of the western universities and presses that generate so much of the postcolonial theory that in turn circulates like a precious currency, with its enormous buying power. *Listening again* involves rereading the new and not-so-new postcolonial canons, and being open to voices that are only just beginning to be heard, locating in the process 'other sites of meaning'[17] that have the capacity to trigger dialogue and debate. *Listening again*, however, also generates a problem, one which Jacqueline Rose ponders in her study of Bessie Head: '. . . how to listen to the . . . writer from a dif-ferent culture when any moment of felt recognition may be mere appro-priation or projection on the reader's part . . .'?[18] Rose expands upon this problem by noting that Head's novel raises 'questions about communication inside and across cultures' which

can serve to expose or lay bare the delusional component behind any uncritical belief that text or speaker simply speak. To put it another way, don't the questions of who is speaking in the text and how I should listen – the issues of race, class, and gender as they have become louder and louder in contemporary critical debate . . . carry an anxiety that the text might be speaking with a hostile voice, one which is alien or unfriendly to *me*?[19]

In other words, it would be wrong for the western reader to assume that *listening again* will necessarily be a comfortable experience, an expectation that causes myriad interpretive and existential problems, as seen above, with the example of the reactions to *Obasan* in the classroom. The discomfort generated by reading postcolonial literature may be, as Rose suggests in relation to Head, an effect of 'the way universality as a concept starts to break up under scrutiny'.[20]

Notes

PREFACE AND ACKNOWLEDGEMENTS

1. Robert Eaglestone, *Doing English: A Guide for Literature Students*, London and New York: Routledge, 2002.
2. See, for example, the comments on performance and ritual in my 'Performing History: The Reconstruction of Gender and Race in British Columbian Drama,' in Sherrill Grace and Albert-Reiner Glaap, eds, *Performing National Identities: International Perspectives on Contemporary Canadian Theatre*, Vancouver: Talon, 2003, pp. 265–77.

CHAPTER 1   INTRODUCING THE POSTCOLONIAL NOVEL IN ENGLISH: WILSON HARRIS'S *PALACE OF THE PEACOCK*

1. David Punter, in his introduction to his *Postcolonial Imaginings: Fictions of a New World Order* (Edinburgh: Edinburgh University Press, 2000), quotes Ketu Katrak, who notes that a study 'that focuses only on English-language post-colonial writers involves some loss, even distortion in terms of the complex reality of linguistic situations in post-colonial areas', p. 7; see Ketu Katrak, 'Post-Colonial Women Writers and Feminisms', in Bruce King, ed., *New National and Post-Colonial Literatures: An Introduction*, Oxford: Clarendon Press, 1996, pp. 230–44.
2. Richard J. Lane, 'Edward Wadie Said', in *Fifty Key Twentieth-Century Literary Theorists*, London and New York: Routledge, forthcoming; see Edward W. Said, *Beginnings: Intention and Method* (first published 1975), New York: Basic Books and New York: Columbia University Press Morningside Edition, 1985; see Michel Foucault, 'Nietzsche, Genealogy, History', in *Language, Counter-Memory, Practice: Selected Essays and Interviews*, ed. Donald F. Bouchard, trans. Donald F. Bouchard and Sherry Simon, Ithaca, NY: Cornell University Press, 1988, pp. 139–64.
3. Wilson Harris, *Palace of the Peacock* (first published 1960), London and Boston: Faber and Faber, 1988. All further page references are cited in the text.
4. Jakob Lothe, *Narrative in Fiction and Film: An Introduction*, Oxford: Oxford University Press, 2000, pp. 42–3.
5. Shifting narrational perspectives can be utilized as a structuring device in prose fiction; see as an example, the analysis of Virginia Woolf's *Mrs Dalloway* in Richard J. Lane, *Literary Masterpieces: Mrs Dalloway*, Detroit and New York: Gale, 2001, pp. 14–27.

6. The difference between narrative modes – called 'document' and 'figment' – offers another way of reading the text here; see John McDowell, 'Duality of Language in *Palace of the Peacock*', *Commonwealth Novel in English*, 4.1 (Spring 1991): 62–8. For analysis of narration, metaphor and symbols in *Palace*, see Gay Wilentz, 'Wilson Harris's Divine Comedy of Existence: Miniaturizations of the Cosmos in *Palace of the Peacock*', *Kunapipi*, 8.2 (1986): 56–66.

7. For a theory of complementarity between the narrator and Donne, see Graham Huggan, 'Anxieties of Influence: Conrad in the Caribbean', *Commonwealth: Essays and Studies*, 11.1 (Autumn 1988): 1–12.

8. Wayne C. Booth, *The Rhetoric of Fiction*, second edition, Chicago and London: University of Chicago Press, 1983, pp. 174–5. See the discussion concerning 'unreliable' narrators and Margaret Atwood in chapter six of this study.

9. Ibid., p. 175.

10. Andrew Gibson, *Postmodernity, Ethics and the Novel: From Leavis to Levinas*, London and New York: Routledge, 1999, p. 6.

11. Richard Ruland and Malcolm Bradbury, *From Puritanism to Postmodernism: A History of American Literature*, London and New York: Penguin, 1992, p. 383; see Linda Hutcheon, *The Canadian Postmodern: A Study of Contemporary English-Canadian Fiction*, Ontario: Oxford University Press, 1988, p. 2.

12. For a powerful yet amusing critique of some of the worse excesses of postmodernism and theory, see Alan Sokal and Jean Bricmont, *Intellectual Impostures: Postmodern Philosophers' Abuse of Science*, London: Profile, 1999.

13. Frantz Fanon, *The Wretched of the Earth* (first published 1961), New York: Grove, 1968, p. 227.

14. Ibid., p. 58.

15. John Thieme, *Postcolonial Con-Texts: Writing Back to the Canon*, London and New York: Continuum, 2001, pp. 27 and pp. 28–9.

16. Ania Loomba, *Colonialism/Postcolonialism*, London and New York: Routledge, 2000, p. 136; see Chinua Achebe, 'An Image of Africa: Racism in Conrad's *Heart of Darkness*', in Chinua Achebe, *Hopes and Impediments: Selected Essays*, New York: Doubleday/Anchor, 1989, pp. 269–74.

17. Edward W. Said, *Culture and Imperialism*, London: Vintage, 1994, p. 26.

18. Ibid.

19. Thieme, *Postcolonial Con-Texts*, p. 31.

20. Ibid., p. 32.

21. Fredric Jameson, *The Political Unconscious: Narrative as a Socially Symbolic Act*, London: Methuen, 1986, p. 219.

22. T.J. Cribb, 'T.W. Harris – Sworn Surveyor', *Journal of Commonwealth Literature*, XXIX.1 (1993): 33–46; p. 38.

23. Ibid.

24. Ibid.

25. Eden Robinson, *Monkey Beach*, London: Abacus, 2000; Richard J. Lane, 'Reclaiming Maps and Metaphors: Canadian First Nations and Narratives of Place', in Deborah Madsen, ed., *Beyond the Borders: American Literature and Post-Colonial Theory*, London: Pluto 2003, pp. 184–94; p. 190.

26. Richard J. Lane, 'The Dangers of "Dumb Talk": Eurocentric Translations of the Potlatch', *Commonwealth: Essays and Studies*, 21.2 (1999): 75–82; an interesting feminist reading of 'The Two Sisters' is hinted at in Veronica Strong-Boag and Carole Gerson, *Paddling Her Own Canoe: The Times and*

Texts Of E. Pauline Johnson (Tekahionwake), Toronto: University of Toronto Press, 2000.

27. Bill Ashcroft, Gareth Griffiths and Helen Tiffin, *The Empire Writes Back: Theory and Practice in Post-Colonial Literatures*, London and New York: Routledge, 1994, p. 151; for discussion of the montage form utilized to critique the concept of 'history as progress', see Susan Buck-Morss, *The Dialectics of Seeing: Walter Benjamin and the Arcades Project*, Cambridge, MA: MIT Press, 1999; for literary-critical applications and further analysis of montage and aesthetics, see Richard J. Lane, *Reading Walter Benjamin: Writing through the Catastrophe*, Manchester: Manchester University Press, 2005.

28. Paula Burnett stresses that Wilson Harris has remained a poet throughout his career; the more recent downplaying of his earlier poems does not recognize his overall poetic approach to language. See Paula Burnett, 'Caribbean', in William Bauer and Kenneth Womack, eds. *The Year's Work in English Studies*, Vol. 80, Oxford: Oxford University Press, 2001, section two of chapter XVII, pp. 840–50; pp. 847–8.

29. Thieme, *Postcolonial Con-Texts*, p. 35.

30. Ibid; see Hena Maes-Jelinek, *The Naked Design: A Reading of 'Palace of the Peacock'*, Århus: Dangaroo Press, 1976, pp. 46–7; Hena Maes-Jelinek, *Wilson Harris*, Boston: Twayne, 1982, p. 10.

31. Bill Ashcroft, Gareth Griffiths and Helen Tiffin, *Key Concepts in Post-Colonial Studies*, London and New York: Routledge, 1999, p. 229.

32. Ibid.

33. For a study of Harris and redemption, see Samuel Durrant, 'Hosting History: Wilson Harris's Sacramental Narratives', *Jouvert: A Journal of Postcolonial Studies*, 1.41 (Autumn 2000). Available on-line: *http://social.chass.ncsu.edu/jouvert/v51/samdur.htm*, accessed 8/12/05.

34. Thieme, *Postcolonial Con-Texts*, p. 33.

35. David Daniel, *The Bible in English: Its History and Influence*, New Haven and London: Yale University Press, 2003, p. 417.

36. Ibid.

37. Ashcroft et al., *The Empire Writes Back*, p. 153.

38. Ibid.

39. Bart Moore-Gilbert, *Postcolonial Theory: Contexts, Practices, Politics*, London and New York: Verso, 1997, pp. 183–4; see the entire section on these two pages for a more in-depth series of comparisons.

40. John McLeod, *Beginning Postcolonialism*, Manchester: Manchester University Press, 2000, p. 10.

41. Ibid., pp. 10–11.

42. A.L. McLeod, ed., *The Commonwealth Pen: An Introduction to the Literature of the British Commonwealth*, Ithaca, NY: Cornell University Press, 1961, p. 2.

43. McLeod, *Beginning Postcolonialism*, p. 14.

44. McLeod, ed., *The Commonwealth Pen*, p. 5.

45. Ibid., p. 7.

46. Ibid.

47. Ibid., pp. 7–8.

48. Ato Quayson, *Postcolonialism: Theory, Practice or Process?*, Cambridge: Polity, 2000, p. 2.

49. Ibid.

50. Deborah Madsen, ed., *Post-Colonial Literatures: Expanding the Canon*, London: Pluto, 1999, p. 2; see also Deborah Madsen, ed., *Beyond The Borders: American Literature and Post-Colonial Theory*, London: Pluto 2003, for a related discussion.

51. Rowland Smith, ed., *Postcolonizing the Commonwealth: Studies in Literature and Culture*, Waterloo, Ont.: Wilfrid Laurier University Press, 2000, p. 4.

52. Thomas King, 'Godzilla vs Post-Colonial', in Ajay Heble, Donna Palmateer Pennee and J.R. (Tim) Struthers, eds, *New Contexts of Canadian Criticism*, Peterborough, Ontario: Broadview, 1997, pp. 241–8; pp. 242–3.

53. Ibid., p. 243.

54. Judith Leggatt, 'Native Writing, Academic Theory: Post-Colonialism across the Cultural Divide', in Laura Moss, ed., *Is Canada Postcolonial? Unsettling Canadian Literature*, Waterloo, Ont.: Wilfrid Laurier Press, 2003, pp. 111–26; pp. 111–12.

55. Punter, *Postcolonial Imaginings*, p. 188.

CHAPTER 2   THE COUNTER-CANONICAL NOVEL: J.M. COETZEE'S *FOE* AND JEAN RHYS'S *WIDE SARGASSO SEA*

1.   *Foe* also writes back against Daniel Defoe's *Roxana* (1724), although this intertextual relationship is less often explored by critics. See, as a comprehensive critical example, Gayatri Chakravorty Spivak's 'Theory in the Margin: Coetzee's *Foe* Reading Defoe's *Crusoe/Roxana*', in Jonathan Arac and Barbara Johnson, eds, *Consequences of Theory: Selected Papers from the English Institute, 1987–88*, New Series, no. 14, Baltimore and London: Johns Hopkins University Press, 1991, pp. 154–80.

2.   Ashcroft et al., *Key Concepts in Post-Colonial Studies*, pp. 56–7.

3.   The critical relationship between Derrida and Hegel is a more complex, if not extreme, example of the stakes between old and new, and the differences between 'dialectical' and 'deconstructive' modes of critique; see the 'Hegel' section of Richard J. Lane, *Functions of the Derrida Archive: Philosophical Receptions*, Budapest: Akadémiai Kiadó, 2003, pp. 73–81.

4.   Strictly speaking, used as a term for a printing process whereby the printer can move from left-to-right and from right-to-left as it prints a page of text.

5.   Richard J. Lane, 'Appropriating the Signifier in J.M. Coetzee's *Foe*', *Commonwealth: Essays and Studies*, 13.1 (Autumn 1990): 106–11.

6.   *Collins English Dictionary*, Glasgow: HarperCollins, 1998.

7.   Ibid.

8.   Dana Dragunoiu, 'Existential Doubt and Political Responsibility in J.M. Coetzee's *Foe*', *Critique*, 42.3 (Spring 2001): 309–26.

9.   Ian Watt, *The Rise of the Novel* (first published 1957) Harmondsworth: Penguin, 1963, p. 65, quoted in Thieme, *Postcolonial Con-Texts*, p. 54.

10. Thieme, *Postcolonial Con-Texts*, p. 56. See the entire quotation and the following more complex argument; Thieme examines the regional responses as being contrary to what might be expected.

11. Said, *Culture and Imperialism*, p. 83.

12. J.M. Coetzee, *Foe*, London: Penguin, 1988. All further references shall be cited in the text by page number.

13. Spivak, 'Theory in the Margin', p. 163.

14. Ibid., p. 161.

15. Lane, 'Appropriating the Signifier in J.M. Coetzee's *Foe*', p. 108; Jonathan Swift, *Gulliver's Travels* (first published 1726), Oxford: Oxford University Press, 1988, p. 84.

16. Edward W. Said, *Orientalism*, New York: Vintage, 1979, p. 177.

17. Maximillian E. Novak notes that when Daniel Defoe's 'bones were disinterred on 16 September 1871 for the purpose of erecting a monument to his achievements, newspaper accounts seemed to be incapable of agreeing about very much. Was there a plaque on his coffin with the name "Daniel Defoe", as stated by the *Daily News*, or did it, as the *Daily Telegraph* insisted, merely say "Foe"?' *Daniel Defoe: Master of Fictions*, Oxford: Oxford University Press, 2001, pp. 2–3.

18. Sylvie Maurel, 'Across the "Wide Sargasso Sea": Jean Rhys's Revision of Charlotte Brontë's Eurocentric Gothic', *Commonwealth: Essays and Studies*, 24.2 (2002): 107–18; p. 112.

19. See the opening page of Novak's *Daniel Defoe: Master of Fictions*.

20. Spivak, 'Theory in the Margin', p. 162.

21. Ibid.

22. Ibid.

23. Virginia Woolf, 'Defoe', in Max Byrd, ed., *Daniel Defoe: A Collection of Critical Essays*, Englewood Cliffs, NJ: Prentice-Hall, 1976, pp. 15–22; p. 21.

24. Lane, 'Appropriating the Signifier in J.M. Coetzee's *Foe*', p. 110.

25. Thieme, *Postcolonial Con-Texts* p. 66.

26. Richard J. Lane, 'Theorizing the Gendered Space of Auto/Biographical Performance via Samuel Beckett and Hans Bellmer', in Sherrill Grace and Jerry Wasserman, eds, *Theatre and Autobiography: Essays on the Theory and Practice of Writing and Performing Lives*, Vancouver, BC: Talon, 2006, pp. 72–88.

27. Spivak, 'Theory in the Margin', p. 174.

28. Ibid, p. 175.

29. Thieme, *Postcolonial Con-Texts*, p. 69.

30. John J. Su, '"Once I Would Have Gone Back . . . But Not Any Longer": Nostalgia and Narrative Ethics in *Wide Sargasso Sea*', *Critique*, 44.2 (Winter 2003): 157–74.

31. Ibid, pp. 158–9. See also Ellen G. Friedman, 'Breaking the Master Narrative: Jean Rhys's *Wide Sargasso Sea*', in Ellen G. Friedman and Miriam Fuchs, eds, *Breaking the Sequence: Women's Experimental Fiction*, Princeton: Princeton University Press, pp. 117–28; and Carine Melkom Mardorossian, 'Double (De)colonization and the Feminist Criticism of *Wide Sargasso Sea*', *College Literature*, 26.2 (Spring 1999): 79–95.

32. Ashcroft, et al., *The Empire Writes Back*, p. 189.

33. Ibid.

34. Su, '"Once I would Have Gone Back . . . But Not Any Longer"', p. 158.

35. Ibid.

36. Jean Rhys, *Wide Sargasso Sea*, London and New York: Norton, 1982, p. 17. All further references shall be cited in the text by page number.

37. A more theoretical reading could examine Antoinette's 'absolute negativity' via the work of Žižek, e.g., the notion that the subject must remain open to Hegelian negativity to escape from the ideological falsehood of a 'full subjectivity that would overcome alienation' – see Ian Parker, *Slavoj Žižek: A Critical Introduction*, London: Pluto, 2004, p. 108.

120

38. Romita Choudhury, '"Is There a Ghost, a Zombie There?" Postcolonial Inter-textuality and Jean Rhys's *Wide Sargasso Sea*', *Textual Practice*, 10.2 (Summer 1996): 315–27; p. 322.
39. Maurel, 'Across the "Wide Sargasso Sea"', p. 111; see also Punter, *Postcolonial Imaginings*, p. 44.
40. Maurel, 'Across the "Wide Sargasso Sea"', p. 114; see Gayatri Chakravorty Spivak, 'Three Women's Texts and a Critique of Imperialism', *Critical Inquiry*, 12.1 (Autumn 1985): 243–61; pp. 252–3.
41. This difference in focus – i.e., that of the structural implications – is derived from Spivak's assessment of Subaltern Studies research. See Gayatri Chakravorty Spivak, *In Other Worlds: Essays in Cultural Politics*, London and New York: Routledge, 1988, p. 219. Spivak's feminist reading of 'the effaced itinerary of the subaltern subject' is also of relevance in 'Can the Subaltern Speak?', in Patrick Williams and Laura Chrisman, eds, *Colonial Discourse and Postcolonial Theory: A Reader*, New York: Columbia University Press, 1994, pp. 66–111; p. 82.
42. Richard J. Lane, 'Performing Gender: First Nations, Feminism, and Trickster Writing in Eden Robinson's *Monkey Beach*', *Hungarian Journal of English and American Studies*, 9.1 (Spring 2003): 161–71; p. 163.
43. Choudhury, '"Is There a Ghost, a Zombie There?"', p. 325.
44. Ibid.
45. See Trenton Hickman, 'The Colonized Woman as Monster in *Jane Eyre*, *Wide Sargasso Sea*, and *Annie John*', *Journal of Caribbean Studies*, 14.3 (Summer 2000): 181–98.
46. R. McClure Smith, '"I Don't Dream About It Any More": The Textual Unconscious in Jean Rhys's *Wide Sargasso Sea*', *Journal of Narrative Technique*, 26.2 (Spring 1996): 113–36; p. 119.
47. Mardorossian, 'Double (De)colonization and the Feminist Criticism of *Wide Sargasso Sea*', p. 79.
48. Samuel Durrant, 'Bearing Witness to Apartheid: J.M. Coetzee's Inconsolable Works of Mourning', *Contemporary Literature*, 40.3 (Fall 1999): 430–63; p. 434.
49. Mardorossian, 'Double (De)colonization and the Feminist Criticism of *Wide Sargasso Sea*', p. 80.
50. Ibid., pp. 80–1.
51. Ibid., p. 83. For analysis of the text's conscious and/or unconscious, see Kathy Mezei, '"And It Kept Its Secret": Narration, Memory, and Madness in Jean Rhys' *Wide Sargasso Sea*', *Critique*, 28.4 (Summer 1987): 195–209, and Jan Curtis, 'The Secret of *Wide Sargasso Sea*', *Critique*, 31.3 (Spring 1990): 185–97.
52. Laura E. Ciolkowski, 'Navigating the *Wide Sargasso Sea*: Colonial History, English Fiction, and British Empire', *Twentieth Century Literature*, 43.3 (Fall 1997): 339–59; p. 351.
53. Durrant, 'Bearing Witness to Apartheid', p. 439.
54. Ibid., pp. 439–46.

CHAPTER 3   ALTERNATIVE HISTORIOGRAPHIES: CHINUA ACHEBE'S *THINGS FALL APART*

1. Simon Gikandi, 'Chinua Achebe and the Invention of African Culture', *Research in African Literatures*, 32.3 (Fall 2001): 3–8; pp. 4–5.
2. Ibid., p. 5.

3. Ibid. See also Ato Quayson, *Strategic Transformations in Nigerian Writing: Orality and History in the Work of Rev. Samuel Johnson, Amos Tutuola, Wole Soyinka and Ben Okri*, Oxford and Bloomington: James Currey and Indiana University Press, 1997.

4. Phillip Darby argues that the publication in 1991 of Simon Gikandi's study of Achebe was a powerful response to those who had criticized Achebe's 'realism', leading to a new wave of critical interest in Achebe's work. See Phillip Darby, *The Fiction of Imperialism: Reading Between International Relations and Postcolonialism*, London and Washington: Cassell, 1998, p. 143, and Simon Gikandi, *Reading Chinua Achebe*, London: James Currey, 1991.

5. Ato Quayson, 'Realism, Criticism, and the Disguises of Both: A Reading of Chinua Achebe's *Things Fall Apart* with an Evaluation of the Criticism Relating to It', *Research in African Literatures*, 25.4 (Winter 1994): 117–36; p. 119; see also the comments on Achebe and 'normativity' in chapter three of Quayson, *Postcolonialism: Theory, Practice or Process?*

6. Quayson, 'Realism, Criticism, and the Disguises of Both', p. 120.

7. Fanon, *The Wretched of the Earth*, p. 219.

8. Ibid., p. 224.

9. Gikandi, 'Chinua Achebe and the Invention of African Culture', p. 3.

10. Chinua Achebe, *Things Fall Apart*, Oxford: Heinemann, 1986, p. 3. All further references shall be cited in the text by page number.

11. Quayson, 'Realism, Criticism, and the Disguises of Both', p. 125.

12. Ibid., p. 126.

13. Wole Ogundele, 'Devices of Evasion: The Mythic versus the Historical Imagination in the Postcolonial African Novel', *Research in African Literatures*, 33.3 (Fall 2002): 125–39; p. 134.

14. Ibid.

15. David Carroll, *Chinua Achebe*, New York: Twayne, 1970, p. 37.

16. Ibid., p. 39.

17. Ibid., p. 41.

18. Ibid.

19. Ogundele, 'Devices of Evasion', p. 134.

20. Ibid.

21. Ibid., p. 135.

22. Ibid.

23. Ibid.

24. See also Joseph McLaren, 'Missionaries and Converts: Religion and Colonial Intrusion in *Things Fall Apart*', *The Literary Griot: International Journal of Black Expressive Cultural Studies*, 10.2 (Fall 1998): 48–60.

25. Thieme, *Postcolonial Con-Texts*, p. 18 and p. 19.

26. Kurt Hoffman, 'The Basic Concepts of Jaspers' Philosophy', in Paul Arthur Schilpp, ed., *The Philosophy of Karl Jaspers*, The Library of Living Philosophers, New York: Tudor, 1957, pp. 95–114; pp. 102–3.

27. Slavoj Žižek, *Tarrying with the Negative: Kant, Hegel, and the Critique of Ideology*, Durham, NC: Duke University Press, 1993, p. 157.

28. Mark Mathuray argues that *Arrow of God* has received the most critical attention among Achebe's novels. See his 'Realizing the Sacred: Power and Meaning in Chinua Achebe's *Arrow of God*', *Research in African Literatures*, 34.3 (Fall 2003): 46–65; p. 49. Mathuray also points out the parallels between the two novels on p. 50.

29. F. Abiola Irele, 'Homage to Chinua Achebe', *Research in African Literatures*, 32.3 (Fall 2001): 1–2.

30. Ibid., p. 2.

31. Quoted in Clayton G. MacKenzie, 'The Metamorphosis of Piety in Chinua Achebe's *Things Fall Apart*', *Research in African Literatures*, 27.2 (Summer 1996): 128–38; p. 134.

32. Ibid.

33. Ibid.

34. Ibid.

35. David Hoegberg, 'Principle and Practice: The Logic of Cultural Violence in Achebe's *Things Fall Apart*', *College Literature*, 26.1 (Winter 1999): 69–79; p. 69.

36. Ibid., pp. 69–70.

37. Kwadwo Osei-Nyame, 'Gender and the Narrative of Identity in Chinua Achebe's *Arrow of God*', *Commonwealth*, 22.2 (March 2000): 25–34; p. 26.

38. Kwadwo Osei-Nyame, 'Chinua Achebe Writing Culture: Representations of Gender and Tradition in *Things Fall Apart*', *Research in African Literatures*, 30.2 (Summer 1999): 148–64; p. 159. Ekwefi is Okonkow's second wife, and Ezinma is her daughter; they are both very independent characters in the patriarchal world of the novel.

39. Biodun Jeyifo, 'Okonkwo and His Mother: *Things Fall Apart* and Issues of Gender in the Constitution of African Postcolonial Discourse', *Callaloo*, 16.4 (1993): 847–58.

40. Richard Begam, 'Achebe's Sense of an Ending: History and Tragedy in *Things Fall Apart*', *Studies in the Novel*, 29.3 (Fall 1997): 396–411.

41. Neil Ten Kortenaar, 'Becoming African and the Death of Ikemefuna', *University of Toronto Quarterly*, 73.2 (Spring 2004): 773–94.

CHAPTER 4   NATIONAL CONSCIOUSNESS: NGŨGĨ WA THIONG'O'S *A GRAIN OF WHEAT*

1. See Bu-Buakei Jabbi, 'Conrad's Influence on Betrayal in *A Grain Of Wheat*', *Research in African Literatures*, 11.1 (Spring 1980): 50–83; see also Alissa Hamilton, 'The Construction and Deconstruction of National Identities through Language in the Narratives of Ngũgĩ Wa Thiong'o's *A Grain Of Wheat* and Joseph Conrad's *Under Western Eyes*', *African Languages and Cultures*, 8.2 (1995): 137–51.

2. Kofi Owusu, 'Point of View and Narrative Strategy in Nguge's [*sic*] *A Grain Of Wheat*', *Notes on Contemporary Literature*, 17.1 (1987): 2–3; 2.

3. Ngũgĩ wa Thiong'o, *A Grain of Wheat*, London: Heinemann, 1988, p. 19. All further references shall be cited in the text by page number.

4. Owusu, 'Point of View and Narrative Strategy in Nguge's [*sic*] *A Grain Of Wheat*', p. 2.

5. Ibid.

6. Ibid.

7. McLeod, *Beginning Postcolonialism*, p. 93.

8. Simon Gikandi, *Ngugi Wa Thiong'o*, Cambridge: Cambridge University Press, 2000, p. 108.

9. Ibid., pp. 108–9.

10. Ibid., p. 109.

11. Ibid., p. 113.

12. Ibid.
13. Ibid.
14. John Lutz, 'Ngugi's Dialectical Vision: Individualism and Revolutionary Consciousness in *A Grain of Wheat*', *Ufahamu*, 29.2–3 (Winter/Spring 2003): 171–98; p. 184.
15. See Frantz Fanon, *Black Skin, White Masks* (first published 1952), London: Pluto, 1986.
16. Lutz, 'Ngugi's Dialectical Vision', pp. 185–6.
17. Gikandi, *Ngugi Wa Thiong'o*, p. 118.
18. Ibid., p. 120.
19. Ibid.
20. Ibid., p. 119.
21. Delia Krause, 'A Grain Of Wheat: Ngugi's Tribute to the Armed Rebellion', *Wasafiri*, 9 (1988): 6–10; p. 7.
22. Ibid.
23. Ibid.
24. Joyce Johnson, 'Character and Circumstance in Ngugi Wa Thiong'o's *A Grain of Wheat*', *Commonwealth Novel in English*, 3.1 (1984): 21–38; p. 26.
25. Jacqueline Bardolph, 'Moving Away from the Mission: Ngugi wa Thiongo'o's Versions of *A Grain of Wheat*', in Gerhard Stilz, ed., *Missions of Interdependence: A Literary Directory*, ASNEL Papers 6, Amsterdam and New York: Rodopi, 2002, pp. 133–41; p. 133.
26. Ibid., p. 140.
27. Ibid., p. 136.
28. Ibid, pp. 137–8.
29. Govind Narain Sharma, 'Ngugi's Christian Vision: Theme and Pattern in *A Grain of Wheat*', *African Literature Today*, 10 (1979): 167–76; p. 169. See also R.L. Townsend, 'The Heroism of Mugo: A Study of Ngugi's "*A Grain of Wheat*"', *Fort Hare Papers*, 8.2 (1987): 46–53.
30. Ashcroft et al., *Key Concepts in Post-Colonial Studies*, p. 229.
31. Bu-Buakei Jabbi, 'The Structure of Symbolism in *A Grain of Wheat*', *Research in African Literatures*, 16.2 (Summer 1985): 210–242; p. 220.
32. See also the analysis by Kenneth Harrow, 'Ngugi wa Thiong'o's *A Grain of Wheat*: Season of Irony', *Research in African Literatures*, 16.2 (1985): 243–63; p. 260.
33. Ibid., p. 243.
34. Byron Caminero-Santangelo, 'Neocolonialism and the Betrayal Plot in *A Grain of Wheat*: Ngũgĩ wa Thiong'o's Re-Vision of *Under Western Eyes*', *Research in African Literatures*, 29.1 (Spring 1998): 139–52; p. 140.
35. Gikandi, *Ngugi Wa Thiong'o*, p. 100.
36. Ibid.
37. Ibid.
38. Kathy Kessler, 'Rewriting History in Fiction: Elements of Postmodernism in Ngugi wa Thiong'o's Later Novels', *Ariel*, 25.2 (1994): 75–90; p. 75; quoting Henry A. Giroux, 'Postmodernism as Border Pedagogy: Redefining the Boundaries of Race and Ethnicity', in Henry A. Giroux, ed., *Postmodernism, Feminism, and Cultural Politics: Redrawing Educational Boundaries*, Albany: SUNY Press, 1991, pp. 217–56.
39. Ibid.

CHAPTER 5   INTERROGATING SUBJECTIVITY:
BESSIE HEAD'S *A QUESTION OF POWER*

1. Linda Anderson, *Autobiography*, London and New York: Routledge, 2001, p. 17. For new ways of theorizing the auto/biographical subject, see Lane, 'Theorizing the Gendered Space of Auto/Biographical Performance via Samuel Beckett and Hans Bellmer'.

2. For the debate concerning autobiographical narratives in Head's work, see Susan Gardner, '"Don't Ask for the True Story": A Memoir of Bessie Head', *Hecate*, 12.1–2 (1986): 110–29 and Teresa Dovey, '*A Question of Power*: Susan Gardner's Biography versus Bessie Head's Autobiography', *English in Africa*, 16 (May 1989): 29–38.

3. Charles Ponnuthurai Sarvan, 'Bessie Head: *A Question of Power* and Identity', *African Literature Today*, 15 (1987): 82–8; p. 82.

4. Jacqueline Rose, 'On the "Universality" of Madness: Bessie Head's *A Question of Power*', *Critical Inquiry*, 20 (Spring 1994): 401–18; p. 409.

5. Ibid.

6. Sarvan, 'Bessie Head', p. 83.

7. Manus Vicki Briault, 'The Lever Out of Hell: Autobiographical Footholds to Read Bessie Head's *A Question of Power*', *Commonwealth: Essays & Studies*, 24.1 (2001): 25–30; p. 25.

8. Rose, 'On the "Universality" of Madness', p. 415.

9. Patrick Colm Hogan, 'Bessie Head's *A Question of Power*: A Lacanian Psychosis', *Mosaic*, 27.2 (1994): 95–112.

10. Rose, 'On the "Universality" of Madness', p. 403.

11. Desiree Lewis, 'Bessie Head's Freedoms', *Chimurenga Online*, http://www.chimurenga.co.za/modules.php?name=News&file=article&sid=51,   accessed 2/12/05.

12. See Hogan, 'Bessie Head's *A Question of Power*'.

13. James M. Garrett, 'Writing Community: Bessie Head and the Politics of Narrative', *Research in African Literatures*, 30.2 (Summer 1999): 122–35; p. 123.

14. Ibid.

15. Joanne Chase, 'Bessie Head's *A Question Of Power*: Romance or Rhetoric?', *ACLALS Bulletin*, 6.1 (1982): 67–75; pp. 70–1.

16. Gilles Deleuze and Félix Guattari, *Anti-Oedipus: Capitalism and Schizophrenia*, trans. Robert Hurley, Mark Seem and Helen R. Lane, Minneapolis: University of Minnesota Press, 1989, p. 2. For an introductory account, see Claire Colebrook, *Gilles Deleuze*, London and New York: Routledge, 2003.

17. Bessie Head, *A Question of Power*, London: Heinemann, 1987, p. 11. All further references shall by cited in the text by page number.

18. Margaret E. Tucker, 'A "Nice-Time Girl" Strikes Back: An Essay on Bessie Head's *A Question of Power*', *Research in African Literatures*, 19.2 (Summer 1988): 170–81; p. 172.

19. Julia Kristeva, *Powers of Horror: An Essay on Abjection*, trans. Leon S. Roudiez, New York: Columbia University Press, 1982, p. 1.

20. Ibid., p. 2.

21. Briault, 'The Lever out of Hell', p. 26.

22. Ibid.

23. Eleni Coundouriotis, 'Authority and Invention in the Fiction of Bessie Head', *Research in African Literatures*, 27.2 (Summer 1996): 17–32; p. 19.

24. Ibid., pp. 19–20.

25. Ibid., p. 20.

26. Ibid.

27. Shoshana Felman, *Writing and Madness: Literature/ Philosophy/ Psychoanalaysis* trans. Martha Noel Evans, Palo Alto, CA: Stanford University Press, 2003, p. 38. See also Michel Foucault, *Discipline and Punish: The Birth of the Prison*, trans. Alan Sheridan, New York: Vintage, 1979.

28. Ibid; my italics.

29. Tucker, 'A "Nice-Time Girl" Strikes Back', p. 172.

30. Ibid., p. 180.

31. Ibid.

32. Ibid.

33. See Deleuze and Guattari, *Anti-Oedipus*.

34. Ibid., p. 9. See also Edward Scheer, ed., *Antonin Artaud: A Critical Reader*, London and New York: Routledge, 2004.

35. Deleuze and Guattari, *Anti-Oedipus*, p. 9.

36. Ibid.

37. Roberta Rubenstein, *New Republic*, 27 April 1974, quoted in 'Bessie Head, 1937–1986', *Contemporary Authors Online*, Gale, 2003 (electronic resource).

38. For alternative readings of gender and sexuality in the novel, see, for example, Earl G. Ingersoll, 'Reconstructing Masculinity in the Postcolonial World of Bessie Head', *Ariel*, 29.3 (July 1998): 95–116.

39. Angelo Fick, 'Beyond Bodies and Texts and Prisons in Bessie Head's Negotiation of Impossible Subjectivity through Allegory: *A Question of Power*', in Hermann Wittenberg, G. Baderoon and Y. Steenkamp, eds, *Inter Action 6: Proceedings of the Fourth Postgraduate Conference*, Bellville: UWC Press, 1998, pp. 144–51. Available on-line: http://www.uwc.ac.za/arts/english/interaction/97af.htm, accessed 5/12/05.

40. Sope Maithufi, 'Fanon's African Ontology, Post-Colonial Ideological Stage and the Liberation of Africa', *APA Newsletters*, 97.1 (Fall 1997). Available on-line: http://www.apa.udel.edu/apa/archive/newsletters/v97n1/black/fanon.asp, accessed 5/12/05.

41. Ibid.

42. Hogan, 'Bessie Head's *A Question of Power*', p. 95.

43. Adetokunbo Pearse, 'Apartheid and Madness: Bessie Head's *A Question of Power*', *Kunapipi*, 2 (1983): 81–93; p. 81.

44. Maxine Sample, 'Introduction', in Maxine Sample, ed., *Critical Essays on Bessie Head*, London and Westport, CT: Praeger, 2003, pp. ix–xii; p. ix. See also Helen Kapstein, '"A Peculiar Shuttling Movement": Madness, Passing, and Trespassing in Bessie Head's *A Question of Power*', in Sample, ed., *Critical Essays on Bessie Head*, pp. 71–98.

45. Natasha C. Vaubel, 'The Battlefield of Politics and Selfhood in Bessie Head's *A Question of Power*', *ALA Bulletin: A Publication of the African Literature Association*, 23.1 (1 December 1997): 83–106; p. 86. See also Rhondha Cobham, 'Introduction' to *Research in African Literatures*, Special Issue on African Women Writes, 19.2 (Summer 1988): 137–42; pp. 140–1.

CHAPTER 6　RECODING NARRATIVE: MARGARET ATWOOD'S *SURFACING*

1.　M. Prabhakar, 'Margaret Atwood's *Surfacing*: Blue-Print of Revolt', *The Literary Half-Yearly*, 36.1 (January 1995): 70–9; p. 71.

2.　Margaret Atwood, *Survival: A Thematic Guide to Canadian Literature*, Concord, Ont.: Anansi, 1991.

3.　Prabhakar, 'Margaret Atwood's *Surfacing*', p. 71.

4.　Erinç Özdemir, 'Power, Madness, and Gender Identity in Margaret Atwood's *Surfacing*: A Feminist Reading', *English Studies*, 84.1 (2003): 57–79; p. 58.

5.　Ibid.

6.　Hutcheon, *The Canadian Postmodern*, p. 144.

7.　For a theoretical analysis and overview of postmodernism, see Linda Hutcheon, *The Politics of Postmodernism*, second edition, London and New York: Routledge, 2002.

8.　Margaret Atwood, *Surfacing*, London: Virago, 1988, pp. 47 and 148. All further references shall be cited in the text by page number.

9.　Shlomith Rimmon-Kenan, *Narrative Fiction: Contemporary Poetics*, London and New York: Methuen, 1986, p. 100.

10.　Ibid.

11.　Ibid., p. 103.

12.　Booth, *The Rhetoric of Fiction*, p. 316.

13.　Ibid., pp. 316, 320, 322.

14.　Ibid., p. 324.

15.　Ibid.

16.　Ibid., pp. 174–5.

17.　Ibid., p. 346.

18.　John Thieme, 'Beyond History: Margaret Atwood's *Surfacing* and Robert Kroetsch's *Badlands*', in Shirley Chew, ed., *Re-visions of Canadian Literature*, Leeds: University of Leeds Institute of Bibliography and Textual Criticism, 1984, pp. 71–87; pp. 75–6.

19.　Gibson, *Postmodernity, Ethics and the Novel*, p. 54.

20.　Ibid.

21.　Shuli Barzilai, 'Who Is He? The Missing Persons Behind the Pronoun in Atwood's *Surfacing*', *Canadian Literature*, 164 (Spring 2000): 57–79; p. 60.

22.　Ibid.

23.　Andrew Benjamin, *Present Hope: Philosophy, Architecture, Judaism*, London & New York: Routledge, 1997, p. 49.

24.　Ibid.

25.　Gérard Genette, *Narrative Discourse*, trans. Jane E. Lewin, Oxford: Basil Blackwell, 1986, p. 35.

26.　Ibid., p. 36.

27.　Michel Foucault, *The Archaeology of Knowledge and the Discourse on Language*, Trans. A.M. Sheridan Smith, New York: Pantheon, 1971.

28.　Mary Ann Caws, 'The Poetics of the Manifesto: Nowness and Newness', in Mary Ann Caws, ed., *Manifesto: A Century of Isms*, Lincoln and London: University of Nebraska Press, 2001, pp. xix–xxxii; pp. xiv–xx.

29.　Barbara C. Ewell, in 'The Language of Alienation in Margaret Atwood's *Surfacing*', *The Centennial Review*, 25.2 (1981): 185–202, reads abortion in the novel via the 'mistaken belief in the self-sufficiency of categories', where the narrator's first lover names abortion as 'reasonability, goodness'; thus: 'Given the right articulation, the abortion achieves validity, at least in the terms of masculine logic. The problem is that the narrator herself does not experience the event as positive' (pp. 189–90). For a poststructuralist account, see Erin Soros, 'If You Die It Will Kill Me: Aborting Maternal History', in Sharon Abbey and Andrea O'Reilly, eds, *Redefining Motherhood: Changing Identities and Patterns*, Toronto: Second Story Press, 1988, pp. 227–43.

30. Caws, 'The Poetics of the Manifesto', p. xxi.
31. Caroline Rosenthal, 'Canonizing Atwood: Her Impact on Teaching in the US, Canada, and Europe', in Reingard M. Nischik, ed., *Margaret Atwood: Works and Impact*, NY: Camden House, 2000, pp. 41–56; p. 53.
32. Alice M. Palumbo, 'On the Border: Margaret Atwood's Novels', in Nischik, ed., *Margaret Atwood: Works and Impact*, pp. 73–85; p. 75.
33. Peter Klovan, '"They Are Out of Reach Now": The Family Motif in Margaret Atwood's *Surfacing*', *Essays on Canadian Writing*, 33.1 (September 1986): 1–28; p. 2.
34. Henry C. Phelps, 'Atwood's *Edible Woman* and *Surfacing*', *Explicator*, 55.2 (Winter 1997): 112–14; p. 113.
35. Ibid., p. 114.
36. Bruce King, 'Margaret Atwood's *Surfacing*', *Journal of Commonwealth Literature*, 12.1 (January 1977): 23–32; p. 23.
37. Ibid., p. 28.
38. Rosenthal, 'Canonizing Atwood', p. 41.
39. Ibid., p. 53.
40. A useful related critical text here to take this interpretation further is Brenda R. Silver, *Virginia Woolf: Icon*, Chicago and London: University of Chicago Press, 1999.
41. Sharon Hengen/WN [W.H. New], 'ATWOOD, Margaret Eleanor', in, W.H. New, ed., *Encyclopedia of Literature in Canada*, Toronto: University of Toronto Press, 2002, pp. 48–51; p. 48.
42. Ibid.
43. Claire Buck, ed., *Bloomsbury Guide to Women's Literature*, Bungay: QPD, 1992, pp. 300 and 301. For a comprehensive bibliographical approach to the impact of women writers in Canada, see the Subject Index entry on 'Women', in Joseph Jones, *Reference Sources for Canadian Literary Studies*, Toronto: University of Toronto Press, 2005, pp. 441–2.
44. Christina Strobel, 'On the Representation of Representation in Margaret Atwood's *Surfacing*', *Zeitschrift für Anglistik und Amerikanistik: A Quarterly of Language, Literature and Culture*, 40.1 (January 1992): 35–43; p. 39.
45. Özdemir, 'Power, Madness, and Gender Identity in Margaret Atwood's *Surfacing*', pp. 73–4; quoting from Atwood, *Surfacing*, p. 165.
46. Sue Thomas, 'Mythic Reconception and the Mother/Daughter Relationship in Margaret Atwood's "*Surfacing*"', *Ariel*, 19.2 (1988): 73–85; p. 73. For a related discussion of the 'myth-quest' schema, see Josie P. Campbell, 'The Woman as Hero in Margaret Atwood's *Surfacing*', *Mosaic*, 11.3 (1978): 17–28. See also Sherrill Grace, *Violent Duality: A Study of Margaret Atwood*, Montreal: Véhicule Press, 1980.

CHAPTER 7   THE RUSHDIE AFFAIR: SALMAN RUSHDIE'S
THE SATANIC VERSES

1. Pnina Werbner, 'Allegories of Sacred Imperfection: Magic, Hermeneutics, and Passion in *The Satanic Verses*', *Current Anthropology*, 37, Supplement (February 1996): S55–S86 (includes critical responses to Werbner's article); p. S59.
2. Ibid.
3. For an excellent discussion of literary critical responses, see K.M. Newton, 'Literary Theory and the Rushdie Affair', *English: The Journal of the English Association*, 41.171 (1992): 235–47.
4. Pnina Werbner's more sophisticated version of this paraphrase is as follows: 'Pakistanis in Britain, and many Muslims worldwide, responded to the novel in a politically violent manner out of a sense of deep offence, a conviction that the novel was enjoyed by Westerners because it was an attack on Islam and its values. It is therefore *politically* necessary and expedient to demonstrate that from a Western perspective, the novel can be read quite differently, as a serious attempt to explore the possibility of a liberal more "open" Islam rather than as a mockery. *The Satanic Verses* compels Westerners to engage seriously with Islam as a great, global, monotheistic religion.' Werbner, 'Allegories of Sacred Imperfection', However, this begs the question as to why Islam has to be denigrated *before* Westerners will take it seriously? Furthermore, much of the 'engagement' with Islam can hardly be called 'serious' in the sense of an ongoing, comprehensive interfaith or transcultural analysis. For example, Tim Brennan notes, admittedly in a different context, that some of the more 'informative, even thoughtful' Western responses 'explained key Quranic names, [and] translated imported Urdu terms from *The Satanic Verses*'. See Tim Brennan, 'Rushdie, Islam, and Postcolonial Criticism', *Social Text*, 31–2 (1992): 271–6; p. 271.
5. Alex Knönagel, '*The Satanic Verses*: Narrative Structure and Islamic Doctrine', *International Fiction Review*, 18.2 (1991): 69–75; p. 69.
6. Ibid., p. 70.
7. Stephen Baker, 'Salman Rushdie: History, Self and the Fiction of Truth', in Richard J. Lane, Rod Mengham and Philip Tew, eds, *Contemporary British Fiction*, Cambridge: Polity, 2003, pp. 145–57; p. 146.
8. Dominic Head, *The Cambridge Introduction to Modern British Fiction, 1950–2000*, Cambridge: Cambridge University Press, 2002, p. 179.
9. Werbner, 'Allegories of Sacred Imperfection', p. S60.
10. Ibid.
11. Sue Vice, *Introducing Bakhtin*, Manchester and New York: Manchester University Press, 1997, pp. 201–2.
12. Werbner, 'Allegories of Sacred Imperfection', p. S60.
13. Ibid.
14. Daniel Pipes, 'The Ayatollah, the Novelist, and the West', *Commentary*, 87.6 (1989): 9–17; p. 10.
15. Aamir Mufti, 'Reading the Rushdie Affair: An Essay on Islam and Politics', *Social Text*, 29 (1991): 95–116; p. 103.
16. Salman Rushdie, *The Satanic Verses*, New York: Viking, 1988, p. 364. All further references shall be cited in the text by page number only.
17. Franz Rosenzweig, *The Star of Redemption*, trans. William W. Hallo, Notre Dame, IN: University of Notre Dame Press, 1985, p. 117.

18. Mufti, 'Reading the Rushdie Affair', p. 97.

19. Ibid., p. 98.

20. Ibid.

21. Ibid.

22. Ibid.

23. Ibid., p. 109. Jean Franco, 'Pastiche in Contemporary Latin American Literature', *Studies in Twentieth Century Literature*, 14.1 (Winter 1990): 95–107. Fredric Jameson, 'Postmodernism, or the Cultural Logic of Late Capitalism', *New Left Review*, 146 (July–August 1986): 59–92.

24. Mufti, 'Reading the Rushdie Affair', pp. 109–10.

25. Ibid., p. 111.

26. As Ashcroft *et al.* write, 'The significance of Orientalism is that as a mode of *knowing* the other it was a supreme example of the *construction* of the other, a form of authority. The Orient is not an inert fact of nature, but a phenomenon constructed by generations of intellectuals, artists, commentators, writers, politicians, and, more importantly, constructed by the naturalizing of a wide range of Orientalist assumptions and stereotypes.' *Key Concepts in Postcolonial Studies*, p. 168.

27. Homi Bhabha, *The Location of Culture*, London and New York: Routledge, 1994, p. 224.

28. Ibid.

29. Head, *The Cambridge Introduction to Modern British Fiction, 1950–2000*, p. 179.

30. Bhabha, *The Location of Culture*, p. 225.

31. Head, *The Cambridge Introduction to Modern British Fiction, 1950–2000*, p. 180.

32. Ibid.

33. Valance's words here are an echo of Deep Throat, the shady underground informant in the Watergate exposé *All the President's Men*. For a brief discussion concerning the significance of this text from Nixon era, see Richard J. Lane, *Jean Baudrillard*, London and New York: Routledge, 2000, pp. 83–5.

34. Bhabha, *The Location of Culture*, p. 225. For a critique of Bhabha's concept of hybridity, see Feroza Jussawalla, 'Are Cultural Rights Bad for Multicultural Societies?', *The South Atlantic Quarterly*, 100.4 (Fall 2001): 967–80. For a critique of postcolonial theory and the location of specific theorists, see Anouar Majid, 'Can the Postcolonial Critic Speak? Orientalism and the Rushdie Affair', *Cultural Critique*, 32.5 (Winter 1995–6): 5–42.

35. Pipes, 'The Ayatollah, the Novelist, and the West', p. 12.

36. Ibid.

37. Both Pipes and Lewis re-focus the 'impact' discussion in relation to America; ibid. and Bernard Lewis, 'Behind the Rushdie Affair', *The American Scholar*, 60.2 (Spring 1991): 185–96.

38. Bridget Fowler, 'A Sociological Analysis of the *Satanic Verses* Affair', *Theory, Culture & Society*, 17.1 (2000): 39–61; p. 40.

39. Ibid.

40. Ibid., pp. 48–50; see Lisa Appignanesi and Sara Maitland, eds, *The Rushdie File*, London: Fourth Estate, 1989.

41. Fowler, 'A Sociological Analysis of the *Satanic Verses* Affair', p. 49.

42. Ibid, pp. 49–50.

43. Ibid., p. 51.

44. Ibid., p. 52.

45. Ibid., p. 55.
46. Shailja Sharma, 'The Ambivalence of Migrancy', *Twentieth Century Literature*, 47.4 (Winter 2001): 596–618; p. 597.
47. Ibid., pp. 596–7.
48. Ibid., pp. 615–16.
49. Feroza Jussawalla, 'Rushdie's Dastan-E-Dilruba: *The Satanic Verses* as Rushdie's Love Letter to Islam', *diacritics*, 26.1: 50–73; p. 54.
50. Rufus Cook, 'The Art of Uncertainty: Cultural Displacement and the Devaluation of the World', *Critique*, 41.3 (Spring 2000): 227–35. Cook gives an extended and in-depth analysis of the trope of 'transubstantiation' in Rushdie's work.
51. Sabina Sawhney and Simona Sawhney, 'Reading Rushdie after September 11, 2001', *Twentieth Century Literature*, 47.4 (Winter 2001): 431–43; pp. 431–2.
52. Simona Sawhney, 'Satanic Choices: Poetry and Prophecy in Rushdie's Novel', *Twentieth Century Literature*, 45.3 (Fall 1999): 253–77; p. 273.
53. See Joel Kuortti, '"Nomsense": Salman Rushdie's *The Satanic Verses*', *Textual Practice*, 13.1 (1999): 137–46; the term 'language-games' originally derives from Ludwig Wittgenstein, *Philosophical Investigations* (first published 1953), trans. G.E.M. Anscombe, Oxford: Basil Blackwell, 1991.

CHAPTER 8   THE OPTICAL UNCONSCIOUS: *ARUNDHATI ROY'S THE GOD OF SMALL THINGS*

1. Carole and Jean-Pierre Durix make this point in the opening of their introduction to their edited collection of essays on Roy; see *Reading Arundhati Roy's The God of Small Things*, Éditions Universitaires de Dijon, Collection U21, 2002.
2. Jean-Pierre Durix, 'The "Post-Coloniality" of *The God of Small Things*', in Durix and Durix, eds, *Reading Arundhati Roy's The God of Small Things*, pp. 7–22; p. 14.
3. Marta Dvorak, 'Translating the Foreign into the Familiar: Arundhati Roy's Postmodern Sleight of Hand', in Durix and Durix, eds, *Reading Arundhati Roy's The God of Small Things*, pp. 41–61; p. 46.
4. Durix, 'The "Post-Coloniality" of *The God of Small Things*', p. 16.
5. Alex Tickell, '*The God of Small Things*: Arundhati Roy's Postcolonial Cosmopolitanism', *Journal of Commonwealth Literature*, 38.1 (2003): 73–89; p. 74.
6. Ibid., quoting Arnab Chakladar, 'The Postcolonial Bazaar: Marketing/Teaching Indian Literature', *ARIEL*, 31.1–2(2000): 183–201; p. 189. Tickell comments on Graham Huggan's *The Postcolonial Exotic*, '. . . in which he agrees that "links clearly exist between postcoloniality as a global regime of value and a cosmopolitan alterity industry". For Huggan, the most noticeable aspect of writing by authors such as Rushdie and Roy is the skill with which they manipulate the expectations and the familiar, "commercially viable" literary codes of this alterity industry.' Ibid., p. 75, quoting Graham Huggan, *The Postcolonial Exotic: Marketing the Margins*, London: Routlege, 2001, p. 12.
7. Tickell, '*The God of Small Things*', p. 87.
8. Arundhati Roy, *The God of Small Things*, New York: Viking, 1997, p. 3. All further references shall be cited in the text by page number.
9. Dvorak, 'Translating the Foreign into the Familiar', p. 56.
10. Christine Vogt-William, '"Language is the Skin of My Thought": Language Relations in *Ancient Promises* and *The God of Small Things*', in Christian Mair, ed., *The*

Politics of English as a World Language: New Horizons in Postcolonial Cultural Studies, ASNEL Papers 7, Amsterdam and New York: Rodopi, 2003, pp. 393–404; p. 397.

11. Chanda Tirkankar, 'Sexual/Textual Strategies in *The God of Small Things*', *Commonwealth: Essays and Studies*, 20.1 (1997): 38–44; p. 39.

12. Cynthia Carey, 'The Architecture of Place in *The God of Small Things*', in Durix and Durix, eds, *Reading Arundhati Roy's The God of Small Things*, pp. 101–10; p. 102.

13. Ibid., p. 103.

14. René Girard, *The Scapegoat*, trans. Yvonne Freccero, Baltimore: Johns Hopkins University Press, 1989, p. 22.

15. Ibid., p. 18.

16. Carey, 'The Architecture of Place in *The God of Small Things*', p. 103.

17. Anthony Vidler, *The Architectural Uncanny: Essays in the Modern Unhomely*, Cambridge, MA and London: MIT Press, 1992, p. 3.

18. Pumla Dineo Gqola, '"History Was Wrong-Footed, Caught Off Guard": Gendered Caste, Class and Manipulation in Arundhati Roy's *The God of Small Things*', *Commonwealth: Essays and Studies*, 26.2 (2004): 107–19; p. 107.

19. Vidler, *The Architectural Uncanny*, p. 7.

20. Ibid., p. 8.

21. Anderson, *Autobiography*, p. 114.

22. Dvorak, 'Translating the Foreign into the Familiar', p. 42.

23. Ibid., p. 47.

24. Walter Benjamin, 'The Work of Art in the Age of Its Technological Reproducibility (Third Version)', in, *Selected Writings Volume 4, 1938–1940*, ed. Howard Eiland and Michael W. Jennings, trans. Edmund Jephcott and others, Cambridge, MA and London: The Belknap Press of Harvard University Press, 2003, pp. 251–83; pp. 265–6; for a discussion of this essay see chapter seven of Lane, *Reading Walter Benjamin*. See also the discussion of montage and orality in Richard Cavell, *McLuhan in Space: A Cultural Geography*, Toronto: University of Toronto Press, 2003, pp. 40–1.

25. Dvorak, 'Translating the Foreign into the Familiar', p. 53.

26. Ibid., p. 61.

27. Ibid.

28. Janet Thormann, 'The Ethical Subject of *The God of Small Things*', *JPCS: Journal for the Psychoanalysis of Culture and Society*, 8.2 (Fall 2003): 299–307; p. 300.

29. Dvorak, 'Translating the Foreign into the Familiar', p. 59.

30. Cavell, *McLuhan in Space*, p. 41.

31. King, 'Godzilla vs Post-Colonial', p. 244.

32. Thormann, 'The Ethical Subject of *The God of Small Things*', p. 300.

33. Ibid.

34. Elisabeth Roudinesco, *Jacques Lacan: An Outline of a Life and a History of a System of Thought*, trans. Barbara Bray, Cambridge: Polity, 1999, p. 360.

35. Ellie Ragland-Sullivan, *Jacques Lacan and the Philosophy of Psychoanalysis*, Urbana and Chicago: University of Illinois Press, 1987, p. 206.

36. See, 'Arundhati Roy, 1960–', in *Contemporary Authors Online*, Gale, 2004 (electronic resource).

37. Chelva Kanaganayakam, 'Religious Myth and Subversion in *The God of Small Things*', in, Erik Borgman, Bart Philipsen and Lea Verstricht, eds, *Literary Canons and Religious Identity*, Aldershot: Ashgate, 2004, pp. 141–9; p. 141.

38. Ibid.
39. Ibid., p. 147.
40. Tickell, '*The God of Small Things*', p. 83.
41. R. Hema Nair, '"Remembrance of Things Past": A Reading of Arundhati Roy's *The God of Small Things*', *Central Institute of English and Foreign Languages Bulletin*, 9.2 (1998): 49–56; p. 51.

CONCLUSION: ENDING WITH JOY KOGAWA'S *OBASAN* AND PHYLLIS GREENWOOD'S *AN INTERRUPTED PANORAMA*

1. Joy Kogawa, *Obasan*, New York: Anchor, 1994.
2. Susan Knutson, 'Kogawa, Joy Nozomi', in W.H. New, ed., *Encyclopedia of Literature in Canada*, Toronto: University of Toronto Press, 2002, pp. 587–589; p. 587.
3. Teruyo Ueki, '*Obasan*: Revelations in a Paradoxical Scheme', *MELUS*, 18.4 (Winter 1993): 5–20; p. 7. See also Carol Fairbanks, 'Joy Kogawa's *Obasan*: A Study in Political Efficacy', *The Journal of American and Canadian Studies*, 5 (Spring 1990): 73–92.
4. Laurie Ricou, *The Arbutus/Madrone Files: Reading the Pacific Northwest*, Edmonton: NeWest Press, 2002, p. 69.
5. Ibid., pp. 69–70.
6. Roy Miki, 'Asiancy: Making Space for Asian Canadian Writing', in Gary Y. Okihino, Marilyn Alguizola, Dorothy Fujita Rong and K. Scott Wong, eds, *Privileging Positions: The Sites of Asian American Studies*, Washington: Pullman, 1995, pp. 135–51.
7. Smaro Kamboureli, *Scandalous Bodies: Diasporic Literature in English Canada*, Don Mills, Ont.: Oxford University Press Canada, 2000, p. 175.
8. Ricou, *The Arbutus/Madrone Files*, p. 181.
9. Phyllis Greenwood, *An Interrupted Panorama: An Installation Revealing Selected Views of the Fraser River*, Vancouver, BC: Phyllis Greenwood, 1997, UBC Rare Books & Special Collections, no page number.
10. Jeff Wall, *Jeff Wall*, London: Phaidon, 1996, p. 129.
11. Greenwood, *An Interrupted Panorama*, p. 21.
12. Ibid., pp. 21–2.
13. Ibid., p. 26.
14. Kogawa, *Obasan*, p. 291.
15. Moore-Gilbert, *Postcolonial Theory*, p. 8.
16. Helen Gilbert and Joanne Tompkins, *Post-Colonial Drama: Theory, Practice, Politics*, London and New York: Routledge, 1996, p. 2.
17. Homi K. Bhabha, ed., *Nation and Narration*, London and New York: Routledge, 1991, p. 4.
18. Rose, 'On the "Universality" of Madness', p. 403.
19. Ibid., pp. 403–4, punctuation as in the original.
20. Ibid., p. 412.

Bibliography

Achebe, Chinua, *Things Fall Apart*, London: Heinemann, 1986.
——'An Image of Africa: Racism in Conrad's *Heart of Darkness*', in Chinua Achebe, *Hopes and Impediments: Selected Essays*, New York: Doubleday/Anchor, 1989, pp. 269–74.
Anderson, Linda, *Autobiography*, London and New York: Routledge, 2001.
Appignanesi, Lisa and Sara Maitland, eds, *The Rushdie File*, London: Fourth Estate, 1989.
'Arundhati Roy, 1960–', *Contemporary Authors Online*, Gale, 2004 (electronic resource).
Ashcroft, Bill, Gareth Griffiths and Helen Tiffin, *The Empire Writes Back: Theory and Practice in Post-Colonial Literatures*, London and New York: Routledge, 1994.
——*Key Concepts in Post-Colonial Studies*, London and New York: Routledge, 1999.
Atwood, Margaret, *Surfacing*, London: Virago, 1988.
——, *Survival: A Thematic Guide to Canadian Literature*, Concord, Ont.: Anansi, 1991.
Baker, Stephen, 'Salman Rushdie: History, Self and the Fiction of Truth', in Richard J. Lane, Rod Mengham and Philip Tew, eds, *Contemporary British Fiction*, Cambridge: Polity, 2003, pp. 145–57.
Bardolph, Jacqueline, 'Moving Away from the Mission: Ngugi wa Thiongo'o's Versions of *A Grain of Wheat*', in Gerhard Stilz, ed., *Missions of Interdependence: A Literary Directory*, ASNEL Papers 6, Amsterdam and New York: Rodopi, 2002, pp. 133–41.
Barzilai, Shuli, 'Who is He? The Missing Persons Behind the Pronoun in Atwood's *Surfacing*', *Canadian Literature*, 164 (Spring 2000): 57–79.
Begam, Richard, 'Achebe's Sense of an Ending: History and Tragedy in *Things Fall Apart*', *Studies in the Novel*, 29.3 (Fall 1997): 396–411.
Benjamin, Andrew, *Present Hope: Philosophy, Architecture, Judaism*, London and New York: Routledge, 1997.
Benjamin, Walter, 'The Work of Art in the Age of Its Technological Reproducibility (Third Version)', in *Selected Writings Volume 4, 1938–1940*, ed. Howard Eiland and Michael W. Jennings, trans. Edmund Jephcott and others, Cambridge, MA and London: The Belknap Press of Harvard University Press, 2003, pp. 251–83.
'Bessie Head, 1937–1986', *Contemporary Authors Online*, Gale, 2003 (electronic resource).
Bhabha, Homi, ed., *Nation and Narration*, London and New York: Routledge, 1991.
——*The Location of Culture*, London and New York: Routledge, 1994.

Booth, Wayne C., *The Rhetoric of Fiction*, second edition, Chicago and London: University of Chicago Press, 1983.

Brennan, Tim, 'Rushdie, Islam, and Postcolonial Criticism', *Social Text*, 31–2 (1992): 271–6.

Briault, Manus Vicki, 'The Lever Out of Hell: Autobiographical Footholds to Read Bessie Head's *A Question of Power*', *Commonwealth: Essays & Studies*, 24.1 (2001): 25–30.

Buck, Claire, ed., *Bloomsbury Guide to Women's Literature*, Bungay: QPD, 1992.

Buck-Morss, Susan, *The Dialectics of Seeing: Walter Benjamin and the Arcades Project*, Cambridge, MA: MIT Press, 1999.

Burnett, Paula, 'Caribbean', in William Baker and Kenneth Womack, eds, *The Year's Work in English Studies*, Vol. 80, Oxford: Oxford University Press, 2001, section two of chapter XVII, pp. 840–50.

Caminero-Santangelo, Byron, 'Neocolonialism and the Betrayal Plot in *A Grain of Wheat*: Ngũgĩ wa Thiong'o's Re-Vision of *Under Western Eyes*', *Research in African Literatures*, 29.1 (Spring 1998): 139–52.

Campbell, Josie P., 'The Woman as Hero in Margaret Atwood's *Surfacing*', *Mosaic*, 11.3 (1978): 17–28.

Carey, Cynthia, 'The Architecture of Place in *The God of Small Things*', in Carole and Jean-Pierre Durix, eds, *Reading Arundhati Roy's The God of Small Things*, Éditions Universitaires de Dijon, Collection U21, 2002, pp. 101–10.

Carroll, David, *Chinua Achebe*, New York: Twayne, 1970.

Cavell, Richard, *McLuhan in Space: A Cultural Geography*, Toronto: University of Toronto Press, 2003.

Caws, Mary Ann, 'The Poetics of the Manifesto: Nowness and Newness', in Mary Ann Caws, ed., *Manifesto: A Century of Isms*, Lincoln and London: University of Nebraska Press, 2001.

Chakladar, Arnab, 'The Postcolonial Bazaar: Marketing/Teaching Indian Literature', *ARIEL*, 31.1–2 (2000): 183–201.

Chase, Joanne, 'Bessie Head's *A Question Of Power*: Romance or Rhetoric?', *ACLALS Bulletin*, 6.1 (1982): 67–75.

Choudhury, Romita, '"Is There a Ghost, a Zombie There?" Postcolonial Intertextuality and Jean Rhys's *Wide Sargasso Sea*', *Textual Practice*, 10.2 (Summer 1996): 315–27.

Ciolkowski, Laura E., 'Navigating the *Wide Sargasso Sea*: Colonial History, English Fiction, and British Empire', *Twentieth Century Literature*, 43.3 (Fall 1997): 339–59.

Cobham, Rhonda, 'Introduction' to *Research in African Literatures*, Special Issue on African Women Writes, 19.2 (Summer 1988): 137–42.

Coetzee, J.M., *Foe*, London: Penguin, 1988.

Colebrook, Claire, *Gilles Deleuze*, London and New York: Routledge, 2003.

Cook, Rufus, 'The Art of Uncertainty: Cultural Displacement and the Devaluation of the World', *Critique*, 41.3 (Spring 2000): 227–35.

Coundouriotis, Eleni, 'Authority and Invention in the Fiction of Bessie Head', *Research in African Literatures*, 27.2 (Summer 1996): 17–32.

Cribb, T.J., 'T.W. Harris – Sworn Surveyor', *Journal of Commonwealth Literature*, XXIX.1 (1993): 33–46.

Curtis, Jan, 'The Secret of *Wide Sargasso Sea*', *Critique*, 31.3 (Spring 1990): 185–97.

Daniel, David, *The Bible in English: Its History and Influence*, New Haven and London: Yale University Press, 2003.

Darby, Phillip, *The Fiction of Imperialism: Reading Between International Relations and Postcolonialism*, London and Washington: Cassell, 1998.

Defoe, Daniel, *Robinson Crusoe* (first published 1719), London: Penguin, 1986.

—— *Roxana* (first published 1724), Oxford: Oxford University Press, 1996.

Deleuze, Gilles and Félix Guattari, *Anti-Oedipus: Capitalism and Schizophrenia*, trans. Robert Hurley, Mark Seem and Helen R.Lane, Minneapolis: University of Minnesota Press, 1989.

Dovey, Teresa, 'A Question of Power: Susan Gardner's Biography versus Bessie Head's Autobiography', *English in Africa*, 16 (May 1989): 29–38.

Dragunoiu, Dana, 'Existential Doubt and Political Responsibility in J.M. Coetzee's *Foe*', *Critique*, 42.3 (Spring 2001): 309–26.

Durix, Carole and Jean-Pierre Durix, eds, *Reading Arundhati Roy's The God of Small Things*, Éditions Universitaires de Dijon, Collection U21, 2002.

Durix, Jean-Pierre, 'The "Post-Coloniality" of *The God of Small Things*', in Carole and Jean-Pierre Durix, eds, *Reading Arundhati Roy's The God of Small Things*, Éditions Universitaires de Dijon, Collection U21, 2002, pp. 7–22.

Durrant, Samuel, 'Bearing Witness to Apartheid: J.M. Coetzee's Inconsolable Works of Mourning', *Contemporary Literature*, 40.3 (Fall 1999): 430–63.

—— 'Hosting History: Wilson Harris's Sacramental Narratives', *Jouvert: A Journal of Postcolonial Studies*, 1.41 (Autumn 2000). Available on-line: *http://social.chass. ncsu.edu/jouvert/v51/samdur.htm*, accessed 8/12/05.

Dvorak, Marta, 'Translating the Foreign into the Familiar: Arundhati Roy's Postmodern Sleight of Hand', in Carole and Jean-Pierre Durix, eds, *Reading Arundhati Roy's The God of Small Things*, Éditions Universitaires de Dijon, Collection U21, 2002, pp. 41–61.

Eaglestone, Robert, *Doing English: A Guide for Literature Students*, London and New York: Routledge, 2002.

Ewell, Barbara C., 'The Language of Alienation in Margaret Atwood's *Surfacing*', *The Centennial Review*, 25.2 (1981): 185–202.

Fairbanks, Carol, 'Joy Kogawa's *Obasan*: A Study in Political Efficacy', *The Journal of American and Canadian Studies*, 5 (Spring 1990): 73–92.

Fanon, Frantz, *Black Skin, White Masks* (first published 1952), London: Pluto, 1986.

—— *The Wretched of the Earth* (first published 1961), New York: Grove, 1968.

Felman, Shoshana, *Writing and Madness: Literature/Philosophy/Psychoanalysis*, trans. Martha Noel Evans, Palo Alto, CA: Stanford University Press, 2003.

Fick, Angelo, 'Beyond Bodies and Texts and Prisons in Bessie Head's Negotiation of Impossible Subjectivity through Allegory', in Hermann Wittenberg, G. Baderoon and Y. Steenkamp, eds, *Inter Action 6: Proceedings of the Fourth Postgraduate Conference*, Bellville: UWC Press, 1998, pp. 144–51; available on-line: *http://www.uwc.ac.2a/arts/english/interaction/97af.htm*, accessed 5/12/05.

Foucault, Michel, *The Archaeology of Knowledge and the Discourse on Language*, trans. A.M. Sheridan Smith, New York: Pantheon, 1971.

——, *Discipline and Punish: The Birth of the Prison*, trans. Alan Sheridan, New York: Vintage, 1979.

—— *Language, Counter-Memory, Practice: Selected Essays and Interviews*, ed. Donald F. Bouchard, trans. Donald F. Bouchard and Sherry Simon, Ithaca, NY: Cornell University Press, 1988.

Fowler, Bridget, 'A Sociological Analysis of the *Satanic Verses* Affair', *Theory, Culture & Society*, 17.1 (2000): 39–61.

Franco, Jean, 'Pastiche in Contemporary Latin American Literature', *Studies in Twentieth Century Literature*, 14.1 (Winter 1990): 95–107.

Friedman, Ellen G., 'Breaking the Master Narrative: Jean Rhys's *Wide Sargasso Sea*', in Ellen G. Friedman and Miriam Fuchs, eds, *Breaking the Sequence: Women's Experimental Fiction*, Princeton: Princeton University Press, 1989, pp. 117–28.

Gardner, Susan, '"Don't Ask for the True Story": A Memoir of Bessie Head', *Hecate*, 12.1–2 (1986): 110–29.

Garrett, James M., 'Writing Community: Bessie Head and the Politics of Narrative', *Research in African Literatures*, 30.2 (Summer 1999): 122–35.

Genette, Gérard, *Narrative Discourse*, trans. Jane E. Lewin, Oxford: Basil Blackwell, 1986.

Gibson, Andrew, *Postmodernity, Ethics and the Novel: From Leavis to Levinas*, London and New York: Routledge, 1999.

Gikandi, Simon, *Reading Chinua Achebe*, London: James Currey, 1991.

——*Ngugi Wa Thiong'o*, Cambridge: Cambridge University Press, 2000.

——'Chinua Achebe and the Invention of African Culture', *Research in African Literatures*, 32.3 (Fall 2001): 3–8.

Gilbert, Helen and Joanne Tompkins, *Post-Colonial Drama: Theory, Practice, Politics*, London and New York: Routledge, 1996.

Girard, René, *The Scapegoat*, trans. Yvonne Freccero, Baltimore: Johns Hopkins University Press, 1989.

Giroux, Henry A., 'Postmodernism as Border Pedagogy: Redefining the Boundaries of Race and Ethnicity', in Henry A. Giroux, ed., *Postmodernism, Feminism, and Cultural Politics: Redrawing Educational Boundaries*, Albany: SUNY Press, 1991, pp. 217–56.

Gqola, Pumla Dineo, '"History Was Wrong-Footed, Caught Off Guard": Gendered Caste, Class and Manipulation in Arundhati Roy's *The God of Small Things*', *Commonwealth: Essays and Studies*, 26.2 (2004): 107–19.

Grace, Sherrill, *Violent Duality: A Study of Margaret Atwood*, Montreal: Véhicle Press, 1980.

Greenwood, Phyllis, *An Interrupted Panorama: An Installation Revealing Selected Views of the Fraser River*, Vancouver, BC: Phyllis Greenwood, 1997, UBC Rare Books & Special Collections.

Hamilton, Alissa, 'The Construction and Deconstruction of National Identities through Language in the Narratives of Ngũgĩ Wa Thiong'o's *A Grain of Wheat* and Joseph Conrad's *Under Western Eyes*', *African Languages and Cultures*, 8.2 (1995): 137–51.

Harris, Wilson, *Palace of the Peacock* (first published 1960), London and Boston: Faber and Faber, 1988.

Harrow, Kenneth, 'Ngugi wa Thiong'o's *A Grain of Wheat*: Season of Irony', *Research in African Literatures*, 16.2 (1985): 243–63.

Head, Bessie, *A Question of Power*, London: Heinemann, 1987.

Head, Dominic, *The Cambridge Introduction to Modern British Fiction, 1950–2000*, Cambridge: Cambridge University Press, 2002.

Hengen, Sharon and WN [W.H. New], 'ATWOOD, Margaret Eleanor', in W.H. New, ed., *Encyclopedia of Literature in Canada*, Toronto: University of Toronto Press, 2002, pp. 48–51.

Hickman, Trenton, 'The Colonized Woman as Monster in *Jane Eyre*, *Wide Sargasso Sea*, and *Annie John*', *Journal of Caribbean Studies*, 14.3 (Summer 2000): 181–98.

Hoegberg, David, 'Principle and Practice: The Logic of Cultural Violence in Achebe's *Things Fall Apart*', *College Literature*, 26.1 (Winter 1999): 69–79.

Hoffman, Kurt, 'The Basic Concepts of Jaspers' Philosophy', in Paul Arthur Schilpp, ed., *The Philosophy of Karl Jaspers*, The Library of Living Philosophers, New York: Tudor, 1957, pp. 95–114.

Hogan, Patrick Colm, 'Bessie Head's *A Question of Power*: A Lacanian Psychosis', *Mosaic*, 27.2 (1994): 95–112.

Huggan, Graham, 'Anxieties of Influence: Conrad in the Caribbean', *Commonwealth: Essays and Studies*, 11.1 (Autumn 1988): 1–12.

—— *The Postcolonial Exotic: Marketing the Margins*, London: Routledge, 2001.

Hutcheon, Linda, *The Canadian Postmodern: A Study of Contemporary English-Canadian Fiction*, Ontario: Oxford University Press, 1988.

—— *The Politics of Postmodernism*, second edition, London and New York: Routledge, 2002.

Ingersoll, Earl G., 'Reconstructing Masculinity in the Postcolonial World of Bessie Head', *Ariel*, 29.3 (July 1998): 95–116.

Irele, F. Abiola, 'Homage to Chinua Achebe', *Research in African Literatures*, 32.3 (Fall 2001): 1–2.

Jabbi, Bu-Buakei, 'Conrad's Influence on Betrayal in *A Grain Of Wheat*', *Research in African Literatures*, 11.1 (Spring 1980): 50–83.

—— 'The Structure of Symbolism in *A Grain of Wheat*', *Research in African Literatures*, 16.2 (Summer 1985): 210–42.

Jameson, Fredric, 'Postmodernism, or the Cultural Logic of Late Capitalism; *New Left Review*, 146 (July–August 1984): 59–92.

—— *The Political Unconscious: Narrative as a Socially Symbolic Act*, London: Methuen, 1986.

Jeyifo, Biodun, 'Okonkwo and His Mother: *Things Fall Apart* and Issues of Gender in the Constitution of African Postcolonial Discourse', *Callaloo*, 16.4 (1993): 847–58.

Johnson, Joyce, 'Character and Circumstance in Ngugi Wa Thiong'o's *A Grain of Wheat*', *Commonwealth Novel in English*, 3.1 (1984): 21–38.

Jones, Joseph, *Reference Sources for Canadian Literary Studies*, Toronto: University of Toronto Press, 2005.

Jussawalla, Feroza, 'Rushdie's Dastan-E-Dilruba: *The Satanic Verses* as Rushdie's Love Letter to Islam', *diacritics*, 26.1 (1996): 50–73.

—— 'Are Cultural Rights Bad for Multicultural Societies?', *The South Atlantic Quarterly*, 100.4 (Fall 2001): 967–80.

Kamboureli, Smaro, *Scandalous Bodies: Diasporic Literature in English Canada*, Don Mills, Ont.: Oxford University Press Canada, 2000.

Kanaganayakam, Chelva, 'Religious Myth and Subversion in *The God of Small Things*', in Erik Borgman, Bart Philipsen and Lea Verstricht, eds, *Literary Canons and Religious Identity*, Aldershot: Ashgate, 2004, pp. 141–9.

Kapstein, Helen, ' "A Peculiar Shuttling Movement": Madness, Passing, and Trespassing in Bessie Head's *A Question of Power*', in Maxine Sample, ed., *Critical Essays on Bessie Head*, London and Westport, Connecticut: Praeger, 2003, pp. 71–98.

Katrak, Ketu, 'Post-Colonial Women Writers and Feminisms', in Bruce King, ed., *New National and Post-Colonial Literatures: An Introduction*, Oxford: Clarendon Press, 1996, pp. 230–44.

Kessler, Kathy, 'Rewriting History in Fiction: Elements of Postmodernism in Ngugi wa Thiong'o's Later Novels', *Ariel*, 25.2 (1994): 75–90.

King, Bruce, 'Margaret Atwood's *Surfacing*', *Journal of Commonwealth Literature*, 12.1 (January 1977): 23–32.

King, Thomas, 'Godzilla vs Post-Colonial', in Ajay Heble, Donna Palmateer Pennee and J.R. (Tim) Struthers, eds, *New Contexts of Canadian Criticism*, Peterborough, Ont.: Broadview, 1997, pp. 241–8.

Klovan, Peter, '"They Are Out of Reach Now"': The Family Motif in Margaret Atwood's *Surfacing*', *Essays on Canadian Writing*, 33.1 (September 1986): 1–28.

Knönagel, Alex, '*The Satanic Verses*: Narrative Structure and Islamic Doctrine', *International Fiction Review*, 18.2 (1991): 69–75.

Knutson, Susan, 'Kogawa, Joy Nozomi', in W.H. New, ed., *Encyclopedia of Literature in Canada*, Toronto: University of Toronto Press, 2002.

Kogawa, Joy, *Obasan*, New York: Anchor, 1994.

Krause, Delia, 'A Grain of Wheat: Ngugi's Tribute to the Armed Rebellion', *Wasafari*, 9 (1988): 6–10.

Kristeva, Julia, *Powers of Horror: An Essay on Abjection*, trans. Leon S. Roudiez, New York: Columbia University Press, 1982.

Kuortti, Joel, '"Nomsense": Salman Rushdie's *The Satanic Verses*', *Textual Practice*, 13.1 (1999): 137–46.

Lane, Richard J., 'Appropriating the Signifier in J.M. Coetzee's *Foe*'. *Commonwealth: Essays and Studies*, 13.1 (Autumn 1990): 106–11.

—— 'The Dangers of "Dumb Talk": Eurocentric Translations of the Potlatch', *Commonwealth: Essays and Studies*, 21.2 (1999): 75–82.

—— *Jean Baudrillard*, London and New York: Routledge, 2000.

—— *Literary Masterpieces: Mrs Dalloway*, Detroit and New York: Gale, 2001.

—— *Functions of the Derrida Archive: Philosophical Receptions*, Budapest: Akadémiai Kiadó, 2003.

—— 'Performing Gender: First Nations, Feminism, and Trickster Writing in Eden Robinson's *Monkey Beach*', *Hungarian Journal of English and American Studies*, 9.1 (Spring 2003): 161–71.

—— 'Performing History: The Reconstruction of Gender and Race in British Columbian Drama,' in Sherrill Grace and Albert-Reiner Glaap, eds, *Performing National Identities: International Perspectives on Contemporary Canadian Theatre*, Vancouver: Talon, 2003, pp. 265–77.

—— 'Reclaiming Maps and Metaphors: Canadian First Nations and Narratives of Place', in Deborah Madsen, ed., *Beyond the Borders: American Literature and Post-Colonial Theory*, London: Pluto 2003, pp. 184–94.

—— *Reading Walter Benjamin: Writing through the Catastrophe*, Manchester: Manchester University Press, 2005.

—— 'Theorizing the Gendered Space of Auto/Biographical Performance via Samuel Beckett and Hans Bellmer', in Sherrill Grace and Jerry Wasserman, eds, *Theatre and Autobiography: Essays on the Theory and Practice of Writing and Performing Lives*, Vancouver: Talon, 2006, pp. 72–88.

—— 'Edward Wadie Said', in *Fifty Key Twentieth-Century Literary Theorists*, London and New York: Routledge, forthcoming.

Leggatt, Judith, 'Native Writing, Academic Theory: Post-Colonialism across the Cultural Divide', in Laura Moss, ed., *Is Canada Postcolonial? Unsettling Canadian Literature*, Waterloo, Ont.: Wilfrid Laurier Press, 2003, pp. 111–26.

Lewis, Bernard, 'Behind the Rushdie Affair', *The American Scholar*, 60.2 (Spring 1991): 185–96.

Lewis, Desiree, 'Bessie Head's Freedoms', *Chimurenga Online*, *http://www.chimurenga.co.za/modules.php?name=News&file=article&sid=51*, accessed 2/12/05.

Loomba, Ania, *Colonialism/Postcolonialism*, London and New York: Routledge, 2000.

Lothe, Jakob, *Narrative in Fiction and Film: An Introduction*, Oxford: Oxford University Press, 2000.

Lutz, John, 'Ngugi's Dialectical Vision: Individualism and Revolutionary Consciousness in *A Grain of Wheat*', *Ufahamu*, 29.2–3 (Winter/Spring 2003): 171–98.

McDowell, John, 'Duality of Language in *Palace of the Peacock*', *Commonwealth Novel in English*, 4.1 (Spring 1991): 62–8.

MacKenzie, Clayton G., 'The Metamorphosis of Piety in Chinua Achebe's *Things Fall Apart*', *Research in African Literatures*, 27.2 (Summer 1996): 128–38.

McLaren, Joseph, 'Missionaries and Converts: Religion and Colonial Intrusion in *Things Fall Apart*', *The Literary Griot: International Journal of Black Expressive Cultural Studies*, 10.2 (Fall 1998): 48–60.

McLeod, A.L., ed. *The Commonwealth Pen: An Introduction to the Literature of the British Commonwealth*, Ithaca, NY: Cornell University Press, 1961.

McLeod, John, *Beginning Postcolonialism*, Manchester: Manchester University Press, 2000.

Madsen, Deborah, ed., *Post-Colonial Literatures: Expanding the Canon*, London: Pluto, 1999.

——*Beyond the Borders: American Literature and Post-Colonial Theory*, London: Pluto 2003.

Maes-Jelinek, Hena, *The Naked Design: A Reading of 'Palace of the Peacock'*, Århus: Dangaroo Press, 1976.

——*Wilson Harris*, Boston: Twayne, 1982.

Maithufi, Sope, 'Fanon's African Ontology, Post-Colonial Ideological Stage and the Liberation of Africa', *APA Newsletters*, 97.1 (Fall 1997); available on-line: *http://www.apa.udel.edu/apa/archive/newsletters/v97n1/black/fanon.asp*, accessed 5/12/05.

Majid, Anouar, 'Can the Postcolonial Critic Speak? Orientalism and the Rushdie Affair', *Cultural Critique*, 32.5 (Winter 1995–96): 5–42.

Mardorossian, Carine Melkom, 'Double (De)colonization and the Feminist Criticism of *Wide Sargasso Sea*', *College Literature*, 26.2 (Spring 1999): 79–95.

Mathuray, Mark, 'Realizing the Sacred: Power and Meaning in Chinua Achebe's *Arrow of God*', *Research in African Literatures*, 34.3 (Fall 2003): 46–65.

Maurel, Sylvie, 'Across the "Wide Sargasso Sea": Jean Rhys's Revision of Charlotte Brontë's Eurocentric Gothic', *Commonwealth: Essays and Studies*, 24.2 (2002): 107–18.

Mezei, Kathy, '"And It Kept Its Secret": Narration, Memory, and Madness in Jean Rhys' *Wide Sargasso Sea*', *Critique*, 28.4 (Summer 1987): 195–209.

Miki, Roy, 'Asiancy: Making Space for Asian Canadian Writing', in Gary Y. Okihino, Marilyn Alguizola, Dorothy Fujita Rong and K. Scott Wong, eds, *Privileging Positions: The Sites of Asian American Studies*, Washington: Pullman, 1995, pp. 135–51.

Moore-Gilbert, Bart, *Postcolonial Theory: Contexts, Practices, Politics*, London and New York: Verso, 1997.

Mufti, Aamir, 'Reading the Rushdie Affair: An Essay on Islam and Politics', *Social Text*, 29 (1991): 95–116.

Nair, R. Hema, '"Remembrance of Things Past": A Reading of Arundhati Roy's *The God of Small Things*', *Central Institute of English and Foreign Languages Bulletin*, 9.2 (1998): 49–56.

Newton, K.M., 'Literary Theory and the Rushdie Affair', *English: The Journal of the English Association*, 41.171 (1992): 235–47.

Ngũgĩ wa Thiong'o, *A Grain of Wheat*, London: Heinemann, 1988.

Novak, Maximillian E., *Daniel Defoe: Master of Fictions*, Oxford: Oxford University Press, 2001.

Ogundele, Wole, 'Devices of Evasion: The Mythic versus the Historical Imagination in the Postcolonial African Novel', *Research in African Literatures*, 33.3 (Fall 2002): 125–39.

Osei-Nyame, Kwadwo, 'Chinua Achebe Writing Culture: Representations of Gender and Tradition in *Things Fall Apart*', *Research in African Literatures*, 30.2 (Summer 1999): 148–64.

——'Gender and the Narrative of Identity in Chinua Achebe's *Arrow of God*', *Commonwealth*, 22.2 (March 2000): 25–34.

Owusu, Kofi, 'Point of View and Narrative Strategy in Nguge's [*sic*] *A Grain Of Wheat*', *Notes on Contemporary Literature*, 17.1 (1987): 2–3.

Özdemir, Erinç, 'Power, Madness, and Gender Identity in Margaret Atwood's *Surfacing*: A Feminist Reading', *English Studies*, 84.1 (2003): 57–79.

Palumbo, Alice M., 'On the Border: Margaret Atwood's Novels', in Reingard M. Nischik, ed., *Margaret Atwood: Works and Impact*, New York: Camden House, 2000, pp. 73–85.

Parker, Ian, *Slavoj Žižek: A Critical Introduction*, London: Pluto, 2004.

Pearse, Adetokunbo, 'Apartheid and Madness: Bessie Head's *A Question of Power*', *Kunapipi*, 2 (1983): 81–93.

Phelps, Henry C., 'Atwood's *Edible Woman* and *Surfacing*', *Explicator*, 55.2 (Winter 1997): 112–14.

Pipes, Daniel, 'The Ayatollah, the Novelist, and the West', *Commentary*, 87.6 (1989): 9–17.

Prabhakar, M., 'Margaret Atwood's *Surfacing*: Blue-Print of Revolt', *The Literary Half-Yearly*, 36.1 (January 1995): 70–9.

Punter, David, *Postcolonial Imaginings: Fictions of a New World Order*, Edinburgh: Edinburgh University Press, 2000.

Quayson, Ato, 'Realism, Criticism, and the Disguises of Both: A Reading of Chinua Achebe's *Things Fall Apart* with an Evaluation of the Criticism Relating to It', *Research in African Literatures*, 25.4 (Winter 1994): 117–36.

——*Strategic Transformations in Nigerian Writing: Orality and History in the Work of Rev. Samuel Johnson, Amos Tutuola, Wole Soyinka and Ben Okri*, Oxford and Bloomington: James Currey and Indiana University Press, 1997.

——*Postcolonialism: Theory, Practice or Process?*, Cambridge: Polity, 2000.

Ragland-Sullivan, Ellie, *Jacques Lacan and the Philosophy of Psychoanalysis*, Urbana and Chicago: University of Illinois Press, 1987.

Rhys, Jean, *Wide Sargasso Sea*, London and New York: Norton, 1982.

Ricou, Laurie, *The Arbutus/Madrone Files: Reading the Pacific Northwest*, Edmonton: NeWest Press, 2002.

Rimmon-Kenan, Shlomith, *Narrative Fiction: Contemporary Poetics*, London and New York: Methuen, 1986.

Robinson, Eden, *Monkey Beach*, London: Abacus, 2000.

Rose, Jacqueline, 'On the "Universality" of Madness: Bessie Head's *A Question of Power*', *Critical Inquiry*, 20 (Spring 1994): 401–18.

Rosenthal, Caroline, 'Canonizing Atwood: Her Impact on Teaching in the US, Canada, and Europe', in Reingard M. Nischik, ed., *Margaret Atwood: Works and Impact*, New York: Camden House, 2000, pp. 41–56.

Rosenzweig, Franz, *The Star of Redemption*, trans. William W. Hallo, Notre Dame, IN: University of Notre Dame Press, 1985.

Roudinesco, Elisabeth, *Jacques Lacan: An Outline of a Life and a History of a System of Thought*, trans. Barbara Bray, Cambridge: Polity, 1999.

Roy, Arundhati, *The God of Small Things*, New York: Viking, 1997.

Ruland, Richard and Malcolm Bradbury, *From Puritanism to Postmodernism: A History of American Literature*, London and New York: Penguin, 1992.

Rushdie, Salman, *The Satanic Verses*, New York: Viking, 1988.

Said, Edward W., *Beginnings: Intention and Method* (first published 1975), New York: Basic Books and New York: Columbia University Press Morningside Edition, 1985.

—— *Orientalism*, New York: Vintage, 1979.

—— *Culture and Imperialism*, London: Vintage, 1994.

Sample, Maxine, ed., *Critical Essays on Bessie Head*, London and Westport, CT: Praeger, 2003.

Sarvan, Charles Ponnuthurai, 'Bessie Head: *A Question of Power* and Identity', *African Literature Today*, 15 (1987): 82–8.

Sawhney, Sabina and Simona Sawhney, 'Reading Rushdie after September 11, 2001', *Twentieth Century Literature*, 47.4 (Winter 2001): 431–43.

Sawhney, Simona, 'Satanic Choices: Poetry and Prophecy in Rushdie's Novel', *Twentieth Century Literature*, 45.3 (Fall 1999): 253–77.

Scheer, Edward, ed., *Antonin Artaud: A Critical Reader*, London and New York: Routledge, 2004.

Sharma, Govind Narain, 'Ngugi's Christian Vision: Theme and Pattern in *A Grain of Wheat*', *African Literature Today*, 10 (1979): 167–76.

Sharma, Shailja, 'The Ambivalence of Migrancy', *Twentieth Century Literature*, 47.4 (Winter 2001): 596–618.

Silver, Brenda R., *Virginia Woolf: Icon*, Chicago and London: University of Chicago Press, 1999.

Smith Rowland, ed., *Postcolonizing the Commonwealth: Studies in Literature and Culture*, Waterloo, Ont.: Wilfrid Laurier University Press, 2000.

Smith, R. McClure, ' "I Don't Dream About It Any More": The Textual Unconscious in Jean Rhys's *Wide Sargasso Sea*', *Journal of Narrative Technique*, 26.2 (Spring 1996): 113–36.

Sokal, Alan and Jean Bricmont, *Intellectual Impostures: Postmodern Philosophers' Abuse of Science*, London: Profile, 1999.

Soros, Erin, 'If You Die It Will Kill Me: Aborting Maternal History', in Sharon Abbey and Andrea O'Reilly, eds, *Redefining Motherhood: Changing Identities and Patterns*, Toronto: Second Story Press, 1988, pp. 227–43.

Spivak, Gayatri Chakravorty, 'Three Women's Texts and a Critique of Imperialism', *Critical Inquiry*, 12.1 (Autumn 1985): 243–61.

—— *In Other Worlds: Essays in Cultural Politics*, London and New York: Routledge, 1988.

—— 'Theory in the Margin: Coetzee's *Foe* Reading Defoe's *Crusoe/Roxana*', in Jonathan Arac and Barbara Johnson, eds, *Consequences of Theory: Selected Papers from the English Institute, 1987–88*, New Series, no. 14, Baltimore and London: Johns Hopkins University Press, 1991, pp. 154–80.

——'Can the Subaltern Speak?', in Patrick Williams and Laura Chrisman, eds, *Colonial Discourse and Postcolonial Theory: A Reader*, New York: Columbia University Press, 1994, pp. 66–111.

Strobel, Christina, 'On the Representation of Representation in Margaret Atwood's *Surfacing*', *Zeitschrift für Anglistik und Amerikanistik: A Quarterly of Language, Literature and Culture*, 40.1 (January 1992): 35–43.

Strong-Boag, Veronica and Carole Gerson. *Paddling Her Own Canoe: The Times And Texts of E. Pauline Johnson (Tekahionwake)*, Toronto: University of Toronto Press, 2000.

Su, John J. '"Once I Would Have Gone Back . . . But Not Any Longer": Nostalgia and Narrative Ethics in *Wide Sargasso Sea*', *Critique*, 44.2 (Winter 2003): 157–74.

Swift, Jonathan, *Gulliver's Travels* (first published 1726), Oxford: Oxford University Press, 1988.

Ten Kortenaar, Neil, 'Becoming African and the Death of Ikemefuna', *University of Toronto Quarterly*, 73.2 (Spring 2004): 773–94.

Thieme, John, 'Beyond History: Margaret Atwood's *Surfacing* and Robert Kroetsch's *Badlands*', in Shirley Chew, ed., *Re-visions of Canadian Literature*, Leeds: University of Leeds Institute of Bibliography and Textual Criticism, 1984, pp. 71–87.

——*Postcolonial Con-Texts: Writing Back to the Canon*, London and New York: Continuum, 2001.

Thomas, Sue, 'Mythic Reconception and the Mother/Daughter Relationship in Margaret Atwood's "Surfacing"', *Ariel*, 19.2 (1988): 73–85.

Thormann, Janet, 'The Ethical Subject of *The God of Small Things*', *JPCS: Journal for the Psychoanalysis of Culture and Society*, 8.2 (Fall 2003): 299–307.

Tickell, Alex, '*The God of Small Things*: Arundhati Roy's Postcolonial Cosmopolitanism', *Journal of Commonwealth Literature*, 38.1 (2003): 73–89.

Tirkankar, Chanda, 'Sexual/Textual Strategies in *The God of Small Things*', *Commonwealth: Essays and Studies*, 20.1 (1997): 38–44.

Townsend, R.L., 'The Heroism of Mugo: A Study of Ngugi's "A Grain of Wheat"', *Fort Hare Papers*, 8.2 (1987): 46–53.

Tucker, Margaret E., 'A "Nice-Time Girl" Strikes Back: An Essay on Bessie Head's *A Question of Power*', *Research in African Literatures*, 19.2 (Summer 1988): 170–81.

Ueki, Teruyo, '*Obasan*: Revelations in a Paradoxical Scheme', *MELUS*, 18.4 (Winter 1993): 5–20.

Vaubel, Natasha C., 'The Battlefield of Politics and Selfhood in Bessie Head's *A Question of Power*', *ALA Bulletin: A Publication of the African Literature Association*, 23.1 (1 December 1997): 83–106.

Vice, Sue, *Introducing Bakhtin*, Manchester and New York: Manchester University Press, 1997.

Vidler, Anthony, *The Architectural Uncanny: Essays in the Modern Unhomely*, Cambridge, MA and London: MIT Press, 1992.

Vogt-William, Christine, '"Language is the Skin of My Thought": Language Relations in *Ancient Promises* and *The God of Small Things*', in Christian Mair, ed., *The Politics of English as a World Language: New Horizons in Postcolonial Cultural Studies*, ASNEL Papers 7, Amsterdam and New York: Rodopi, 2003, pp. 393–404.

Wall, Jeff, *Jeff Wall*, London: Phaidon, 1996.

Watt, Ian, *The Rise of the Novel* (first published 1957), Harmondsworth: Penguin, 1963.

Werbner, Pnina, 'Allegories of Sacred Imperfection: Magic, Hermeneutics, and Passion in *The Satanic Verses*', *Current Anthropology*, 37, Supplement (February 1996): S55–S86 (includes critical responses to Werbner's article).

Wilentz, Gay, 'Wilson Harris's Divine Comedy of Existence: Miniaturizations of the Cosmos in *Palace of the Peacock*', *Kunapipi*, 8.2 (1986): 56–66.

Wittgenstein, Ludwig, *Philosophical Investigations* (first published 1953), trans. S.E.M. Anscombe, Oxford: Basil Blackwell, 1991.

Woolf, Virginia, 'Defoe', in Max Byrd, ed., *Daniel Defoe: A Collection of Critical Essays*, Englewood Cliffs, NJ: Prentice-Hall, 1976, pp. 15–22.

Žižek, Slavoj, *Tarrying with the Negative: Kant, Hegel, and the Critique of Ideology*, Durham, NC: Duke University Press, 1993.

Index

Note: the index does not cover the authors who are the subject(s) of each chapter of this book, except where they are given significant mention elsewhere.

abject, the 63–4
African literary tradition,
    establishment of 32, 34, 44
apartheid 30–1, 59–60, 69–70
Artaud, Antonin 68
Ashcroft, Bill, Gareth Griffiths and
    Helen Tiffin 9, 11, 27
    Empire Writes Back, The 14
    *Key Concepts in Post-Colonial
    Studies* 18
Atwood, Margaret
    Edible Woman, The 80
    Survival 71, 80–1
autobiography 59–60
    and narrative analysis 64–5, 74

Bhabha, Homi 11–12, 14–15, 90–1, 93
    third space 12
Beckett, Samuel
    Not I 26
Benjamin, Walter
    critical constellation 27
    'differentia of time'/temporal
    montage 78–9
    Spielraum/field of action 105–7
    translation, theories of 90
    'Work of Art in the Age of Its
    Technological Reproducibility,
    The' 104
*Bloomsbury Guide to Women's
    Literature* 81–2
Booth, Wayne C.
    on the unreliable narrator 3–4, 73–6

Bourdieu, Pierre 94
Brontë, Charlotte
    Jane Eyre 18, 27–30

canon 7, 12–13, 15, 18–19, 25,
    27–28, 30, 37, 58, 109
caste system 97, 100–3
    as scapegoating 101
Castres, Édouard
    *Panorama of the French Army
    Entering Switzerland* 111
Caws, Mary Ann
    on manifestos 79–80
Chandra, Vikram
    Red Earth and Pouring Rain 98
chronotope 85–7
Cixous, Hélène 70
Commonwealth literature 12–14
Conrad, Joseph 5
    Heart of Darkness 5–8, 14, 102
    Lord Jim 7
    Nigger of the Narcissus 14
    Under Western Eyes 47, 50, 58
counter-discourse 7–8, 16,
    18–31, 46, 58, 113

deconstruction 11
defamiliarization 102–3
Defoe, Daniel
    Journal of the Plague Year, The
    21
    Robinson Crusoe 18–27
    Roxana 20, 24–5

Deleuze, Gilles and Félix Guattari
  *Anti-Oedipus: Capitalism and
    Schizophrenia* 63
  'body without organs' 68–9
  desiring machines 68–9
  machinic assemblages 68
Derrida, Jacques 11, 103
  Of Grammatology 11
  Writing and Difference 11
Desani, G.V.
  All about H. Hatterr 97
Donne, John 10–11
Durix, Jean-Pierre
  on Rushdie and Roy 97
Dutch West India Company 4
Dvorak, Marta
  on logocentrism 103
  on Roy and Rushdie 97
  on Roy's cinematic structure 104
  on Roy's 'exoticist strategy' 104–5
  on Roy's language 97, 99
  on Roy's postmodernism 105

Encyclopedia of Literature in Canada 81
ethico-religious difference 45

Fanon, Frantz 5, 15, 51, 53, 58, 60,
    69–70
  Black Skin, White Masks 14
  Wretched of the Earth, The 5,
    33–4, 58
fatwa 83, 93
Forster, E.M.
  Passage to India, A 13
Foucault, Michel 1, 14, 55
  Archaeology of Knowledge, The 79
Franco, Jean
  on pastiche 88
Fraser, Simon 111
Fraser River 111–12
Freud, Sigmund
  Interpretation of Dreams, The 10
  Oedipus Complex 63
  Uncanny, the 102

Genette, Gérard
  analepsis/flashback 53–4
  focalization 65
  sabotage 78

Ghosh, Amitav
  Circle of Reason, The 98
Gibson, Andrew 3–4
  *Postmodernity, Ethics and the
    Novel* 75–6
Gikandi, Simon
  on *A Grain of Wheat* 51–2, 54–5,
    58
  on *Things Fall Apart* 32, 34
Girard, René
  scapegoat concept 101
gothic novel, the 29
Griffiths, Gareth, *see* Ashcroft, Bill
Guattari, Félix, *see* Deleuze, Gilles

Haisla First Nation (Canada) 8
Head, Dominic
  on the British Nationality Act
    (1981) 92
  on Rushdie 91–2
Hutcheon, Linda
  on *Surfacing* 72
hybridity 9–11, 15, 59, 88, 90–3,
    95–7

intertextuality 7, 27, 57–8, 97–8,
    102
Islamic ethics and aesthetics 84, 94

James, Henry
  Turn of the Screw, The 73–4
Jameson, Fredric
  on Joseph Conrad 7
  parody and pastiche 61
  political unconscious 88
Jaspers, Karl 14, 44, 60

King, Thomas 15–16
  'interfusional literature' 106
Kristeva, Julia 63–4

Lacan, Jacques 14, 27, 60–1
  'lalangue' 106
linguistic turn, the 103
logocentric discourse 11, 103–4
  deconstruction of
    logocentrism 103–4
Loomba, Ania 6
Lothe, Jakob 2

McLeod, John 12–13
    on *A Grain of Wheat* and Fanon 51
    on Commonwealth literature 12
Madsen, Deborah 15
manifesto writing 78–80
montage 8–9, 77, 105–6
Moore-Gilbert, Bart 11–12, 113
Mufti, Aamir
    on *The Satanic Verses* 86–9
Mulroney, Brian 109

narrated monologue 64–5
Nelson, Viscount Horatio 28
Nietzsche, Friedrich 1

Okada, John
    No-No Boy 109
optical unconscious, the 104–5

parataxis 34–5
pastiche 88
political consciousness 109–10
psycho-narration 65

Quayson, Ato 14–15
    on Chinua Achebe 33
    on realism 33
    on *Things Fall Apart* 35

Richardson, Samuel
    Pamela 23
Ricou, Laurie
    on *An Interrupted Panorama* 111
    on *Obasan* 110
Rimmon-Kenan, Shlomith
    on reliable/unreliable narrators 73
Robinson, Eden
    Monkey Beach 8
Rose, Jacqueline
    on *A Question of Power* 59–61,
        113–14
Rushdie, Salman
    compared with Roy 97, 107
    Grimus 97
    Midnight's Children 97–8

Said, Edward
    beginnings 1
    on *Heart of Darkness* 6–7
    on *Robinson Crusoe* 20
    Orientalism, concept of 14
Sardar Sarovar Dam 107
Sartre, Jean-Paul 14
Schreiner, Olive
    Story of an African Farm, The
        13
Spivak, Gayatri
    'Can the Subaltern Speak?' 14
    on *Foe* 20, 24–6
    on *Robinson Crusoe* 21
    on *Wide Sargasso Sea* 29, 31
Swift, Jonathan 4, 22
syncretism 9–10, 57
syncretist vision 9–10, 113

Thatcher, Margaret 92–3
Thieme, John vi, 5–6, 7, 9
    on Chinua Achebe 43–4
    on *Foe* 27
    on parallels between *Heart of
        Darkness* and *Foe* 25
    on *Surfacing* 75
Tiffin, Helen, *see* Ashcroft, Bill

unreliable narrator, the 72–9

Vancouver, Canada 8, 109–10
    Lions/Two Sisters, The 8

Wall, Jeff
    on Édouard Castres 111–12
    Restoration 111–12
Watt, Ian
    Rise of the Novel, The 20
Werbner, Pnina
    on *The Satanic Verses* 83–6
Woolf, Virginia
    on *Robinson Crusoe* 25

Žižek, Slavoj 44
zombies 5, 30